Charles Washington Baird

History of the Huguenot Emigration to America

Charles Washington Baird

History of the Huguenot Emigration to America

ISBN/EAN: 9783337290689

Printed in Europe, USA, Canada, Australia, Japan

Cover: Foto ©ninafisch / pixelio.de

More available books at **www.hansebooks.com**

HISTORY

OF THE

Huguenot Emigration

TO

America

BY
CHARLES W. BAIRD, D.D.

Volume I

NEW YORK
DODD, MEAD & COMPANY
PUBLISHERS

COPYRIGHT, 1885,
BY
DODD, MEAD & COMPANY.

ILLUSTRATIONS.

VOLUME I.

Bay of Rio de Janeiro. Villegagnon's Island	Facing title-page.	
Mouth of St. John's River, Florida	Page	64
Fort Caroline ; from a view in the *Brevis Narratio* of Jacques Lemoyne de Mourgues	"	73
Map: Acadia and part of Canada	Facing page	79
Fac-simile : Signatures of the Walloon and French Petitioners	" "	162
Map: St. Christopher (St. Kitts), Guadeloupe, and Martinique, West Indies	" "	201
Basse-Terre, St. Kitts ; and the Island of Nevis	" "	204
La Rochelle ; from the Outer Port	" "	264
The "Temple" of La Rochelle ; built in the year 1630, and demolished March 1, 1685	" "	276
La Rochelle ; from the Inner Port	" "	318
Map: Provinces of Saintonge, Aunis and Poitou, France	End.	

PREFACE.

I have undertaken to narrate the coming of the persecuted Protestants of France to the New World, and their establishment, particularly in the seaboard provinces now comprehended within the United States. This movement and settlement took place principally at the time of the Revocation of the Edict of Nantes. But before that period, important emigrations had already occurred; emigrations to Acadia, or Nova Scotia, to Canada, to the French West Indies, and, by way of Holland, to the Dutch possession of New Netherland—now New York. And still earlier, the effort had been made by Coligny—unsuccessfully, indeed—to plant a colony and provide a retreat for the French Calvinists, first in Brazil, and afterward in Florida.

The volumes now submitted to the public treat first of these antecedent movements, and then take up the narrative of the events that led to the more considerable and more effective emigration, in the latter years of the seventeenth century. The attempt has been made, in connection with a brief account of the Huguenots, before their exodus from France,[1] to trace the fortunes of many who ultimately reached this country. The recital is by no means to be regarded as exhaustive. It is presented rather as illustrative of the subject. Yet the number of families whose places of

---

[1] Of the works devoted to the consideration of this topic, the latest—the History of the Rise of the Huguenots of France, by my brother Professor Henry M. Baird—is already widely known. Two volumes, on The Huguenots and Henry the Fourth, will soon succeed that publication, to be followed—it is hoped—by others, covering the period of struggle and suffering, down to the Edict of Toleration.

origination I have ascertained, and of whose flight from France some particulars at least have been gathered, constitutes no small portion of the whole number known to have come to America : and the exemplification of their adventures here given, may be taken, it is believed, as a picture, tolerably correct, of the entire history.

Of the settlement in America, at the period of the Revocation, the present work includes only the part relating to New England. In another work I propose to treat of the settlement in the Middle and Southern provinces or States— in New York, New Jersey, Pennsylvania and Delaware— and in Maryland, Virginia and South Carolina.

The story of the Huguenot emigration to America has remained, till now, unwritten. This has not been due to a lack of interest in the subject, nor to a failure to recognize its importance. Many a glowing tribute has been paid to the memory of the persecuted exiles, and many a thoughtful estimate has been formed, of the value of the contribution made by them to the American character and spirit. No traditions have been more fondly and reverently cherished among us, than those concerning the hardships and sufferings of the fugitives from France : and no names are more honored than the names, of foreign cast, that indicate descent from them. Yet there has scarcely been a serious attempt to set in order the facts that have been known with reference to this theme ; much less, to delve into the mass of documentary evidence that might be supposed to exist. The entire literature of the subject, to the present day, may be said to consist of little more than a few newspaper and magazine articles, a few passages of works upon more general themes,[1] and a few valuable monographs relating to local settlements.

---

[1] I do not forget that the episode of "The Huguenots in Florida" has been told by the brilliant historian of New France, in his graphic way, and that a brief account of De Monts' settlement in Acadia is embodied in the same volume. (Pioneers of France in the New World, by Francis Parkman.) But that episode is rather introductory to the history of the Huguenots in America, than a part of it; and both these incidents are related by Mr. Parkman as subordinate to his special theme: France and England in North America.

PREFACE.

My attention was called to this deficiency, more than thirty years ago, when M. Charles Weiss, while preparing his important "History of the French Protestant Refugees, from the Revocation of the Edict of Nantes to our Own Days," applied to my father, the late Reverend Robert Baird, D.D., for direction in the endeavor to obtain materials for an account of the Huguenot colonists in the United States. Little information could at that time be imparted, in addition to the brief but interesting sketch that had already appeared, in my father's book entitled "Religion in America;"[1] and upon that sketch, M. Weiss based the greater part of his chapters on the Refugees in America.

The present work is the fruit of investigations that have been carried on, in this country, and in France and England, during the last ten or twelve years. The materials used have been found largely in unpublished documents. Manuscripts in the possession of the descendants of refugees; memorials, petitions, wills, and other papers, on file in public offices; the records of a few of the early French Churches in America; the registers of the French Churches in England, in the custody of the Registrar-General, London; the letter-books of the Society for the Propagation of the Gospel in Foreign Parts; documents in the British State Paper Office, and in the National Archives of France, have constituted a precious part of this material. Of the published works that have aided me, the most important have been, the volumes—now numbering thirty-three—of the monthly Bulletin of the French Protestant Historical Society; the volumes of La France Protestante, the second edition of which, edited by M. Henri Bordier, is in progress; the histories of Protestantism in several of the provinces and chief towns of France; and the series of volumes printed in this country under government auspices, comprising doc-

---

[1] Religion in the United States of America. By the Rev. Robert Baird. Glasgow and Edinburgh: MDCCCXLIV. Book II., Chapter XII. "Religious Character of the early Colonists: Huguenots from France." A revised edition was published in the year 1857, by Messrs. Harper Brothers, New York.

uments relative to the colonial history of several of the States.

Of traditions, however interesting, I have taken little account, save where they have been substantiated through written testimony, or incidentally confirmed by established facts. It was a remark of Goethe, which Baron Bunsen quotes as verified under his own observation, that tradition ceases, after three generations; in the fourth, already, every thing is either myth, or documentary history.[1] Yet I have found not unfrequently, and sometimes very unexpectedly, that the legends preserved in our Huguenot families for six or seven generations, have agreed, in the main, with historic statements; confirming, in their turn, the accounts preserved in more durable forms, of the perils and sufferings undergone by the exiles.

In the prosecution of these researches, I have been favored with the able and generous assistance of many fellow-laborers, my indebtedness to whom I gladly acknowledge here. To none of them have I owed more, than to M. Henri Bordier, of Paris, whose labors in connection with the revision of La France Protestante are conferring a vast obligation upon the student of Huguenot history; to M. Jules Bonnet, of Paris, the accomplished Editor of the "Bulletin de la société de l'histoire du protestantisme français," and to M. W. N. du Rieu, Director of the University and Walloon Libraries, Leyden. From M. Louis Meschinet de Richemond, of La Rochelle; from M. James Vaucher, of Geneva; and from M. Philippe Plan, Librarian of the Public Library of Geneva, I have also received material help.

During a visit to London, made in the autumn of the year 1879, I experienced the greatest courtesy at the hands of the gentlemen in charge of the collections of documents that I had occasion to consult. My thanks are especially due to Mr. Walford D. Selby, of the Public Record Office; to Mr. John Shoveller, of the General Register Office, Somerset House; and to Mr. S. W. Kershaw, Librarian of

---

[1] Memoirs of Baron Bunsen. Vol. II., p. 305.

Lambeth Palace Library. Since that visit, I have received important aid from these gentlemen, and also from two of the Directors of the French Protestant Hospital in London. Mr. Arthur Giraud Browning, and Mr. Henry Wagner, F. S. A., who have spared no pains to procure for me all needed information upon the subjects of my inquiry.

At home, I have enjoyed the invaluable coöperation of the custodians of various repositories of manuscripts and books. I may particularly mention Dr. George H. Moore, Superintendent of the Lenox Library; Mr. Frederick Saunders, Librarian of the Astor Library; and Mr. B. Fernow, of Albany, and Dr. Edward Strong, of Boston, who have been most helpful to me in the investigation of the historical records of the State of New York and of the State of Massachusetts. I have been greatly indebted to the authorities of the French Protestant Episcopal Church "du St. Esprit," and of the Protestant Reformed Dutch Churches of New York, Kingston, and New Paltz, for the privilege of consulting the ancient records in their keeping. The numerous manuscripts of Gabriel Bernon, perhaps the most remarkable of the Huguenots who came to America after the Revocation, have been kindly intrusted to me for examination, by Mr. Sullivan Dorr, Mrs. William D. Ely, and the late Mrs. Anne Allen Ives, of Providence, Rhode Island, descendants of that distinguished refugee. The Mascarene papers, now published for the first time,[1] have been made accessible to me through the courtesy of their possessor, Miss Mary W. Nichols, of Danvers, Massachusetts. These interesting documents, upon the death of the last male descendant of Jean Mascarene, passed into the hands of Dr. Edward Augustus Holyoke, of Salem, the ancestor of the lady named.

I have received important help, the value of which will appear in future volumes, rather than in these, from Professor Frederick A. Porcher, President of the South Carolina Historical Society, from the Reverend Dr.

---

[1] A translation of one of these papers appeared in the New England Historical and Genealogical Register, No. CXXXIX. (July, 1881.)

Charles S. Vedder, and from Mr. Langdon Cheves, of Charleston. My thanks are also due to Mr. William Kelby, of the New York Historical Society; to the Reverend Dr. Benjamin F. De Costa; to Mr. John William Potts, of Camden, New Jersey, and to Mr. James A. Dupee, and Mr. J. C. J. Brown, of Boston, for their obliging counsel and assistance. To the names of these friends and helpers I must be permitted gratefully to add the name of my brother, Professor Henry M. Baird.

The views of La Rochelle, that illustrate these volumes, have been copied, with the kind consent of Mr. Matthew Clarkson, of New York, from engravings in his possession, made early in the last century, and doubtless representing the city very much as it was at the time of the dispersion. The quaint view of the Huguenot "temple" of La Rochelle, is a fac-simile of a picture contained in the rare work attributed to Abraham Tessereau, a copy of which exists in the British Museum. The petition, bearing the signatures of the Walloons and French, among whom, it is believed, were several of the first colonists of New Netherland, and founders of the city of New York, is a fac-simile of the original, preserved in the British State Paper Office. Permission to reproduce this important document was readily given by the Master of the Rolls, upon the application made in my behalf by Mr. A. G. Browning.

I am indebted to Mr. George F. Daniels, the author of a very valuable account of "The Huguenots in the Nipmuck Country," for a view of Oxford, Massachusetts, the site of one of the most interesting of the French settlements in America.

I offer no apology for the multiplicity of proper names, and of personal details, that will be found in several of these chapters. The value of such a work as the present one must obviously depend in no small degree upon the fullness and the accuracy of information of this nature. On the other hand, it may be necessary that I should explain, that these particulars relate chiefly to the emigrants themselves, except in the case of those who came to New England. Of the families that came to the Middle and Southern provinces, or States, fuller notices will be reserved for a future publication, that will treat of the settlement in those parts of our land.

A general appreciation of the Huguenot character, and of the Huguenot element in the population of this country, will naturally find its place in the concluding chapter of that publication.

RYE, NEW YORK,
    November 1, 1884.

CONTENTS OF VOLUME FIRST.

INTRODUCTION.

	PAGE
ATTEMPTED SETTLEMENTS IN BRAZIL AND FLORIDA	21
Coligny's Plans of Colonization	21
— A Refuge from Persecution	22
Spread of Calvinism in France	23
The Inquisition proposed	24
Reformed Church of France	25
Coligny's Apprehensions	25
The Moment favorable	26
Durand de Villegagnon	27
Projected Colony in Brazil	27
Recruits for the Expedition	28
Rio de Janeiro	29
The Bay of Nitherohy	29
Difficulties encountered	30
The Island Coligny	31
The Settlement	31
Embassy to Geneva	32
First Mission to the Heathen	33
The Sieur du Pont	33
Visit to Coligny	34
Voyage to Antarctic France	35
Affray in Honfleur	35
Villegagnon's Professions	36
First Religious Service	37
Villegagnon's singular Demeanor	38
Glowing Anticipations	39
A sleepless Night	39
Villegagnon a second St. Paul	40
Holy Communion administered	41
Letters to Calvin	41
Plans of Missionary Work	42
Villegagnon writes to Calvin	43
Gathering Clouds	43

Chartier's Mission	44
Change in Villegagnon	45
His Eccentricities	45
Rupture with the Genevese	46
Du Pont leaves the Island	47
Psalm-singing in the Forest	47
A Brazilian Village	48
Preaching to the Savages	49
Attentive Hearers	49
An Indian Tradition	50
Transient Impressions	51
The War-Song	51
The homeward Voyage	52
Villegagnon's Treachery	53
Sufferers for the Faith	53
Jean Boles	54
The Colony broken up	55
Coligny undiscouraged	56
ATTEMPTED SETTLEMENTS: FLORIDA	57
A favorable Juncture	57
Edict of July, 1561	58
Edict of January, 1562	59
The "New Religion" recognized	59
Civil War impending	59
The Expedition	60
The River of May	61
Port Royal	61
Outbreak of the first Civil War	62
Fate of Charlesfort	63
Second Expedition	63
La Caroline	65
Former Mistakes repeated	67
The Leader's Weakness	67
Psalm-singing in Florida	68
Sir John Hawkins	69
Third Expedition	70
A common Danger	71
The Spaniards	71
Council of War	72
Pedro Menendez de Abila	73
Ribaut surrenders	74
No Terms with Heretics	75
Butchery at St Augustine	75
The Crime avenged	76
Dominique de Gourgues	77

CONTENTS.   xiii

CHAPTER I.

	PAGE
UNDER THE EDICT: ACADIA AND CANADA	79
Sully's Statesmanship	79
Henry IV. favors Colonization	80
The Reformation in Western France	81
Spread of the new Doctrines	81
The Mass unsaid	82
The Huguenots insecure	83
Need of a Refuge foreseen	83
Pierre Chauvin, Seigneur de Tontuit	84
New France still unoccupied	85
La Cadie	86
De Monts' Commission	87
The Rights of Conscience secured	87
Pierre du Gua, sieur de Monts	88
Minister and Priest	89
The Coast of Acadia explored	90
Aubry's Adventure	91
Port Royal discovered	92
Annapolis Harbor	93
St. Croix Island	93
Lay Preaching at Port Royal	94
A Missionary Expedition	95
Converts to Christianity	95
"The Christian Faith and Religion"	97
Objections to De Monts' Commission	97
No Guarantee against Heresy	98
Religious Differences	99
Privileges of Trade withdrawn	100
Port Royal abandoned	100
Settlement at Quebec	101
Religious Liberty unrestricted	102
De Monts' Commission surrendered	103
The Jesuit Missions	103
The Bargain closed	104
The Jesuits in Acadia	105
Mount Desert	105
UNDER THE EDICT: CANADA	106
The Compagnie Montmorency	106
Guillaume de Caen	107
The Jesuits enter Canada	107
Company of New France	108
Huguenot Settlers excluded	109
Triumph of the Jesuits	109
Toleration deplored	110

CONTENTS.

	PAGE
No Compromise with Heresy	111
England enters the Lists	112
Expedition to conquer New France	113
Huguenots join it	113
Quebec taken	114
Canada reverts to France	115
The Doom pronounced	116
The Loss to Canada	117
Protestants detected in the Colony	118
A stubborn Heretic	119
Pulverized Relics	120
Relations with La Rochelle	121
Rochellese Merchants	121
Dangerous Proximity of Boston	122
Deserters to New York	123
Protestant Soldiers in Canada	124
False Brethren	125
The Sieur du Buisson	125
Echoes of the Revocation	126
Bernon in Canada	127
UNDER THE EDICT: ACADIA	128
Changing Owners	128
Dealings with the Puritans	129
The "Wonderful Plague"	130
Emigration from La Rochelle	131
Huguenot Families	132
Charles de la Tour	133
Inflexible Loyalty	135
Rival Chieftains	136
Madame de la Tour	137
Acadia reverts to France	139
John Paul Mascarene	140
Heresy in Acadia	143
Bergier, of La Rochelle	144
Huguenots in Newfoundland	145
The Sieur Pasteur's Daughter	146

CHAPTER II.

NEW NETHERLAND	148
The Walloons	149
The Refuge in Holland	151
The Bayards	151
Leyden	152
Walloons and French in Leyden	153

CONTENTS. XV

	PAGE
The Brownists	154
Projects of Emigration	155
Negotiations	156
The Puritans leave Leyden	157
The Walloons prepare to follow	158
Jesse de Forest	159
Petition of the Walloons and French	159
Privileges desired	161
Manorial Rights	161
Promises of Fealty	162
The Virginia Company's Answer	163
Inadmissible Requests	164
The Correspondence ceases	165
The Dutch West India Company	166
Providential Aspects	167
The "New Netherland" sails	169
The Bay of New York	170
Landing on Manhattan Island	171
The Colonists disperse	171
A cheerful Report	172
George de Rapalie	172
First Settlers of New York	173
Jean Mousnier de la Montagne	174
Death of Jesse de Forest	175
Peter Minuit, the Walloon	175
The Church of New Amsterdam	176
Religious Services in French	177
Bay of the Walloons	177
Judith Bayard	178
Arrivals from France	179
Growth of Persecution in France	180
Condition of the French Protestants	181
Emigration from the Northern Provinces	181
Waldenses of Piedmont	183
They take Refuge in Holland	184
Wreck of the "Prince Maurice"	185
Waldenses on Staten Island	186
Louis, the Walloon	187
The Palatinate	188
The New Palatinate	189
Esopus	190
Indian Depredations	191
The Esopus War	191
Dominie Hermanus Blom	192
Site of the Settlement	193

CONTENTS.

	PAGE
The "New Village"	194
Attack upon the Settlements	195
Brave Defense of Wiltwyck	196
Consternation at New Amsterdam	196
The Esopus Indians pursued	197
The Rescue	198
Security of the Settlement	199
New Netherland becomes an English Possession	200
David Provost, and Johannes de Peyster	200

CHAPTER III.

THE ANTILLES	201
Caribbean Islands	202
Occupation of St. Christopher	202
Mount Misery	203
Basse-Terre	204
Early Toleration	205
Heretics always suffered	205
Huguenot Seamen	206
Churches in St. Christopher	206
Protestant Merchants	208
The Protestant Quarter of Guadeloupe	210
American Huguenot Names	211
The Storm approaches	211
Proscriptive Edicts	212
Protestant Officials in the Islands	213
Elie Neau in the West Indies	214
Occasional Severities	215
Methods of Intimidation	217
The "Engagés"	218
Transportation to the Islands dreaded	219
Banishment and Slavery	220
Numbers actually shipped	221
Sympathy awakened in Europe	222
A Transport Ship at Cadiz	223
Horrors of the Passage	224
Large Mortality	225
Martinique	226
"Les Mornes"	227
Quartering of Soldiers	227
Instances of Humane Treatment	228
Flight from the Islands	229
Methods of Escape	230
Arrivals in New York	231

CONTENTS.   xvii

	PAGE
Tardy Change of Policy	233
Protestants remaining in the Islands	234
Bermuda	235

CHAPTER IV.

APPROACH OF THE REVOCATION . . . 238
Fall of La Rochelle 238
Political Importance of the Huguenots . . 239
They cease to form a Party . . 239
Their Devotion to Trade and Manufactures . 240
Their unimpeached Loyalty . . . 241
Testimonies of Louis XIII. and Louis XIV. . 241
Their Relentless Enemy . . 242
The Edict irrevocable 242
Preparing to revoke it 242
The family attacked: Disorder introduced into the Home 243
The Schools attacked: Academies suppressed 245
The Church attacked: Closing of Protestant "Temples" 247
Personal Rights invaded . . . 247
Exclusion from Trades and Professions . . 247
The Dragonnades 249
As in an Enemy's Country 249
Forced Conversions 250
The Exodus 251
Expedients of the Fugitives . . . 251
Flight by Sea and Land 252
The Collapse 253
Doors of Escape 254
England's Welcome 255
The Royal Bounty 255
Other Overtures 255
The Protestant Princes 256
Persecution continues . . . 256
The Edict of Revocation 257
Its Provisions 258
Judgment of the Age, and of Posterity . . 259

CHAPTER V.

THE REVOCATION: FLIGHT FROM LA ROCHELLE AND AUNIS 262
Calvin's first Disciples . . . 262

CONTENTS.

	PAGE
The seaboard Provinces	263
Home of American Huguenots	263
La Rochelle	264
"La Terre d' Aunis"	264
A glorious History	265
The Protestant Capital	266
Second Siege of La Rochelle	267
Its political Importance ceases	268
Three hundred Families ejected from the City	269
Emigrants to America	270
Jean Touton	271
Correspondence with Governor Stuyvesant	272
Homes of the Rochellese	273
Streets of La Rochelle	273
St. Nicolas, and La Lanterne	274
Historic Associations	275
"Le Bastion de l' Evangile"	275
The Pré de Maubec	276
The Huguenot "Prêche"	276
Rochellese Families: Bernon and Jay	277
Gabriel Manigault	279
Baudouin, Sieur de la Laigne	280
Allaire and Faneuil	281
The Sigourneys	282
The Protestant "Noblesse" of Aunis	283
The Sieur de Rivedoux	283
Bruneau de la Chabossière	284
The Seigneurs de Cramahé	285
Daniel Robert	286
Rochellese Emigrants to Boston	287
Emigrants to the City of New York	288
The Ancestor of John Morin Scott	290
Emigrants to New Rochelle,	291
Settlers in Ulster County	293
Settlers on Staten Island	294
Antoine Pintard	295
Settlers in South Carolina	296
Marans in Aunis	297
The Seigneur de Cressy	598
Elie Boudinot's Will	299
Benon and Mauzé, in Aunis	300
The Gallaudets	301
The Isle of Ré	302
Descendants of the "New Converts"	303
Emigrants from the Isle of Ré	303

CONTENTS.

	PAGE
Emigrants from the Isle of Ré to New England	304
To New York	305
Pierre Bontecou	307
Emigrants to South Carolina	308
Isaac Mazyck	310
The Intendant Demuyn	312
The "Temple" of La Rochelle demolished	313
Bernon's Letter to a Friend in Boston	314
Fusileers from Béarn	315
Pillage in La Rochelle	315
"Bowing the Knee to Baal"	316
Pierre Jay	317
Escape of Jay's Family	317
A Prisoner in La Lanterne	318
André Bernon	319
Brutality of the Intendant Arnou	320
Samuel and Jean Bernon	321
Fervent Proselytes	322
Gabriel Bernon	323
His Escape to Holland	324
Relatives in the Convents and Galleys	325
APPENDIX	327
Letter of the Ministers Richer and Chartier to Calvin	329
Translation	330
Letter of the Minister Richer to an unknown Correspondent	332
Translation	333
Letter of Villegagnon to Calvin	335
Translation	338
Commission of Henry IV. to De Monts	341
Translation. "The Patent of the French Kinge to Mounsieur De Monts"	344
Petition of the Walloons and French	348
Answer of the Virginia Company	350
The Walloon and French Petitioners	351
Notes from the Walloon Records of Leyden	353

INTRODUCTION.

ATTEMPTED SETTLEMENTS

IN

BRAZIL AND FLORIDA.

The project of establishing colonies of French Protestants in America, was entertained and advocated, as early as the middle of the sixteenth century, by the illustrious Gaspard de Coligny. A patriotic and a religious zeal alike prompted him to favor the measure. Intent on furthering the prosperity of France through the development of her industrial resources, the great Admiral, a hundred years before Colbert, pleaded for colonization. Whenever released from the more pressing cares of political and military life, his mind was occupied with plans of this nature, hoping, as he expressed it, "so to manage that in a little while we may have the finest trade in all Christendom." Coligny's views of the foreign policy of France also led him to favor a colonial system. Spain, foremost in the discovery and exploration of the New World, was now nearly without a rival upon its continents and waters. The vast empires of Mexico and Peru had fallen an easy prey to her captains; and the riches which the conquest poured into the royal treasury, enabled Charles

Introd.
1555.

Coligny's plans of Colonization.

the Fifth to carry on the wars which disturbed the peace of Europe, and which especially humiliated France. Coligny had already distinguished himself in arms against the Spaniard. Devoted to his country's interests, he could not but approve a plan for weakening her inveterate foe by planting settlements and trading posts along the American shore, and contesting the commerce and the sovereignty of the New World with Spain.

But there was another consideration, perhaps more potent, appealing to Coligny's religious sympathies. Though not yet an avowed adherent of the Reformed faith, he was in accord with the Protestant movement, and was preparing to be the fearless champion of religious freedom and of the rights of conscience that he proved himself ever after. At this moment, the outlook for Protestantism in France was an anxious one. The doctrines of the Reformation, proclaimed in Germany by Luther, had soon spread into the neighboring territory of France, and made converts among the learned and the titled, as well as among the common people. For a time it seemed probable that the evangelical faith might enjoy toleration, if not patronage and acceptance, from the great. The king, Francis the First, himself professed a desire to see the abuses of the Church corrected. His sister, Margaret of Angoulême, afterwards Queen of Navarre, early came into sympathy with the teachings of the reformers, and showed herself their zealous and steadfast friend. Motives of state policy prompted Francis to seek alliance with the Protestant princes of Germany, and to conciliate the Lutherans among his own subjects. But it was not long before, influenced by other considerations, he forsook the course of moderation upon which he had entered, and acknowledged himself the implacable foe of the Reformation. His hostility was reflected and intensified in the legislation of the period. Parliamentary enactments pronounced the profession of the new doctrines a crime, to be punished with death; and executions for heresy became frequent throughout the kingdom. The last years of Francis I. were stained by the massacre of the Protestant inhabitants of twenty-two towns and villages in southeastern France, and by the burning at the stake of fourteen members of the newly organized church of Meaux. Under the reign of his son, Henry II., the laws that aimed at the extirpation of heresy became increasingly severe. The edict of Châteaubriand enjoined upon the civil and ecclesiastical courts of the kingdom to combine for the detection and punishment of heretics. Persons convicted of heresy were denied the right of appeal from the decisions of these courts. Suspected persons were excluded from every public preferment, and from all academic honors. Heavy penalties were imposed upon any who should harbor them, connive at their escape, or present petitions in their behalf. Informers were awarded one-third part of the goods of persons informed against. The property of those who fled from the kingdom was to be confiscated. The same edict forbade the introduction of heretical books from abroad, and established a rigid censorship of the press at home, to prevent the publication of such works within the realm.

Yet in spite of these harsh repressive measures, the Protestant faith continued to spread in France. Its enemies, finding that the torture and the fagot, as applied under the sanction of civil law, availed nothing to deter multitudes from embracing the new religion, now urged the introduction of the Spanish Inquisition, which had proved so effectual in destroying heresy on the other side of the Pyrenees. It was, however, at the very time when this proposal was under consideration in the Parliament of Paris, that the first Protestant church in France was organized in a private house of that city; and it was soon after this that the foundations of an ecclesiastical system destined to unite and consolidate the scattered congregations of believers throughout the kingdom, were laid by a handful of obscure and persecuted men.

The first National Synod of the Reformed Churches of France met in Paris, in May, 1559. The form of ecclesiastical discipline adopted was that already existing in the Reformed Church of Geneva; and it was substantially the same with that which was established in the following year by the first General Assembly of the Church of Scotland. The parity of the Holy Ministry was recognized. In each congregation the minister or ministers, together with the "anciens," (elders,) chosen by the people, formed the "Consistoire" or Church Session, having the oversight of the flock. From the decisions of this court, appeal could be made to the "Colloque," or Provincial Synod, which met twice every year, and which was composed of all the pastors of the churches within a certain territory, together with elders representing the congregations. The National Synod was the supreme ecclesiastical court.

Coligny knew the temper of the religious party to which he was already bound in sympathy, and of which he was soon to become the military leader. Sagacious and far-sighted, this eminent man—"one of the largest, firmest, and most active spirits that have ever illustrated France"—dreaded the effect of persecution upon a body of men, steadily growing in numbers, swayed by the most powerful convictions, conscious of their strength, yet denied the liberty either to enjoy their rights of conscience at home or to seek room for the enjoyment of them in foreign lands. The plan of founding a French colony in America, where the adherents of the Reformed religion might freely profess and exercise their faith,[1] while at the same time enlarging the possessions and increasing the resources of the kingdom,[2] commended itself strongly to

---

[1] "Le but étoit bien moins d'acquérir à la France une partie du Brésil, que d'y assurer une ressource au Calvinisme, proscrit et persecuté par le Souverain."—Histoire de la Nouvelle France, par le P. de Charlevoix. Vol. I., p. 35.

[2] "La colonisation par les protestants des régions qu'on

his judgment: and upon his representations, the king, Henry II., consented to the scheme.¹

The moment seemed favorable. A series of military reverses had inclined Charles the Fifth to terms of peace with France and with her allies, the Protestant States of Germany. Spain was resting from a long and an exhaustive war. Among the countries beyond the seas which had been discovered by Spanish adventurers, Brazil remained almost unnoticed. A companion of Christopher Columbus had taken possession of it, fifty years before, in the name of the King of Castile: but the claim had not been pressed. By the line of demarkation which the Roman See had drawn, dividing all lands as yet undiscovered between the crowns of Spain and Portugal, Brazil was found to belong to the lat-

---

nommait alors les Indes était un des rêves favoris de l'amiral."—De Grammont: Relation de l' expédition de Charles-Quint contre Alger par Villegaignon. P. 8.

¹ "On disoit ouvertement que c'étoit-là le moyen d'étendre la gloire du nom François, & d' affoiblir les forces des ennemis, qui tiroient de ces contrées de puissans secours, pour faire la guerre: Que l' exemple des François serviroit beaucoup à ouvrir aux nations étrangères le chemin de cette partie du monde: de sorte qu' en rendant la liberté aux Américains, on y établiroit un commerce public et commun à toutes les nations, dont les seuls Espagnols, par le joug insupportable qu' ils avoient imposé à ces peuples, tiroient tout le profit. Voilà ce qu' on publioit par tout. Mais Villegagnon avoit traité secretement avec Coligny, et comme il sçavoit que l' Amiral favorisoit sourdement les sectateurs de la Religion des Suisses et de Geneve, dont il y avoit déja un grand nombre en France, il lui avoit fait espérer qu' il établiroit cette Religion dans les païs dont il se rendroit le maître."—Histoire Universelle de Jaques Auguste de Thou. Tome II., p. 381.

ter power. The Portuguese indeed, at an early day, formed a few settlements along the coast. But it was not until the discovery of gold in that country, that Portugal herself showed any great interest in this occupation. Meanwhile, the French, who had never admitted the right of the Pope to apportion a hemisphere between their rivals the Spaniards and Portuguese, were exploring the coast of Brazil, and trading with its inhabitants, upon their own account.

It was now that a French soldier of fortune, Durand de Villegagnon, proposed to Coligny the establishment of a Protestant colony in Brazil. Villegagnon was well known as a brave soldier, and an accomplished naval commander, and was particularly recommended for such an expedition by his acquaintance with the Brazilian coast. He also represented himself to the Protestants as in sympathy with their views; and if he did not himself originate the plan of emigration to the New World, willingly lent himself to Coligny's scheme in behalf of his persecuted brethren.[1]

---

[1] Jurieu, Apologie pour la Réformation, I. 552, maintains that Coligny fixed upon Villegagnon to carry out his own design, and prepare a retreat in America for the persecuted Protestants. Bayle, Hist. & Crit. Dictionary (v. Villegagnon) quotes Beza in opposition to this statement. Count Delaborde (Gaspard de Coligny, Amiral de France, I. 145, 146,) adopts the former view. "Coligny avait conçu le projet d'y fonder [en Brésil] une colonie, dans la double pensée de servir les intérêts de la France en lui assurant, au delà de l'Océan, la possession d'une contrée propre à favoriser son commerce, et d'ouvrir un asile à ceux des protestants français qui pourraient se soustraire aux persécutions dirigées contre eux sur le sol natal."

28 ATTEMPTED SETTLEMENTS: BRAZIL.

Introd.
July 12, 1555.

It was in July, 1555, that two ships and a transport, furnished and fitted out at the royal charges,¹ set forth under the auspices of Admiral Coligny, from the port of Havre de Grace. The company of emigrants was considerable. Villegagnon's ship alone carried one hundred persons. Some of these were Protestants, of various conditions—noblemen, soldiers, and mechanics. But there were others who probably cared little either for the "new" doctrines or for the old.

Recruits for the Expedition.

Villegagnon had availed himself of the king's permission to visit the prisons of Paris, and select any of the criminals whom he might judge to be suitable as recruits. This was no uncommon way of securing colonists for the settlement of lands beyond the seas. It may be doubted whether the experiment ever proved a successful one.

The band of volunteers was soon reduced in number by desertions. Scarcely had the vessels gained the Channel, before a severe gale set in, driving them back to the coast of Normandy. At Dieppe, where they put in for shelter and repairs, many of the voyagers, satisfied with their brief experience of the perils and discomforts of the ocean, abandoned the enterprise. Only eighty persevered, of whom thirty were artisans and common workmen.

A long and stormy voyage brought the adventurers to the wonderful Bay, which its discoverer,

---

¹ In addition to this outfit, the king granted the sum of ten thousand *livres* for the first expenses of the enterprise. (De Léry.)

supposing it to be the mouth of some great river, had misnamed Rio de Janeiro. As their ships approached the narrow entrance to this landlocked sheet of water, the Frenchmen looked with admiring eyes upon scenery unsurpassed for magnificence and beauty by any other in either hemisphere. On each side of this entrance, a granite mountain stood, as if forbidding access. Beyond these giant sentinels, and through a deep vista of wooded hills, the vast harbor was seen, its expanse broken by palm-clad islands, and framed in with dense forests, behind which rose lofty ranges of mountains, strangely contorted in abrupt, fantastic forms. Nearing the shore, the voyagers beheld for the first time the splendors of a tropical vegetation. The atmosphere was heavy with the odor of flowers, and sight and hearing were together regaled by the incessant song and the brilliant plumage of countless varieties of birds.

Villegagnon landed with his men upon the shore near the entrance of the bay. The arrival of the party was greeted by the savages in the neighborhood with every demonstration of joy. These tribes were friendly to the French, with whom they had long traded; and they regarded their visitors as allies, come to protect them against the Portuguese, whom they hated for their cruelty and rapacity. But neither the friendliness of the savages nor the grandeur and loveliness of the scenes of nature around them, could blind the strangers to the fact that a laborious and discouraging work awaited them. The

Introd.
1555.

Bay of Nitheroby.

country was utterly uncultivated. The natives, though disposed to be helpful, were improvident, and had no sufficient stores of food for their supply. It was necessary to begin without delay the building of some kind of fortification, not only as a precaution against the Indians, whose fidelity could not be greatly relied on, but especially in view of the proximity of the Portuguese, who, though they had not been able to retain possession of the land, were enraged by the intrusion of the French, and might at any moment make a descent upon them from their settlement at San Salvador, in the north. But the difficulties in the way of building were many. There were no beasts of burden, and timber must be carried on the shoulders of men, up the steep hillsides of the wild broken country. Villegagnon himself was at a loss to decide upon the best course to be pursued: and his companions, the better portion of them especially, were completely discouraged, and only waited till the ships which had brought them over should be ready for the homeward voyage, returning to France with a cargo of Brazil-wood. The leader was soon left with a diminished band, consisting for the most part of the convicts whom he had taken out of the prisons in Paris. Fearing lest they too might desert him, and go over to the savages, with whom they were but too well inclined to consort, he determined to leave the main-land,[1] and establish himself upon

---

[1] So Villegagnon himself intimates in his letter to Calvin,

one of the numerous islands in the beautiful
bay. The little island of Lage, just within the
entrance of the bay, was first chosen. Here
Villegagnon set his men at work to build a temporary fort or block-house. But it was soon
found that the action of the water at flood-tide
in the narrow channel threatened the security of
the building; and the party removed to another
small island, two miles further up the widening
portal of the bay, and directly opposite the site
now occupied by the city of Rio de Janeiro.
This island, known at the present day by Villegagnon's name, is less than a mile in circumference, and lies at the distance of only two furlongs from the shore. It was called in honor of
the patron of the colony, Coligny: a fort was
erected on a rock at the water's edge, and near
by, under shelter of the guns, the rude cabins of
the settlers were hastily constructed.

Even in this isolated spot, Villegagnon found
it difficult to keep his vicious and refractory followers under control. A conspiracy against his

---

(see appendix to this volume,) in which he gives his reasons
for subsequently removing to an island. De Léry, who
arrived more than a year later, and who may not have
known all the particulars of the beginnings of the colony,
says nothing about the unsuccessful attempt to settle on the
main-land.

There is an allusion to it in André Thevet's notices of
the expedition. "Nous trouvasmes une petite isle . . .
dans laquelle quelques deux mois suivans commençames à
fortifier, après avoir pensé à nos affaires et avoir *fait
descente en terre continente*, pour tirer l'amitié de ces barbares." (Histoire de deux voyages par luy faits aux Indes
australes et occidentales, apud Mémoires de Claude Haton:
appendice, p. 1099.)

life, in which all but five joined, was discovered barely in time, and the summary punishment of the ringleader struck terror into the minds of the rest. After this, the work of fortification proceeded, and the little colony enjoyed a tolerable degree of tranquillity for the remainder of the year.

The ship that returned to Europe with some of the discouraged adventurers, carried also a trusty messenger from Villegagnon, charged with the duty of reporting to Coligny and to the king the establishment of the colony, and of seeking re-enforcements, in order to the permanent occupation of "Antarctic France," as the new continent was now denominated. In addition to this embassy, the messenger was instructed to proceed to Geneva, and there to present to the ministers and magistrates of the city an earnest appeal for help to plant the Gospel in America. Calvin himself was absent, having been called to Frankfort for the purpose of endeavoring to settle the serious disputes among the English exiles and the Protestants of that city. But the envoy was heartily welcomed by the other ministers of Geneva, as well as by the magistrates. Solemn religious services were held in the cathedral church of St. Pierre: the Genevese, who were "naturally desirous of the spread of their own religion, giving thanks to God," as the old chronicler Lescarbot relates, "for that they saw the way open to establish their doctrine yonder, and to cause the light of the Gospel to shine forth among those barbarous people, godless, lawless, and without religion." Several pious young students, one of whom was Jean de Léry, offered themselves for the work of instructing the savages in the knowledge of Christianity; and two clergymen of the Church of Geneva, Pierre Richer, called de Lisle, and Guillaume Chartier—the first Protestant ministers to cross the Atlantic—were appointed to this mission.

The other members of the little company were Pierre Bourdon, Mathieu Verneuil, Jean du Bordel, André Lafon, Nicolas Denis, Jean Gardien, Martin David, Nicolas Roviquet, Nicolas Carmeau, and Jacques Rousseau. Three of these were destined to martyrdom for their faith.

A number of mechanics and laborers also joined the party. At its head was the aged Philippe de Corguilleray, sieur du Pont, an old neighbor and friend of Coligny, who had left his estates at Châtillon sur Loing, some years before, that he might live amid the religious privileges to be enjoyed in Geneva. It was at the admiral's own request, seconded by that of Calvin, that this venerable man[1] consented to take the leadership of the enterprise.[2]

---

[1] Ja vieil et caduc.—De Léry.

[2] The particulars of the expedition to Brazil are given by De Léry, who accompanied it, and by Lescarbot, who seems to have derived his information from others who were engaged in it. De Léry's account is to be found in his "Histoire d'un Voyage fait en la Terre du Bresil, autrement dite Amerique. Contenant la Navigation, & choses remarquables, veües sur mer par l' aucteur. Le comportement

Introd.
1556.
September 2.
Visit to Coligny.

The band of volunteers thus organized left Geneva in excellent spirits.¹ Crossing the Jura mountains, they made their way through the provinces of Franche Comté and Burgundy, to the home of Coligny, in the valley of the Loing. Here the admiral graciously entertained them, in his ancient castle of Châtillon, "one of the very finest in France," and encouraged them in their undertaking, setting before them many reasons that led him to hope that God would permit them to see the fruit of their labors, and promising them the help of the naval force at his command. From Châtillon they proceeded to Paris, where they spent a month, and where, to their delight, Richer and Chartier found that "a church had been gathered in the best manner, according to the word of God." Scarcely a year had passed since the organization of this

---

de Villegagnon en ce païs là. Les meurs & façons de vivre estranges des Sauvages Ameriquains: avec un colloque de leur langage. Ensemble la description de plusieurs Animaux, Arbres, Herbes, & autres choses singulieres, & du tout inconues pardeça : dont on verra les sommaires des chapitres au commencement du livre. Non encores mis en lumiere, pour les causes contenues en la preface. Le tout receuilli sur les lieux par Iean De Lery, natif de La Margelle, terre de Sainct Sene, au Duché de Bourgougne. Pseaume CVIII. Seigneur, ie te celebreray entre les peuples, & te diray Pseaumes entre les nations. A Geneve. Pour Antoine Chuppin, M.D. LXXX."—8 vo., pp. 382.

¹ Gallasius writes, September 16th, from Geneva, to Calvin, then in Frankfort, "*Richerius* et *Quadrigarius* [Chartier] cum *Pontano* [du Pont] octavo die hujus mensis in viam se dederunt eadem alacritate animi quam antea prae se ferebant. Unum tantum diem discessum eorum distulit Pontanus, quod torminibus subito correptus itineris laborem ferre non posset."

little flock in the French capital, the first Protestant church in France: and the visit of these ministers was well-timed, as on the way to their mission field, they stopped to speak to their fellow-believers of the prospects of God's kingdom in the heathen world. In Paris the travelers were joined by several noblemen who had heard of the expedition. In due time they reached Honfleur, in Normandy, their appointed place of embarkation. *(Introd. 1556.)*

While waiting for the little fleet of three vessels which the king had promised to furnish for their voyage, the emigrants experienced one of those effects of the popular hatred to which the Protestants of France were perpetually exposed, even in times of peace. Gathered in their lodgings, they were celebrating the Lord's Supper at night, when a mob burst in upon them, and in the affray that followed, one of their number, the captain Saint Denis, was killed. *(Affray in Honfleur.)*

It was on the twentieth of November that the adventurers launched upon "that great and impestuous sea, the Ocean." A nephew of Vellegagnon, the sieur Bois-le-Compte, was in command. His flag-ship, "la petite Roberge," carried eighty persons. Jean de Léry, and his companions, sailed with Captain de Sainte-Marie; and a third vessel, the "Rosée," had on board six boys, sent over to learn the language of the country, and five young girls, under the care of a matron. The voyage lasted nearly four months. It was disgraced by several acts of piracy, perpetrated by Bois-le-Comte, upon *(November 20.)*

Spanish and Portuguese ships. The emigrants remonstrated in vain with the commander against these lawless acts, which he doubtless sought to justify by the maritime customs of the time.[1]

March 10 — At length, on Wednesday, the tenth of March, the passengers landed on the island Coligny, in the bay of Rio de Janeiro. "The first thing we did," says Jean de Léry, "was to join in thanksgiving to God." The new-comers were led at once into the presence of Villegagnon, who welcomed them warmly. These courtesies over, the aged sieur du Pont addressed him, setting forth the motives which had influenced his companions and himself in undertaking a voyage attended with so many dangers and hardships. It was, he said, to constitute in that country a Church reformed according to the word of God. Villegagnon replied, declaring that inasmuch as this had long been the desire of his own heart, he received them gladly with this understanding. Nay, it was his purpose that their Church should be the best reformed of all, and even far beyond others: and that henceforth vice should be rebuked, extravagance in dress corrected, and in short everything that might hinder the worship of God in its purity removed. Then, clasping his hands, and raising

---

[1] It deserves to be noticed that Coligny himself had earnestly protested against piracy, and had exerted himself for its repression, and for the protection of commerce upon the high seas.—Gaspard de Coligny, Amiral de France; par le comte Jules Delaborde, Paris, 1882. T. III., p. 363.

his eyes toward heaven, he thanked God for sending him the blessing which he had so fervently besought from Him; and turning to the Genevese, he addressed them as his children, assuring them of his unselfish design to provide for their welfare and for that of those who might come to this place for the same purposes. "For," said he, "I am planning to prepare a refuge for the poor believers who may be persecuted in France, in Spain, and elsewhere, beyond the sea, to the end that, without fear of king, emperor or other potentate, they may here serve God in purity according to His will."

Introd. 1557.

This interview ended, Villegagnon led the whole company into a cabin that stood in the middle of the island, and that served both as chapel and as refectory. Here, when they had sung the fifth Psalm, after Marot's version,[1]

First religious service.

---

[1] Aux paroles que je veux dire,
 Plaise toi l'oreille prester :
 Et à cognoistre t'arrester,
 Pourquoi mon cœur pense et soupire,
  Souverain Sire.

Enten à la voix tres-ardente,
De ma clameur, mon Dieu mon Roy,
Veu que tant seulement à toi
Ma supplication presente
  J'offre et presente.

Matin devant que jour il face,
S'il te plaist, tu m'exauceras :
Car bien matin prié seras
De moi, leuant au ciel la face,
  Attendant grace.

Tu es le vrai Dieu qui meschance
N' aimes point, ne malignité :

Introd.
1557.

Villegagnon's singular demeanor.

Richer, one of the two ministers, preached, taking for his text the fourth verse of the xxviith Psalm: One thing have I desired of the Lord, that will I seek after, that I may dwell in the house of the Lord all the days of my life. Doubtless the discourse was eloquent,[1] as the occasion was inspiring. But the preacher's attention, and that of his audience, must have been greatly distracted by the singular conduct of their host. Villegagnon, throughout the sermon, "ceased not to clasp his hands, raise his eyes to heaven, heave deep sighs, and assume other like expressions, insomuch that every one marveled." Less edifying was the surprise that awaited the voyagers, on the same day, when, a few hours later, they were summoned into the cabin, now transformed into a dining-hall. It was a sorry feast to which the austere commander invited them: consisting of boiled fish, and bread prepared after the manner of the savages from dried roots reduced to flour, together with certain other roots baked in the ashes. The rocky island, upon which the little settlement was perched, contained neither spring nor

---

    Et auec qui en verité
Malfaicteurs n' auront accointance,
    Ne demeurance.

Jamais le fol et temeraire
N'ose apparoir devant tes yeux :
Car tousiours te sont odieux
Ceux qui prenent plaisir à faire
    Mauuais affaire.

[1] "Il avoit le talent de la parole," says Arcère.—*Histoire de la ville de la Rochelle*, II., 103.

running stream, and the only beverage provided for the company was drawn from a tank which Villegagnon's men had dug upon their first arrival.

The sober meal concluded, Du Pont and his companions were led to the quarters provided for them. These were small Indian huts, built near the water's edge, which the savages in the governor's employ were just completing, by roofing them over with grass. For beds, they had hammocks, suspended in the air, according to the South American custom.[1] But it was a sleepless night, we may suppose, to some of the party, if not to all. The air was balmy—as mild as that of May in their native land. The cloudless heavens, revealing new constellations—the bay, its irregular shores fringed with graceful palm-trees—the encircling mountains, that recalled to the Genevese their own majestic Alps —must have kept the eyes of more than one of them waking. But to the pious ministers, at least, the mental prospect was still more impressive. This, then, was the New World, where the Gospel of the Son of God, so lately revealed in its purity to the nations of Europe, was to be

---

[1] The Portuguese missionaries who found their way to Brazil about the same time with the French Calvinists, speak of the Indian hammock as a novel but an agreeable contrivance. It is still in use at the present day, among the tribes of the Rio Negro and the Amazon. The hammock is woven from the fibrous portions of certain varieties of the palm-tree.—Brazil and the Brazilians, by Rev. James C. Fletcher and Rev. D. P. Kidder, D.D., sixth edition, pp. 68, 468.

preached to savage tribes still immersed in heathen darkness.[1] Here, in the first mission-field of Protestantism, the pure doctrines of Christianity were to be announced, before the emissaries of Loyola could introduce their corrupted creed. Here, "Antarctic France" was to be possessed for the king, and for that persecuted cause to which the good Coligny was lending his powerful influence.[2] It is not unlikely, however, that these glowing anticipations may have been shaded somewhat by recollections of the past few hours, as the ministers remembered with perplexity the singular demeanor of Villegagnon at the religious service in which they had engaged, and his excessive protestations of zeal for the reformed religion.

Three weeks passed by, and the commander's great show of piety was kept up so admirably, that the good minister Richer, captivated by his eloquence and soundness in the faith, declared to his companions that they ought to esteem themselves happy in having a second Saint Paul in this extraordinary man. To testify his zeal for religion, Villegagnon lost no time in establishing an order of public worship for his colony. Evening prayer was to be said daily, after the

---

[1] "Voyage... qui donna une merveilleuse espérance d'avancer le royaume de Dieu jusques au bout du monde."—Theodore de Bèze, Histoire ecclésiastique, livre II.

[2] "Osant assurer qu' il ne se trouvera a par toute l'antiquité qu' il y ait iamais eu Capitaine François et Chrestien, qui tout à une fois ait estendu le regne de Jesus Christ Roy des Rois, et Seigneur des Seigneurs, et les limites de son Prince Souuerain en pays si lointain."—De Léry.

colonists had left their work:[1] and a sermon, not exceeding one hour in length, was to be preached. It was on Sunday, the twenty-first of March, 1557, that this order of worship was solemnly inaugurated. A preparatory service was held, according to the custom already adopted in the French Reformed Churches; and those who wished to communicate were catechised. At the celebration of the Lord's Supper which followed, Villegagnon insisted that the shipmasters and seamen who were not of the Reformed religion should go out from the assembly; and then, to the amazement of some and the edification of others, he kneeled down, and offered two lengthy prayers. After this he presented himself the first to receive the sacrament, kneeling upon a piece of velvet cloth which a page had spread on the ground before him.

The two ministers were perhaps the last to see any occasion for uneasiness in the governor's conduct. The ship that sailed early in April on its homeward trip, carried letters from Richer and Chartier to Calvin and to another correspondent, extolling in rapturous terms their "brother and father" the sieur de Villegagnon.[2] The colony under his pious care presents the appearance of a Christian household, or rather of a church, like that which in apostolic times gathered in the house of Nymphas. From this nucleus, it is to be hoped, illustrious churches shall spring forth,

---

[1] "Apres qu'on avoit laissé la besongne."—Lescarbot.
[2] See these letters, in the appendix to this volume.

and overspread the vast continent of Antarctic France, which is now waiting for the Gospel. Concerning the barbarous inhabitants of the land, the ministers write with undissembled horror. Not only are they accustomed to eat human flesh, but they seem to be in all respects sunk to the very level of the beasts, not knowing good from evil, and having no conception of the being of a God. The ministers are oppressed with a sense of their inability to reach these perishing heathen, with the good news of Redemption. Their unacquaintance with the language of the aborigines, and the want of competent interpreters, shut them off from immediate effort in this direction. But great things are expected of the young men who have come from Geneva expressly to learn the native dialect, and prepare themselves to preach the Gospel to the savages. They have already begun this work, and are spending their time on shore among the people. God grant, adds Richer, that this may be without peril to their own souls.

Villegagnon himself wrote to the great reformer, by the same ship. His letter is not surpassed by that of Richer and Chartier, in the profusion of its assurances of respect and devotion. He acknowledges the letter which he has received from Calvin by these brethren, and promises for himself and for his colony that the counsels given shall be observed even to the minutest particulars. He rejoices in the coming of the ministers, to relieve him of the burden of care for the spiritual interests of his followers, and to aid him by their advice and sympathy in all things. He recounts the hardships and perplexities of his undertaking, and especially his anxieties for the moral and religious welfare of the colonists. Nothing, indeed, but a regard for his own good name, prevents him from doing as others have done, and abandoning the enterprise. But he is confident that, having a work to do for Christ, he will be sustained and prospered. He closes his long letter with best wishes for the lengthened life and usefulness of the reformer and his colleagues, and sends his special salutations to the pious Renée of France, the daughter of Louis XII., and the warm friend of Calvin and of the Protestant cause.

Before the vessel that bore these letters could reach its destination, the aspect of affairs on the island Coligny had greatly changed. Villegagnon's zeal for orthodoxy and strictness of living had passed into captiousness and querulousness, ending in pronounced opposition. He began by finding fault with the manner of celebrating the Lord's Supper and of administering Baptism, as practiced by the Genevan ministers. Protesting that he wished only to know and to follow the teachings of the Gospel, he sent one of the ministers, Guillaume Chartier, to France, by a vessel homeward bound from the coast of Brazil, in order to confer with the principal Reformed theologians upon certain questions of dogma and casuistry which he had

Introd.
1557.
April.

Gathering clouds.

raised.¹ The same ship carried to France ten young savages, who had been captured in war by one of the native tribes friendly to the French, and sold to Villegagnon as slaves. These were designed as a present to the king, who graciously received them, and distributed them among the nobles of his court. Villegagnon did not wait for the minister's return,² to announce his conclusions with reference to the Protestant doctrines. He soon declared that his opinion of Calvin had been changed, and that he now held the so-called reformer to be an arch-heretic and an apostate. Villegagnon attributed this change in his religious views to the arguments of one Jean Contat,³ a student

---

¹ According to De Léry—who, however, confesses his inability to understand Villegagnon's views—he rejected both the doctrine of Transubstantiation and that of Consubstantiation, and yet held to the bodily presence of Christ in the Lord's Supper, in a sense peculiarly his own. The practical questions upon which he professed a desire for instruction, were such as these: Whether the Lord's Supper should be celebrated with a certain degree of pomp: whether the wine should be mingled with water: whether unleavened bread ought to be used: whether, if any of the consecrated bread should remain after the celebration of the ordinance, it ought to be set aside as sacred, etc.—La France Protestante, deuxième edition. Vol. III., p. 795.

² Chartier, indeed, did not return to Brazil. He incurred Calvin's displeasure by delaying the fulfillment of his mission for several months after his arrival in Europe. His excuse was, that certain important despatches, which he was expecting from Brazil, had been withheld by Villegagnon. Nothing is known positively concerning Chartier's subsequent career; but there are reasons for identifying him with a minister of the same name, who was chaplain to Jeanne d'Albret, about the year 1581.—La France Protestante: ubi supra.

³ "Un nommé Jean Contat étudiant de Sorbonne, aspir-

of the University of Paris, who had abjured the Roman Catholic faith, but who soon began to discuss points of theology with the ministers, generally taking the side of Rome. It was shrewdly suspected, however, that certain letters of warning which the commander received about this time from France had more to do with his conversion.[1] Villegagnon found that in his professions of friendliness toward the Reformed religion he had gone too far. While seeking to ingratiate himself with Coligny and the Protestant party, whose favor he needed for the success of his expedition, he was in danger of incurring the displeasure of the king.

The colonists were sorely disappointed in their leader. But they had still greater cause for uneasiness, in view of the change of temper that accompanied this change of religious profession. Villegagnon became moody and capricious. His eccentric manners, indicating an unbalanced mind, his frequent outbursts of

---

ant secrètement à je ne sais quelle dignité épiscopale aussi fantastique qu'était le royaume de Villegagnon, étant venu le jour destiné pour célébrer la Cène, demanda où étaient les habillemens sacerdotaux, et commença de disputer du pain sans levain, qu'il disait être necessaire, et de mêler de l'eau avec le vin de la Cène, avec autres questions semblables. . . . Le différent ne laissa pas de croître, voire jusques à ce point, que Richer faisant un baptême, condamnant la superstition qu'on y ajoute, Villegagnon démentit tout hautement le ministre, protestant de ne se trouver plus à ses sermons, et de n'adhérer à la secte qu'il appellait calvinienne."—De Bèze, Histoire universelle, livre II.

[1] "Sollicité, comme l' on croit, par les lettres du Cardinal de Lorraine."—De Thou, Histoire Universelle, tome II., p. 383.

Introd.
1557.

violent rage, and the cruel punishments he inflicted on any that displeased him, alienated and disgusted his followers. Several of them abandoned the colony, and went off to seek their fortune in the wilderness. More than one conspiracy against the governor's life was detected among the soldiers and seamen on the island. Toward Du Pont and his associates, he now showed himself haughty and overbearing. At length they declared plainly to the commander, that since he had rejected the Gospel, they considered themselves no longer bound to serve him, and refused to work at the building

Rupture with the Genevese.
of the fort. Thereupon, Villegagnon cut short their provisions, and threatened to put them in irons. The threat precipitated a rupture which could not have been long deferred. Du Pont answered for his brethren, that they would not submit to such treatment; and that inasmuch as he was not disposed to maintain them in the exercise of their religion, they renounced his authority. Villegagnon quailed before this fearless and determined attitude, and made no attempt to execute his threat. But not long after, he resolved to rid himself altogether of the Protestant leaders, and ordered them to leave the island. They obeyed at once—"Although," observes one of them in his narrative of the expedition, "we, ourselves, might have readily driven him from the place, but we would give him no occasion to complain of us." Removing to the main land, they awaited the departure of a ship from the coast of Normandy, which was

then taking in her cargo for the homeward trip.¹

The Genevese had spent eight months on the island Coligny.² Two months more elapsed before the vessel was ready to sail. Meanwhile Du Pont and his companions, who were now at liberty to employ themselves as they pleased, beguiled the time by visiting some of the friendly tribes of Indians in the neighborhood. The savages appear to have been singularly susceptible of religious emotions. One day, Jean de Léry tells us, as he was walking in the forest, accompanied by three or four of the natives, the grandeur and beauty of the tropical scenery so enchanted him that he could not refrain from singing, and he broke forth in the words of the metrical psalm: "*Sus, sus, mon ame, il te faut dire bien.*"³ His companions,

Psalm-singing in the forest.

---

¹ De Léry, Histoire d'un Voyage fait en la Terre du Bresil, p. 95. De Thou, Histoire Universelle, tome II., p. 383.

² Two of Du Pont's followers, the sieurs de la Chapelle and du Boissi, remained with Villegagnon after the departure of the others; but they soon joined their brethren on the main.—(De Léry, p. 378.)

³ Sus, sus, mon ame, il te faut dire bien
De l'Eternel : ô mon vrai Dieu, combien
Ta grandeur est excellent' et notoire !
Tu es vestu de splendeur et de gloire :
Tu es vestu de splendeur proprement,
Ne plus ne moins que d'un accoustrement :
Pour pavillon que d'un tel Roi soit digne,
Tu rends le ciel ainsi qu'une courtine

Lambrisé d'eaux est ton palais vousté :
En lieu de char, sur la nue es porté :
Et les forts vents qui parmi l'air souspirent
Ton chariot avec leurs ailes tirent.

ATTEMPTED SETTLEMENTS: BRAZIL.

Introd.
1557.

filled with surprise and delight, asked the meaning of the words. When this had been explained to them, they exclaimed, using their ordinary expression of wonder and admiration, "*Tch!* O how happy are you, to know so many things that are hidden from us poor miserable creatures!"[1]

A Brazilian village.

On another occasion, a few of the French were entertained with great hospitality in one of the principal villages of the region, some miles back from the coast. The whole population of the place collected around the strangers, as they seated themselves at the feast prepared for them, the old men of the village, proud of the honor shown to their people by the visit of these distinguished guests, constituting themselves a body guard to keep the children from disturbing them. Each of them was armed with a curious weapon, two or three feet long, in the shape of a saw, made of the spine of a large fish. At the close of the feast, one of these old men approached the party, and asked the meaning of a strange procedure which he had noticed. Twice —before partaking of food, and again after eating—he had seen the Frenchmen remove their hats, and remain perfectly still, while one of their

---

Des vents aussi diligens et legers
Fais tes herauts, postes et messagers :
Et foudre et feu fort prompts à ton service,
Sont les sergeans de ta haute justice.   Ps. civ.

[1] "Usant de leur interjection desbahissement *Tch!* ils dirent, O que vous autres Mairs estent heureux de scavoir tant de secrets qui sont cachez à nous chetifs & pouvres miserables."—De Léry. Histoire d'un Voyage fait en la Terre du Bresil, p. 290.

number uttered some words. To whom was he speaking? Was it to them, or to some person not present? The pious Huguenots thought this a providential opening for the instruction of these savages in the true religion; and they hastened to enter it, with the help of the interpreter who accompanied them. They told them of the great God to whom they prayed, and who, though they could not see Him, heard their words and knew their most secret thoughts. It was this God who had brought them in safety across the wide ocean, preserving them during a voyage of many months, while they were out of sight of the solid land; and because they served Him and trusted in Him, they had no fear of being tormented by Aigna—the dreaded demon of these savages—either in this life or in one to come. They exhorted their hearers to abandon the errors taught them by their lying priests, and especially to leave off the barbarous practice of eating the flesh of their enemies, promising them that if they would do this, they should enjoy the same blessings with themselves. The Indians listened with breathless attention to the account of the creation of the world and the fall of man, in which, says Jean de Léry, who was the spokesman, "I endeavored to show them man's lost condition, and so prepare them to receive Jesus Christ." The discourse lasted two hours, and left the audience in a state of great amazement. At length one of the old men replied. "Certainly," said he, "these are wonderful things that you have told us, and things that are very good, though we have never known them till now. Nevertheless, your words have brought to my mind what we have often heard our fathers relate, namely, that long ago, so many moons that we have not been able to keep the reckoning of them, there came a *Mair*—a European—clothed and bearded like some of you, who tried to persuade our people to obey your God, telling them what you have just told us. But our people would not believe his teachings; and when he left there came another, who gave them a sword, in token of a curse,[1] and from that time to this we have slain one another with the sword, insomuch that, having become used to it, if now we should forsake our ancient custom, all the other tribes around us would laugh us to scorn."[2] The French warmly remonstrated with

---

[1] De Léry speculates as to the *Mair* who had come so many hundreds of years before to announce the true God to the natives of Brazil, and somewhat timidly ventures the query, "si c'auroit point esté l'un des Apostres." As for the one who followed, he suggests the apocalyptic vision of the red horse and him that sat thereon, to whom it was given "to take peace from the earth, and that they should kill one another: and there was given unto him a great sword."—Revelation, vi. 4.

[2] "Nous fusmes plus de 2. heures sur ceste matiere de la creation, dont pour brieveté ie ne feray ici plus long discours. Or tous prestans l'oreille, avec grande admiration escoutoyent attentivement de maniere qu'estans entrez en esbahissement de ce qu'ils auoyent ouy, il y eut un vieillard qui prenant la parole dit: Certainement vous nous auez dit merueilles, & choses tres bonnes que nous n'auions iamais entendües: toutesfois, dit-il, vostre harengue m'a fait rememorer ce que nous auõs ouy reciter beaucoup de fois à nos grãds peres: assauoir que des longtemps & dés le nombre de tãt de Lunes que nous n'en auons pus

their hearers. They entreated them to disregard the foolish ridicule to which they might be subjected, and assured them that if they would worship and serve the one living and true God, He would help them; and should their enemies attack them on that account, they should vanquish them all. "In short," says Jean de Léry, "our hearers were so moved by the power which God gave to our words, that some of them promised to follow our teachings, and declared that they would never again eat human flesh: and the interview closed with a prayer offered by one of our company, which our interpreter translated into their language, the savages kneeling together with us." It must be added, however, that the hopes awakened in the hearts of the zealous missionaries were soon grievously disappointed: for in the middle of the night, as they lay in the hammocks which the hospitable savages had provided for them, they heard the whole band singing a war-song, the purport of which was, that to revenge themselves on their enemies, they

Introd.
1557.

The warsong.

---

retenir le conte, un *Mair*, c'est à dire François ou etranger vestu & barbu comme aucuns de vous autres, vint en ce pays ici, lequel pour les penser ranger à l'obeissance de vostre Dieu, leur tint le mesme lãgage que vous nous auez maintenant tenu: mais comme nous tenons aussi de peres en fils, ils ne le voulurent pas croire: & partant il en vint vn autre qui en signe de malediction leur bailla l'espeé, dequoy depuis nous nous sommes tousiours tuez l'vn l'autre; tellement, qu'en estans entrez si auant en possession, si maintenant laissans nostre coustume nous desistions, toutes les nations qui nous sont voisines se moqueroyent de nous."—De Léry, pp. 283, 284.

must slay and eat more victims than ever before. "Such," says De Léry, "is the inconstancy of these poor people, a striking illustration of human depravity. "Notwithstanding," he adds, " I verily believe that if Villegagnon had not proved recreant to the Reformed religion, and had we have remained longer in that country, some of them might have been attracted and won to Christ."[1]

There are few accounts of peril and suffering at sea more frightful than that of the returning voyage of Du Pont and his companions, from the coast of Brazil. The story has been minutely told by two of the sufferers, the minister Richer, and Jean de Léry. The ship on which they had taken passage proved to be a crazy bark, leaky and worm-eaten, and almost waterlogged. Before they were out of sight of land, five of the party losing heart asked to be sent back. They were accordingly put in a boat, and reached the shore safely, but only to meet from Villegagnon a worse fate than that of their brethren. The rest pursued their way; and after five months, in the course of which a number died of sheer starvation, the survivors landed in a state of indescribable misery, upon the coast of Bretagne. But their dangers were not over when they had escaped the perils of the sea. Villegagnon had intrusted the master

---

[1] "Toutesfois i' ay opinion que si Villegagnon ne se fust reuolté de la Religion reformée, & que nous fussions demeurez plus longtemps en ce pays là, qu'on en eust attiré & gagné quelques vns à Iesus Christ."

of the ship with a packet of letters, to be delivered to certain persons on his arrival in France. Among these letters, there was one addressed to the nearest magistrate. It contained a formal accusation against the bearers, as heretics, and recommended that they be forthwith consigned to the stake. Happily, the sieur Du Pont, the leader of the little band, took counsel with some magistrates whom he found to be well affected toward the Protestant cause. These, so far from molesting the travelers, entertained them with the utmost kindness, and sent them on their journey.[1]

Little remains to be said of the unfortunate Brazilian expedition. Three of the five men who had turned back to the ship, were at once sentenced by Villegagnon to be drowned, as heretics and rebels. The names of these sufferers have been preserved, and enrolled in the martyrology of the French Reformation. They were Pierre Bourdon,[2] Jean du Bordel, and Mathieu Verneuil. "Thus," observes Jean de

---

[1] Pierre Richer, dit de Lisle, made his way to La Rochelle, where he found the nucleus of a Protestant congregation, which had been gathered by Charles de Clermont a few months before. He deserves, says Callot, to be regarded as the father of the Rochellese reformation, because of the part he took in the organization of the church in that place. On Sunday, November 17, 1558, he officiated at the formation of the first Consistory of La Rochelle. (La Rochelle protestante, pp. 24, 25.) Richer died in La Rochelle, March 8, 1580. (Ibid. See also Delmas, Eglise réformée de la Rochelle, p. 434.)

[2] Pierre Bourdon was a native of Ambonay in Champagne, France, who had taken refuge at Geneva in September, 1555.

54 ATTEMPTED SETTLEMENTS: BRAZIL.

<small>Introd.
1558.</small>

Léry, "Villegagnon was the first to shed the blood of God's children in that newly-discovered country; and because of that cruel deed, he has well been called *the Cain of America.*"

Of the Protestants who had remained on the island, a number now escaped to the continent. They soon fell into the hands of the Portuguese, who were not more disposed than the treacherous Villegagnon to show mercy to Calvinists. One of the fugitives was induced by threats or by promises to renounce his faith. Three others were thrown into prison. Among <small>Jean Boles.</small> these was a man of note, Jean Boles, a scholar versed in the Greek and Hebrew languages. The Jesuits spared no effort to persuade him to follow his companion's example. Boles, however, remained firm throughout a captivity of eight years. At the end of that time, the Jesuit <small>1567.</small> Provincial ordered him to be brought to the newly-founded city of St. Sebastian—now Rio de Janeiro—and there put to a cruel death, in order that any of his Protestant countrymen, still lingering in that region, might take warning by his fate. The Jesuit writers represent this martyr as having recanted shortly before his execution. If so, his recantation must have been made, according to their own showing, under promise of reprieve, or of an easier mode of death. For they relate, that when the executioner showed awkwardness in the performance of his work, the Provincial interposed, and gave him directions how to dispatch the heretic more speedily, "fearing lest he should become impatient, being an obstinate man, and newly reclaimed."

Meanwhile, Villegagnon's colony had been entirely broken up by the Portuguese. Soon after the departure of Du Pont and the other Protestant leaders for Europe, the commander himself returned to France, where he at once avowed himself a zealous champion of the Church of Rome.[1] It was noticed that this change of faith coincided with Coligny's imprisonment by the Spaniards after the defeat of St. Quentin. The powerful patron upon whose help he had depended for the carrying out of his ambitious plans, was now in captivity; and Villegagnon sought a new master.[2]

Introd. 1567.

August 27, 1557.

---

[1] There seems to be no room for doubt as to Villegagnon's duplicity. That he professed to favor the Reformed doctrines, the accounts given by De Léry, Lescarbot, Théodore de Bèze, and Agrippa d'Aubigné, and his own letter to Calvin (see the appendix to this volume,) abundantly prove. On the other hand, the Roman Catholic writers make no mention of a departure from the Roman faith: and he appears upon his return to France only as a vehement foe of Protestantism, using both sword and pen against its adherents. If Claude Haton is to be credited, Villegagnon carried with him to Brazil all the requisites for the celebration of the Mass ("ornemens d'église pour dire la messe."—Mémoires, I., 38.) An estimate of his character would be incomplete, however, that should not take into account, together with his insincerity, his eccentricities of conduct while in Brazil, indicating apparently some degree of mental aberration.

[2] Villegagnon died January 15, 1571. He was a native of Provins, in Champagne. His fellow-townsman, Claude Haton, eulogizes him as a valiant servant of the king, and defender of the Church, " ennemy capital " of the heretical Huguenots, whom he opposed to his utmost with temporal and spiritual arms. " Il a faict plusieurs beaux livres latins

56 ATTEMPTED SETTLEMENTS: BRAZIL.

Introd.
1560.

Coligny
undis-
couraged.

Early in the year 1560, a Portuguese fleet arrived at Rio de Janeiro. The little garrison which Villegagnon had left in charge of Fort Coligny was overpowered after a brave resistance. Some of the occupants escaped to the main land, where they sought refuge among the savages; others were mercilessly butchered; and soon every trace of the French occupation disappeared from the island.

Coligny's first experiment in colonization had failed, and the hopes that had been awakened throughout Protestant France, of a place of refuge from religious oppression in the New World, lay prostrate. But Coligny himself was not one to be discouraged by failure. There was much to account for the ill success of the expedition to Brazil, especially in the character and conduct of its chief; but for whose faithlessness or imbecility, it must have seemed then as it has seemed since, a French colony might have flourished at Rio de Janeiro, and the dream of an "Antarctic France" might have been realized. Such a settlement would have speedily received large accessions, and would have found itself strong enough to hold its ground against the enemy. Indeed, when the news of Villegagnon's treachery reached Europe, a company of emigrants, numbering seven or eight hund-

---

et françoys, pour confuter la faulse oppinion de son compaignon d'escolle, Jehan Calvin, de Genefve, et autres prédicans de la faulse oppinion luthérienne et huguenoticque." (Mémoires de Claude Haton, publiés par M. Felix Bourquelot. Paris, 1857. Tome II., p. 623.)

red, was preparing to join the colony; and it was estimated by Jean de Léry, that ten thousand French Protestants would soon have crossed the ocean to Brazil.[1]

The baseness of one man had ruined the scheme which promised so much for France and for America. But there were others in the Protestant ranks, tried and trusted leaders, who stood ready for a second venture, upon Coligny's bidding; and the harbors of Bretagne and Normandy swarmed with men as ready to follow. The times also, if not brighter, were more opportune. The *Huguenots*, as they now began to be called, had become a recognized power in the land; with two princes of the blood—Antoine, king of Navarre, and his brother, Louis, prince of Condé—at their head. There was a lull in the storm of persecution. Nearly thirty-seven years had passed since Jean Leclerc, the first conpicuous martyr of the Reformation in France,

---

[1] "Car quoy qu' aucuns disent, veu le peu de temps que ces choses ont duré, & que n'y estoit à present non plus de nouvelle de vraye Religion que de nom de François pour y habiter, qu'on n'en doit faire estime : nonobstant telles allegations, ce que j'ay dit ne laisse pas de demeurer tousiours tellement vray, que tout ainsi que l'Evangile du fils de Dieu a esté de nos jours annoncé en ceste quarte partie du monde dite Amerique, aussi est-il très certain si l' affaire eust esté aussi bien poursuivi qu'il avoit esté heureusement commencé, que l' un & l' autre Regne spirituel & temporel, y avoyent si bien prins pied de nostre temps, que plus de dix mille personnes de la nation Françoise y seroient maintenant en aussi plein & seure possession pour nostre Roy, que les Espagnols y sont au nom de leurs."—Histoire d' un Voyage fait en la Terre du Bresil. P. 2.

had been burned at Metz; and each intervening year had witnessed the sufferings, in every part of the kingdom, of those who had been tried, condemned, and sentenced to the prison, the torture or the stake, for the crime of heresy. Edict after edict of the government had pronounced the penalties of imprisonment, confiscation of goods, and death, upon the followers of Luther and Calvin, and while enforcing persecution under the forms of law, had encouraged the countless deeds of violence which a lawless populace stood always ready to perpetrate. The latest of these edicts was the most severe and sweeping. It inflicted punishment by imprisonment and confiscation upon all who, whether armed or unarmed, should attend any heretical service of worship, public or private. The passage of this law intensified the feelings of hostility, which were soon to break out into open strife, between the two great religious parties. While the Romanists exulted, the Protestants did not conceal their indignation. Even Coligny, pacific, and anxious to avert the impending calamity of civil war, declared plainly that the "Edict of July," as it was called, could never be carried into effect. But meanwhile, as the strength of the Protestant party grew more apparent, and its position more menacing, the necessity of conciliation became obvious to the court. Catharine de Medici, now regent of the kingdom during the minority of her son Charles IX., turned to Coligny for advice. The Admiral counseled toleration; and to show the expediency of toleration, he presented to Catharine a list of the Protestant churches of France, already numbering two thousand one hundred and fifty, that asked for freedom and protection in the exercise of their religion. His advice was heeded; and the "Edict of July" was followed, six months later, by the "Edict of January," 1562. It was now that for the first time the existence of "the new religion" became recognized in France as legal, and as claiming some degree of protection under the laws. The penalties previously pronounced on its adherents were provisionally repealed, until a general Council of the Church could be called for the settlement of all questions of religious faith. Protestants throughout the kingdom were to be exempt from all molestation, while proceeding on their way to their religious assemblies and in returning from them; and the presence of an officer of the government at every ecclesiastical meeting gave dignity and legality to the proceedings of the Protestant consistories, colloquies, and synods.

Such was the favorable juncture which Coligny chose for a second effort to accomplish his cherished plan of American colonization. Little did the sagacious statesman and chieftain dream that the year which was opening so auspiciously would prove one of the darkest in the history of France! Six weeks from the date of the promulgation of the Edict of January, the massacre at Vassy precipitated the outbreak of the First Civil War; and for the next ten months the kingdom

Introd. 1561.

Edict of January, 1562.

Civil war impending.

was a scene of horrible massacre and devastation.

Introd. 1562.

All this was happily unforeseen by the brave men who set sail from the port of Havre, in Normandy, on the eighteenth day of February, 1562, for the coast of Florida. At their head was Jean Ribaut, an experienced officer of the Reformed party, whom Coligny had chosen to lead them. Preparations for the expedition had been going on for some months in that harbor, of which the Admiral had lately been appointed governor; and a goodly number of volunteers had responded to the invitation to join it. Nearly all the soldiers and laborers, as well as a few noblemen who presented themselves, were Calvinists. The only names that have come down to us are those of René de Laudonnière, Nicolas Barré, Nicolas Mallon, Fiquinville, Sale, Albert, Lacaille, the drummer Guernache, and the soldiers Lachère, Aymon, Rouffi, and Martin Atinas. The first of these, René de Laudonnière, was no ordinary man. An experienced navigator, and a man of tried integrity, he enjoyed the full confidence of Coligny, whom he greatly resembled in character. Nicolas Barré had accompanied Villegagnon in the expedition to Brazil. Others of the party were veteran seamen, and were familiar with the region about to be visited.

February 18.

The Expedition.

To avoid the Spaniards, Ribaut took a more direct course across the Atlantic than that which was usually followed; and on the last day of April his little fleet, composed of two staunch

THE RIVER OF MAY. 61

but unwieldy ships, arrived off the coast of Florida. Proceeding northward along the coast, they found themselves the next day at the mouth of a large river, which they named the River of May—now the St. John's. Here they landed; and the first impulse of the Huguenots was to kneel down upon the shore, in thanksgiving to God, and in prayer that he would bless their enterprise, and that he would bring to the knowledge of the Saviour the heathen inhabitants of this new world. Their actions were watched with wonder by a company of the friendly natives, who had gathered fearlessly around them and who sat motionless during the strange ceremonial. After this, Ribaut took formal possession of the country in the name of the King of France, and set up a pillar of stone, engraven with the royal arms, upon a small elevation in a grove of cypress and palm trees near the harbor.

Returning to their ships, the French continued the exploration of the coast, until they reached a broad estuary to which they gave a name which it has retained to the present day. It was the channel of Port Royal. The voyagers had passed the northern limit of Florida, as it was to be defined in later days, and, leaving untried the shallow inlets along the sandy shore of Georgia, found themselves off the coast of South Carolina. Entering the harbor, "one of the largest and fairest of the greatest havens of the world," Ribaut decided here to lay the foundations of a colony. The site of a fort was chosen, not far from the present town of Beau-

Introd.
1562.

May 1.

Port Royal.

> Introd.
> 1562.

fort. It was called Charlesfort, in honor of the boy-king who had lately come to the throne of France. Ribaut did not wait to see the work completed. His present voyage was one of exploration chiefly. Report of the discoveries made and the enterprise begun must be carried to the king; and larger supplies of men and of means for the establishment of the colony must be secured. Leaving, therefore, a few of his followers to garrison the little fort, Ribaut, with Laudonnière and the others, set sail for Europe, and arrived in Dieppe on the twentieth day of July, only five months from the time of their embarkation.

> Outbreak of the first civil war.

Meanwhile, however, civil war had broken out in France. The unprovoked attack of the Duke of Guise upon an assembly of Protestants, met for worship in one of the towns of Champagne, and the slaughter of fifty or sixty inoffensive persons in cold blood, had stirred the long suffering Huguenots as none of the many preceding outrages inflicted upon them had done. For the first time, they took up arms in good earnest to defend their civil and religious rights. The Protestant nobility of the kingdom gathered around the Prince of Condé, their recognized leader. Coligny himself, whose cautious and patriotic spirit shrank from the prospect of a civil conflict, at length decided to join his brethren in the field. The moment was unfavorable, in which to plead for re-enforcements in behalf of a distant colony. Failing in his efforts to do this, or swept against his will into the

FATE OF CHARLESFORT. 63

current of political excitement at home, Ribaut entered the Protestant ranks under his old leader the Admiral, and the next year, upon the return of peace, took refuge, for some reason, in England.

The handful of men left in possession of the fort near Port Royal, met a miserable fate. Undisciplined and improvident, they soon fell into disputes among themselves, murdered their captain, Albert, whom Ribaut had placed in command, consumed all the supplies they had brought with them, and after subsisting for awhile upon the charity of their generous savage neighbors, set themselves in their desperation to build a boat, upon which, after incredible sufferings, they succeeded in reaching Europe.

Coligny was still ignorant of this wretched failure of his second attempt to establish a colony in America, when the peace of Amboise brought the first civil war to a close, and set him free to resume his efforts in behalf of commerce and colonization. Representing to the king that no tidings had yet arrived from the men whom Ribaut had left in Florida, he obtained permission to fit out three ships, of sixty, one hundred, and one hundred and twenty tons respectively, to go in search of them, and to bring them relief. René de Laudonnière was chosen as chief of the new expedition, and a number of noblemen, and of experienced officers and sailors, volunteered to join it. Among the noblemen were d'Ottigny, d'Erlach, officers, and de la Rocheferrière, de Marillac, de Gron-

64 ATTEMPTED SETTLEMENTS: FLORIDA

Introd.

1564.

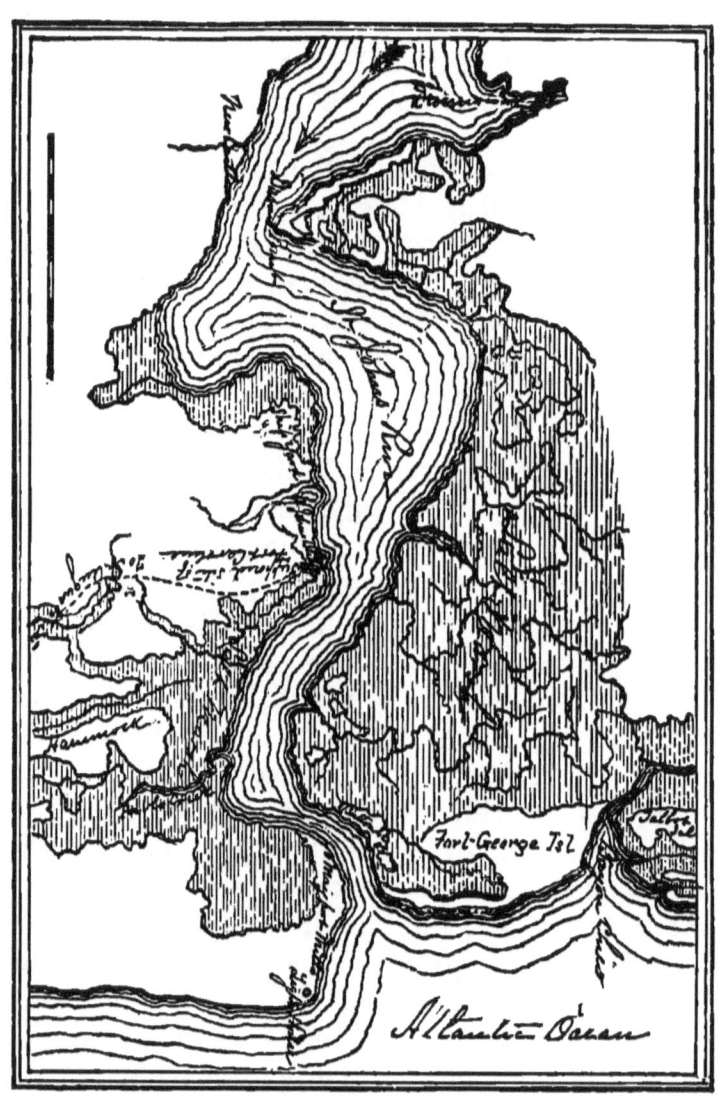

taut, and Normans de Pompierre, who went as volunteers. Michel Vasseur commanded one of the ships—the "Breton;" Jean Lucas commanded the "Elisabeth," and Pierre Marchant the "Faucon." Nicolas Vasseur and Trenchant were pilots; sergeant Lacaille was interpreter, Jean Dehaies, carpenter, and Hance, artificer. Among the seamen were Pierre Gambié, La Roquette, Le Gendre, Martin Chauveau, Bertrand, Sanferrent, La Croix, Estienne Gondeau, Grandpré, Nicholas Lemaistre, Doublet, Fourneaux, Estienne de Gênes, Jacques Salé, Le Mesureur, Barthélemy, Aymon, LaCrète, Grandchemin, Pierre Debray, and three brothers of sergeant Lacaille. The expedition was accompanied by a draughtsman, Jacques Lemoyne de Mourgues.

The adventurers sailed from Havre in April, 1564. A voyage of no more than the usual length brought them to the mouth of the St. John's, where Ribaut had first set up the arms of France. Following the course of the river for a short distance, Laudonnière chose a spot, six miles from the sea, as the site of a projected town, and at once began the building of a fort which he named La Caroline. The locality is now known as St. John's Bluff.[1] The Hugue-

---

[1] "The river St. John's . . . is more like an arm of the sea than a river; from its mouth for a distance of fifteen miles, it is spread over extensive marshes, and there are few points where the channel touches the banks of the river. At its mouth it is comparatively narrow, but immediately extends itself over wide-spread marshes; and the first headland or shore which is washed by the channel is a place

Introd.
1564.
July 1.

nots after their pious usage inaugurated the work with their simple and hearty worship. "There," in the language of the commander himself, "we sang praises to the Lord, beseeching Him that of His holy grace He would be pleased to continue His accustomed goodness to us, and henceforth help us in all our undertakings, in such wise that the whole might redound to His glory, and to the furtherance of our faith. Prayers ended, each one began to take courage."

But the brief history of this expedition was to be one of disappointment and disaster throughout. Not fourteen months from the day when Laudonnière landed upon the bank of St. John's river, full of hope and courage, the spot thus consecrated with prayer and praise was reddened by the blood of his followers; and another of Coligny's experiments of colonization ter-

---

known as St. John's Bluff. Here the river runs closely by the shore, making a bold, deep channel close up to the bank. The land rises abruptly on one side into a hill of moderate height, covered with a dense growth of pine, cedar, etc. This hill gently slopes to the bank of the river, and runs off to the southwest, where, at a distance of a quarter of a mile, a creek discharges itself into the river, at a place called "the shipyard" from time immemorial. I am not aware that any remains of Fort Caroline, or any old remains of a fortress, have ever been discovered here; but it must be recollected that this fort was constructed of sand and pine trees, and that three hundred years have passed away—a period sufficient to have destroyed a work of much more durable character. Moreover, it is highly probable, judging from present appearances, that the constant abrasion of the banks, still going on, has long since worn away the narrow spot where stood Fort Caroline."—History and Antiquities of St. Augustine, Florida, by George R. Fairbanks, M. A. Pp. 26, 27.

minated in a horrible massacre. The events of that hapless year have been related with particularity by the chroniclers of the time, and by later writers. Suffice it to say here, that the French re-enacted the mistakes and the misfortunes of previous undertakings. They neglected the cultivation of the soil, yielded to the seductions of gold, and fell out among themselves. Their policy toward the natives was injudicious. Finding the savage tribes of the interior at war, and anxious to secure the white man's help, Laudonnière at first endeavored to maintain a strict neutrality; but he soon suffered himself to be drawn into alliances that proved disastrous. As a leader, he showed a deplorable lack of firmness. Insubordination and conspiracy were too easily pardoned. The young nobles, who had accompanied the expedition in the hope that they might enrich themselves from the far-famed treasures of the new world, were soured and angered by their failure to discover gold in Florida. They could not stoop to work for their bread, and they took it ill when required to do their part in the labors of fortification. The Protestants, who composed the majority of the expedition, complained of the indifference of their leader to religion. No Huguenot pastor had joined the colony; and those who had been accustomed to religious ministrations in the camp, as well as at home, declared openly that they would take the very first opportunity to leave. But the direst calamity that befell the ill-planned enterprise, was famine. By the second

Introd.
1565.

The leader's weakness.

summer, scarcity prevailed at La Caroline. No crops had been planted in the rich soil of the surrounding lands, and though the river teemed with fish, the colonists depended on their savage neighbors for the food which they would not condescend to obtain for themselves.

From this record of mistakes and calamitous errors, it is pleasant to turn for a moment to some redeeming facts in the story of the French in Florida. Unlike the Spaniards, they treated the savage inhabitants of the country with much gentleness; and their brief occupation left no such memories of cruelty as the earlier visits of the Spanish adventurers had left. The simple-minded children of the forest were greatly impressed with the habitual gayety and good nature of the French, and they were especially captivated by the sonorous singing in which the Huguenots perpetually indulged. Long after the breaking up of Laudonnière's colony, the European, cruising along the coast, or landing upon the shore, would be saluted with some snatch of a French psalm uncouthly rendered by Indian voices, in strains caught from the Calvinist soldier on patrol, or from the boatman plying his oar on the river.[1] No fierce imprecation or profane expletive lingered in the recollection of the red men, as the synonym for a French Protestant.

---

[1] Le Challeux, who states this, gives the words "*Du fond de ma pensée*" and "*Bienheureux est quiconque sert à Dieu volontiers,*" as frequently used by the Indians in this manner.

Laudonnière at length reluctantly decided to abandon the expedition, and return to Europe. Of the three small and frail vessels which had brought his followers over, only one remained that could be made sea-worthy. By the first days of August, the carpenters had completed their work; and the French were making ready for departure, when a fleet appeared off the mouth of the St. John's. The four ships of which it was composed were commanded by the famous English navigator John Hawkins. His coming was friendly; he willingly relieved from his naval stores the most pressing necessities of the French, and he offered to transport them all to France. Laudonnière declined this offer, but availed himself of the Englishman's kindness by purchasing one of his ships at a nominal price. Scarcely had this visitor disappeared, when another fleet was seen in the offing. Its admiral was Jean Ribaut, the leader of the former expedition.

Reports unfavorable to the character of Laudonnière had reached France. Coligny decided to recall him, and at the same time to send a much larger force for the occupation of Florida. Seven ships, some of them of considerable size, were fitted out for this purpose. They carried not far from one thousand men. A number of Huguenot gentlemen joined the expedition as volunteers. Among them were the sieurs de la Blonderie, d'Ully, de Beauchaire, de Lagrange, de San Marain, du Vest, de Jonville. Of the officers, the names of Jacques Ribaut, Maillard,

Introd.
1565.

August 3.

August 27.

Introd.
1565.

de Machonville, Jean Dubois, Valuot, Cosette, Louis Ballaud, Nicolas Verdier, de Saint-Clerk, de la Vigne, Du Lys, and Le Beau have come down to us. Among the artisans, seamen and soldiers, were Nicolas le Challeux, of Dieppe, Nicaise de la Crotte, François Duval, Elie Desplanques, Jacques Tauzé, Christophe Lebreton, Drouet, Jacques Dulac, Masselin, Jehan Mennin, Gros, Bellot, Martin, Pierre Rennat, Jacques, Vincent Simon, and Michel Gonnor. This time, the religious wants of the adventurers were not forgotten. At least one clergyman,[1] Robert by name, accompanied them. The minister had an efficient helper in Le Challeux, the ship-carpenter, a man of advanced years, and well versed in Holy Scripture.[2]

Third expedition.

Jean Ribaut was called home from England to command this fleet, which sailed from the harbor of Dieppe, in the latter part of May, and arrived at the mouth of St. John's river on the twenty-seventh of August. The larger ships remained at anchor, while Ribaut with three smaller vessels sailed up the river to La Caroline. Laudonnière, summoned on board the flag-ship, was soon able to clear himself from the charges which Ribaut brought to his notice, and the old associates were friends once more.

---

[1] Gaffarel intimates that more than one minister was sent.—Histoire de la Floride française, par Paul Gaffard. P. 195. "Maître Robert, qui avoit charge de faire les prieres," is the only one mentioned by Le Challeux.

[2] A graphic account of the expedition from the pen of this pious Huguenot has been preserved.

A COMMON DANGER.

But a common danger was now to cement their fortunes. Five days after Ribaut's arrival, tidings were signaled from the coast that another fleet had come in sight. It was late in the afternoon; a heavy fog was just lifting, and in the dusk the sentinels at the mouth of the river could not distinguish the nationality of the ships. The night of the third of September wore away anxiously at La Caroline. But with the dawn of the following day all uncertainty vanished. Ribaut's larger vessels were now seen to have left their anchorage, and to be making for the open sea. They had descried the approaching fleet, and recognized a dreaded foe. The Spaniards had come. Spain and France were for the time at peace. But Spain had always denied the right of France in the New World. Florida belonged to Spain by virtue of discovery; and though the Spaniards had been unsuccessful heretofore in their attempts to conquer the country, they did not propose to surrender their claim to a rival power. Least of all would they permit the hated Huguenot to establish himself upon those shores. No sooner did Philip the Second learn that such an attempt had actually been made, than he commissioned one of his bravest and most resolute captains to dislodge the audacious intruder. Pedro Menendez de Abila had now come with a strong force to execute this commission. His fleet consisted of some fifteen vessels, several of them ships of large tonnage. They carried twenty-six hundred men, Spanish and Portu-

Introd.
1565.
September 3.

The Spaniards.

March 22.

guese, the latter of whom were to distinguish themselves by their demon-like ferocity.

Menendez hoped to take the French unawares. Failing in this, he landed his men at a spot thirty miles south of the St. John's, near the present city of St. Augustine. Meanwhile the French at La Caroline were consulting as to the course to be pursued in view of this sudden danger. Laudonnière was for strengthening the fort, and harassing the enemy by land, in a series of skirmishes, aided by the friendly savages. The wisdom of this policy seemed obvious to all the members of the council of war, save one. Ribaut alone insisted upon a naval engagement. His plan was to fall upon the enemy's ships, and after disarming them, attack and destroy the forces already landed. Remonstrances and arguments availed nothing. Laudonnière was no longer in command. Had his advice been taken, "Florida," says the enthusiastic historian of *La Floride Française*, "would have remained a French country."

The four ships which had taken flight upon the approach of the Spaniards, now re-appeared. Ribaut ordered all his soldiers on board, together with as many of Laudonnière's men as were fit for service. Only those who had been wounded in a late affray with one of the Indian tribes of the interior, were left at La Caroline, with their late commander, himself disabled at the time by illness.

Heavy-hearted, Laudonnière saw his comrades sail away. His fears for the ill-judged expedition were more than realized. A furious storm soon broke upon the coast: and Ribaut's ships, driven southward, far beyond the spot where Menendez was landing his men, were miserably wrecked on the dangerous shore in the neighborhood of Cape Canaveral.

Menendez was now free to execute the work of butchery for which he had come across the Atlantic. Leaving the bulk of his little army at the fort which he had built and named St. Augustine, he took five hundred picked men and set out for La Caroline. Within three days the

Introd.
1565.
September 20.

French fort was reached.[1] Surprised in their slumbers, the sick and wounded, as well as the able-bodied, were put to the sword. Only the women and children were spared. Laudonnière and a few others fled. Among them was the Huguenot minister Robert. After many hairbreadth escapes, the fugitives reached the coast, and were taken on board one of the smaller ships which Ribaut had left in the river. It was soon joined by another of these vessels, and the two, though poorly fitted for the long voyage, succeeded in making their way across the ocean.

Ribaut surrenders.

A far more wretched fate was reserved for Ribaut and his shipwrecked followers. With great difficulty, they made their way northward through forests and swamps almost impassable, till they came in view of La Caroline, only to see the Spanish flag flying from its wall. Retracing their steps, they found themselves in the neighborhood of the Spanish force at fort St. Augustine. Ribaut sent one of his officers to ask for terms of surrender. Menendez informed the Frenchman of the slaughter of his companions at La Caroline. Even such, he coldly assured him, should be the fate of every man who professed the Protestant religion. Menendez was reminded that his nation was still at peace with France. "True," he answered, "but not so in the case of heretics, with whom I

---

[1] It was occupied by some two hundred and forty persons—invalid soldiers, artisans, women and little children. (Delaborde, Coligny, I., 447, note.)

NO TERMS WITH HERETICS. 75

shall ever carry on war in these parts: and I shall do it with all possible cruelty toward all of that sect, wherever I shall find them, whether by sea or by land. Yield yourselves to my mercy, give up your arms and your colors, and I will do as God may prompt me."

Introd. 1565. October.

We shall not reproduce here the sickening details of the massacre that followed. Ribaut announced the Spaniard's decision to his little army, and gave it as his own opinion that there was no alternative for them but surrender. Two hundred rejected the proposal, and fled into the woods. The others—one hundred and fifty in number—hoping against hope, threw themselves upon the compassion of one to whom the word had no meaning. The French accounts of the affair represent Menendez as resorting to a base subterfuge in order to induce them to submit without a struggle. In an interview with Ribaut's messenger, the Spanish commander caused one of his officers to personate him. The officer made the most solemn promise that the lives of the French should be spared. However this may be, all the authorities agree as to the fact of the surrender, and the wholesale execution. Menendez himself announced it to his government. "I had their hands tied behind their backs," he wrote to the king, "and themselves put to the sword. It appeared to me that by thus chastising them, God our Lord and your Majesty were served. Whereby in future this evil sect will leave us more free to plant the Gospel in these parts."

Butchery at St. Augustine.

Introd.
1565.

The party of two hundred that had refused to surrender with the rest, escaped the butchery. Making their way back to the place of their shipwreck, near Cape Canaveral, they attempted to construct a vessel out of the fragments of the broken ships. Menendez pursued them, but finding that they were prepared to sell their lives dear, he entered into negotiations with them, and engaged to treat them as prisoners of war. Perhaps satiated for the time with human blood, he kept the promise, until word came from the Spanish king, remanding his prisoners to the galleys.

Thus ends the story of the Huguenot expedition to Florida—in carnage, and in slavery worse than death.

Upon the spot where many of his unresisting victims were ignominiously killed, after the capture of La Caroline, Menendez placed a tablet bearing this inscription:

"Hung not as Frenchmen, but as Lutherans."

1567.
The crime avenged.

Two years later, a gallant French officer determined to avenge the slaughter of his countrymen. The horrible brutality of the Spaniards had awakened general indignation in France. The French court had loudly complained of this outrage committed upon its subjects in a time of peace between the two nations. Its remonstrances, however, made no impression upon Philip the Second, nor was any redress obtained for the widows and orphans of the butchered Huguenots. But Dominique de Gourgues, though not of the Huguenot faith, could not rest while the blood of his countrymen cried for vengeance. Through the sale of his little patrimony, and by the help of his brother, he gathered means to purchase and equip three small vessels. After a perilous voyage, De Gourgues reached the coast of Florida, enlisted the friendly Indians of the neighboring region in his service, and falling upon La Caroline, took prisoners the Spanish force by whom it was garrisoned. The greater number of these he put to the sword. The remainder he hung upon the trees from which Menendez had hung his French captives; and upon the other side of the tablet which the Spaniard had placed near by, he inscribed these words:

Introd.
1567.
August 2.

1568.

April 28.

"I do this not as unto Spaniards, nor as unto seamen, but as unto traitors, robbers, and murderers."

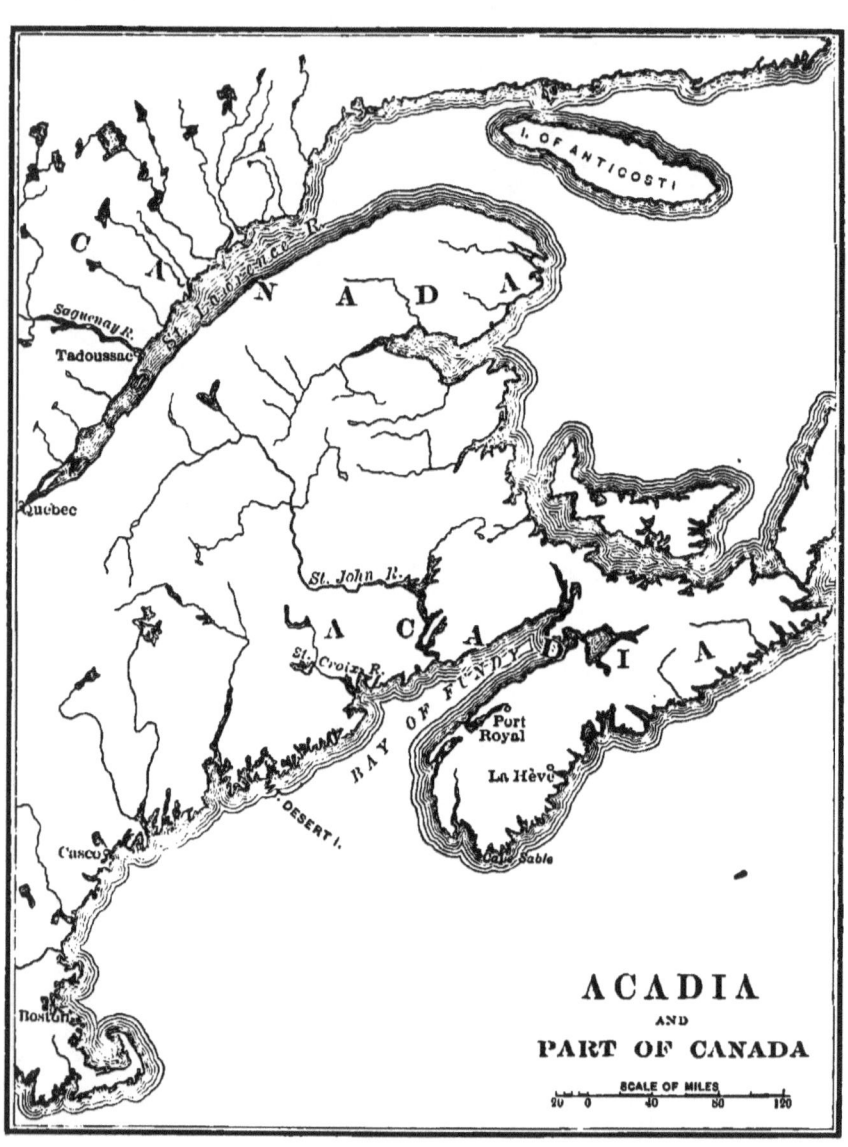

CHAPTER I.

UNDER THE EDICT.

ACADIA AND CANADA.

The Edict of Nantes was signed on the thirteenth day of April, 1598. Never were the justice and expediency of a political measure more promptly vindicated by its effects. The publication of this royal decree was followed by the speedy return of prosperity to France. In one day, says Benoist, the disasters of forty years were repaired. The civil wars had left the country in a deplorable condition. Everywhere the traces of the long struggle were to be seen, in ruined villages and dismantled castles, in farms laid waste, and cities impoverished. Under the Edict, which secured to the Protestants of France the enjoyment of their civil and religious rights, public confidence soon revived, and trade and manufactures began to flourish.

For these advantages, the kingdom was largely indebted to the statesmanship of the great Sully. It was the good fortune of Henry the Fourth to have for his trusty counselor a man of staunch fidelity and of far-sighted wisdom. Sully was a Protestant, and, unlike his master, remained faithful to his religious convictions,

Chap. I.
1598.

through all the changes of his times. In administering the affairs of the country, his principal concern was for the development of its internal resources. Bringing a rigid economy into all the departments of government, he rapidly reduced the enormous debt which had accumulated during the civil wars; whilst at the same time he sought to encourage agriculture as the most assured means of national enrichment.

Henry favors colonization.

Henry shared his minister's views; but he had other plans also, into which Sully did not enter so cordially. The king favored foreign commerce and colonization. It was his ambition to possess a powerful navy; to promote adventure and discovery and trade with distant parts; and especially, to carry out the scheme which had originated with Coligny, his early teacher and companion in arms, for the establishment of a French colony in America. The time for this great undertaking had come at last; and it is to Henry the Fourth that the honor belongs, of having founded the first agricultural colony in the New World, and of having founded it upon principles of religious equality and freedom. •

1504.

Already for a hundred years the banks of Newfoundland had been frequented by French fishermen. From the harbors of Normandy and Bretagne, from La Rochelle, and the low sandy islands along the coast between the Loire and the Gironde, hardy seamen ventured forth annually across the Atlantic, rivaling the English and the Spaniards in discovery and commercial enterprise. Not a few of them were Protestants. Many of the ships that visited the fishing banks, or cruised along the shores of the gulf of St. Lawrence, were owned by Huguenot merchants, and manned by Huguenot sailors, whose loud voices were often heard, in port and at sea, to the indignation of all good Catholics, as they joined lustily in singing Clement Marot's psalms.

<small>Chap. I.
1598.</small>

The Reformation early gained a foothold in the seaboard provinces of western France. It was about the year 1534, that two of Calvin's first and most ardent disciples[1] entered the province of Saintonge, and began to preach the new doctrines. Their success was marked, especially among the humbler classes of the population. In a short time, nearly every village and hamlet had been reached. These missionary labors were aided by recruits from an unexpected quarter. A number of monks, in the central part of France, having heard of Luther, left their monasteries, and crossed the frontier into Germany, to hear the great reformer for themselves. Upon their return to France, they began to preach boldly against the abuses of Rome; but soon, incurring the displeasure of

<small>Spread of the new doctrines.</small>

---

[1] Philippe Véron, called "le Ramasseur," and Albert Babinot, were of the number of those who came under Calvin's influence during his stay in Poitiers for some months, before he went to Geneva.—Histoire des Protestants et des églises réformées du Poitou, par A. Lièvre. Tome I., p. 34.—Histoire des églises réformées de Pons, Gemozac et Mortagne, en Saintonge, par A. Crottet. P. 10, seq.—Bulletin de la Société de l'histoire du protestantisme français, 31e année (1882) p. 6.

the clergy, they were forced to scatter, and hide themselves in the remoter parts of the kingdom. Several of these monks came into Saintonge, and took refuge among the rude fishermen and seamen who inhabited the islands of Oléron, Marennes, and Arvert. Here, cautiously at first, and then more openly, they preached their Lutheran doctrines, protected by a dignitary of the Church who was in sympathy with the Reformation, and finding much acceptance with the people. The persecution that soon arrested the labors of these zealous men, several of whom were burned at the stake, did not prevent the spread of the new faith in Saintonge. By the middle of the sixteenth century, a large part of the population of this province, as of the adjoining provinces, had embraced the Protestant religion.

Chap. I.
1540.

1546.
August.

The mass unsaid.
So rapid and so thorough was the change, that at the time when the Edict of Nantes was published, the Roman mass had not been said openly at La Rochelle for nearly forty years. In many other Huguenot towns, the public exercises of the Roman Catholic worship had been interrupted almost as long: and in lower Normandy, and in Henry's native province of Béarn, it had been formally excluded.

Protestant and Catholic alike, the merchants and seamen of western France were now looking with keen interest toward America as a field of commercial adventure. The fisheries and the fur-trade, pursued hitherto without government aid, by companies of merchants and by

THE HUGUENOTS INSECURE. 83

private individuals, had proved exceedingly lucrative; and the seaport towns of Normandy, Bretagne and Aunis vied with one another in seeking to obtain the exclusive control of the profitable traffic. There were reasons, however, why Protestants especially should welcome the plan of colonization in the New World. They were by no means free from anxiety as to their condition and prospects in France. The Edict of Nantes, whilst it recognized and "irrevocably" confirmed their civil and religious rights, greatly exasperated their enemies. The clergy, and the more extreme among the Roman Catholic party, were bitterly opposed to its execution. The parliaments long refused to register the decree, and yielded only to the express command of the king. Henry himself was viewed with distrust by his former fellow-religionists. Whilst protecting them in the exercise of their religion, he was endeavoring to weaken them as a political party. It was known that the Jesuits, who had been banished from the kingdom, were regaining their influence at court. The day might come, which Coligny had foreseen, when the Protestants of France would need a place of refuge from renewed persecution, and a country where they and their children could enjoy freedom of conscience. It was by considerations like these, that the Protestant subjects of Henry were moved to fall in heartily with his plans of American colonization.

Chap. I.
1603.

Need of a refuge foreseen.

On the eighth of November, 1603, a commission was granted to a Huguenot gentleman of Saintonge, Pierre du Gua, sieur de Monts, authorizing him to possess and settle that part of North America lying between the fortieth and the forty-sixth degrees of north latitude, and granting him the monopoly of trade between Cape Race and the fortieth degree of latitude, for a period of ten years. The coasts of this region had been visited and explored by Jacques Cartier, nearly seventy years before; and during the reign of Francis the First an ineffectual attempt had been made to plant a colony on the bank of the St. Lawrence. Later experiments had not been more fortunate. One of these adventures was conducted by a Huguenot officer. In the year 1599, Pierre Chauvin, seigneur de Tontuit,[1] of Honfleur in Normandy, was commissioned by Henry IV. to colonize America. Chauvin was a captain in the royal navy, "very expert and well versed in matters of navigation," says Champlain, "who had served his Majesty in the late wars, *although* he was of the Pretended Reformed religion."[2] Several vessels were

---

[1] Nouvelles Glanes historiques Normandes, puisées exclusivement dans des documents inédits. Par E. Gosselin, Greffier-Archiviste. Rouen: Imprimerie de H. Boissel, rue de la Vicomté, 55.—1873. P. 17. *Du* Tontuit. Id., p. 35.

[2] "Homme très expert et entendu au faict de la navigation, qui avoit servi sa Majesté aux guerres passées, quoi qu'il fust de la religion prétendue reformée." "Ce qui fut à blasmer en cette entreprise, est d' avoir donné une commission à un homme de contraire religion, pour pulluler la foi c., a. et r., que les hérétiques ont tant en horreur, et abbomination. Voilà les defauts que j'avois à dire sur ceste entreprise." Voyages de Champlain, vol. I., pp. 44, 48.

equipped, and with a force of five hundred men, Chauvin embarked, accompanied by none but Calvinistic ministers.¹ At Tadoussac, on the northern shore of the St. Lawrence, at the mouth of its confluent the Saguenay, a trading-post was established ; and leaving sixteen of his men to gather furs, the leader returned to France. The little colony dragged out a miserable existence through the winter. Several of the men died, and the others were barely kept alive by the compassionate savages, who shared with them their slender provisions. Chauvin made another unsuccessful attempt to effect a settlement in the same place, and was about to start upon a third voyage, when he died. In the following year, the commission which had been granted him was transferred to a Roman Catholic patentee, Aymar de Chastes, governor of Dieppe. But before the ships sent out for the exploration of the country returned, De Chastes too was dead. Thus in the early days of the seventeenth century, scarcely a trace remained of the expeditions of French adventurers to North America. The whole of the vast region claimed by France in virtue of the discoveries of Verrazzano, who as early as the year 1524 had planted her standard upon its soil, was still waiting to be occupied.

De Monts had accompanied Chauvin, " for his own pleasure," on his first visit to the St. Law-

---

¹ " Tout ira assez bien, horsmis qu'il n' y aura que des ministres & pasteurs Calvinistes."—Id., p. 45.

rence. His impressions of the country watered by that great river—influenced perhaps by the unfortunate result of the expedition—were not favorable; and he preferred a more southerly region, and a milder temperature, for his own agricultural colony. For this reason he was attracted to the large peninsula lying south of the gulf of St. Lawrence, now known as Nova Scotia. The discoverer Cartier had given a glowing account of this territory, and had particularly noticed its climate, resembling that of Spain, and in singular contrast with the bleak weather he had encountered on the neighboring coast of Newfoundland. This fertile country, abounding in lakes and rivers and estuaries,[1] had already received the name of La Cadie;[2] and the commission given by Henry IV. to his trusty subject the Sieur de Monts, constituted him its viceroy.

This commission was a characteristic document.[3] It began by setting forth the king's favorite project for the enlargement of his dominions. "It has ever been," reads the preamble of the royal grant, "our principal concern and endeavor, since our accession to this crown, to maintain and preserve it in its ancient dignity, greatness and splendor, and to spread and augment, so far as may be legitimately done, the

---

[1] About one-fifth of the area of Nova Scotia is occupied by these waters.
[2] The earliest mention, however, occurs in De Monts' commission.
[3] See the Appendix to this volume.

bounds and limits thereof." But there was an object of still higher importance to be sought in the present enterprise. The king, "having long since informed himself of the situation and condition of the country and territory of Acadia," professed to be "moved above all things by a singular zeal, and by a devout and firm resolution" which he had taken, "with the help and assistance of God, who is the author, distributor, and protector of all kingdoms and states, to seek the conversion, guidance and instruction of the races that inhabit that country, from their barbarous and godless condition, without faith or religion, to Christianity and the belief and profession of our faith and religion, and to rescue them from the ignorance and unbelief in which they now lie." For these purposes, secular as well as spiritual, Henry appointed the Sieur de Monts his lieutenant-general, with powers "to subject all the peoples of that country and of the surrounding parts to our authority; and by all lawful means to lead them to the knowledge of God and to the light of the Christian faith and religion, and to establish them therein." All other inhabitants were to be maintained and protected in the exercise and profession of the same Christian faith and religion, and in peace, repose and tranquillity.

Thus the foundations of New France were to be laid in religious freedom and toleration. Romanist and Calvinist were equally secured in the enjoyment of the rights of conscience. And the heathen aborigines were to be taught the truths of that common Christianity which Catholic and Protestant alike professed. If the plan was impracticable, it did honor nevertheless to the heart and mind that prompted and devised the Edict of Nantes.

De Monts associated with himself the members of a company which had been organized for one of the previous unsuccessful expeditions; adding to their number some of the merchants of the principal seaports of the kingdom, chiefly of La Rochelle. He himself was well fitted to be the leader of such an enterprise. He had fought bravely under Henry in the late wars, and the king, who trusted him thoroughly, had made him one of the gentlemen of his bed-chamber, and some years after appointed him governor of Pons, in his native province of Saintonge. All the early writers agree in characterizing him as a man of the highest integrity, and the purest patriotism. In courage, energy, perseverance, in tact and firmness, and in unselfish devotion to his country's glory, the Protestant founder of New France was admirably qualified for his mission.[1]

With two well-provisioned ships at his command, De Monts sailed from Havre de Grace

---

[1] "Henry IV. avoit une grande confiance [en lui] pour sa fidelité, comme il a toujours fait paroitre jusques à sa mort."—Voyages du Sieur Champlain, ou Journal ès Decouvertes de la Nouvelle France. Paris, 1830. Vol. I., p. 54.

"C'étoit d' ailleurs un fort honnête homme, et qui avoit du zele pour l'Etat et toute la capacité nécessaire pour réussir dans l'entreprise dont il s'étoit chargé."—Histoire de la Nouvelle France, par le P. de Charlevoix. Vol. I., p. 173.

early in March, 1604. The band of adventurers whom he had gathered for his colony, numbered about one hundred and twenty persons.[1] It was made up of materials very diverse. Some were of noble birth, while others were of low condition. There were Huguenots and Romanists; and for the spiritual care of the settlers, and the proposed conversion of the savages of America, a Protestant minister and a Roman Catholic priest went with them.[2] De Monts' commission authorized him to impress for his expedition any "vagabonds, idlers or vagrants," as well as any criminals condemned to banishment from the realm, whom he might see fit to employ. A like permission had been given to preceding adventurers, and more than one of them had availed himself of it.[3] But it does not appear that the

---

[1] The names of a few of these may be gathered from Champlain's account of the expedition. Mention is made of les Sieurs de Geneston, Sourin, d' Oraille, Chaudoré, de Beaumont, la Motte Bourioli, Fougeray, la Taille, Miquelet; the surgeons des Champs, of Honfleur, and Bonnerme; Messire Aubry, priest, and le Sieur Raleau, secretary of M. de Monts.

[2] It is charitable to presume that these religious teachers may have kept the peace during the voyage, at least. The lively incident related by Champlain (*v. postea*, page 99) did not occur *at sea*, as we might infer from the account of it in "Pioneers of France in the New World," page 223; since it took place in the presence of "the savages," who sometimes sided with the one disputant and sometimes with the other. Their differences doubtless began in earnest when they engaged in efforts to convert the Indians, each to his own religious belief.

[3] In 1540, Francis I. sent Cartier back to Canada, with orders to take with him fifty persons condemned for crime, "hors d' hérésie, et de lèse-majesté divine et humaine," for the settlement of that country. (Nouvelles Glanes historiques

Chap. I.
1604.

The coast of Acadia explored.

Huguenot leader found it necessary to form his company out of such materials. There were good men and true, of his own creed and severe morality, who could easily be drawn into an enterprise so hopeful. Among the gentlemen who accompanied De Monts were two of his former comrades in the service of Henry of Navarre. The one was the famous Samuel de Champlain, like himself a native of Saintonge, and not improbably a Protestant by birth,[1] but who if originally a Protestant had followed the king's example in conforming to the Church of Rome. The other was Jean de Biencourt, baron de Poutrincourt, the future proprietor of Port Royal.

A short and uneventful voyage brought the colonists in sight of Acadia. Some time was consumed in explorations with a view to the discovery of a suitable place for the settlement. On one occasion, the explorers met with an adventure, that came near disturbing the harmony of the expedition. Coasting along the south-eastern shore of the peninsula, De Monts had passed Cape Sable, and then steering northward had entered a bay, to which he gave the name St.

Normandes, par E. Gosselin. P. 4.) The saving clause, "*heresy excepted,*" illustrates the fatuous policy of France, in shutting out from her colonies the only class of people disposed to emigrate, and the class affording the best material for colonization.

[1] The possibility is suggested by the authors of the Histoire de la Colonie française en Canada, in view of the fact that no record of Champlain's birth and baptism is to be found in Brouage, his native place; and in view of his surname, Samuel, "nom inusité alors chez les Catholiques et en honneur chez les Protestants."—Vol. I. Note XXI.

Mary, which it retains. Here, pleased with the appearance of the country, he sent ashore a party to make further examination. Among the men were two, a Protestant, and a young Roman Catholic priest, named Aubry, who had often during the voyage engaged in hot discussion over their differing religious tenets. Straying from his companions, Aubry lost his way in the forest, and when the time came for their return to the ship, he could not be found. Anxious for his safety, De Monts caused a search to be made, not only by his own men, but by the friendly savages also. Trumpets were sounded, and cannon were fired, but in vain. At length all hope of success was abandoned. With heavy hearts the colonists set sail, and leaving St. Mary's bay proceeded on their course. But now their conjectures as to the fate of their unfortunate comrade took the hue of grave suspicion. For it was remembered that Aubry had last been seen in company with the Protestant who had so frequently been his antagonist in sharp debate. Angry words, that might be construed as threats of personal violence, were recalled by the priest's co-religionists. Finally, they openly charged the Calvinist with having secretly murdered his opponent. His earnest denials, and the efforts of the prudent commander to allay the rising storm, deterred them from taking summary vengeance. Great must have been the relief of all, when after many days Aubry reappeared. Wandering in the trackless forest until his strength and courage failed, he had given up all thought of rescue, when finding himself on the shore of the great bay—now known as the Bay of Fundy—he spied a boat. It belonged to De Monts' ship, and was lying off the island that still bears the name of Long Island, where the men were engaged in fishing. Aubry succeeded in attracting their attention, and was taken on board, a mere shadow of his former self, having subsisted for seventeen days upon such edible herbs and berries as he could find in the wilderness.[1]

Proceeding northward in the Bay of Fundy, De Monts came to another inlet. A narrow channel, between two wooded elevations, admitted the ship to a noble harbor, surrounded by sheltering hills. To this beautiful basin—now called Annapolis Harbor—the commander gave the name of Port Royal; and here his associate De Poutrincourt, who was in search of an eligible spot for a settlement of his own, decided to remain and make his home. De Monts approved the choice, and accompanied the consent with a grant of the locality to his friend, who promised at once to bring over a number of families from France to occupy and improve it.

The site chosen for the future town of Port Royal was a point of land jutting out from the eastern shore, between two rivers that flowed into the bay. A wooded island, half a league in circumference, lay directly opposite, in the cen-

---

[1] Histoire de la Nouvelle France, par Marc Lescarbot. A Paris : chez Jean Millot. MDC. XII. P. 453. Œuvres de Champlain, tome II., p. 16.

ter of the basin. The surrounding forests were broken here and there by broad prairies; and along the shore stretched extensive salt marshes, which at a later day were reclaimed and made exceedingly productive. The largest ships could ride in safety within the land-locked harbor, which was, however, difficult of access, owing to the narrowness of the entrance and the shoals within. The place offered every advantage for settlement. The fertile soil, the abundant and excellent timber, the rich fisheries, the salubrious climate, invited the colonist. In no other part of Acadia were the winters so mild.

Accompanied by Champlain, De Monts continued his explorations, passing from headland to headland along the shores of the great bay, and finally fixed upon a place for the establishment of his own colony. It was a small island off the coast, at the mouth of the St. Croix river, on the opposite side of the Bay of Fundy. The site was singularly unsuitable. The island, not more than ten acres in extent, was without water, and ill-supplied with wood. The bitter experiences of a winter passed upon this rocky islet convinced the French of their mistake, and after examining other places along the coast, De Monts resolved to remove his colony to Port Royal, and unite his forces with the settlement which De Poutrincourt had commenced there. Sickness had thinned the numbers of the little company during their stay at St. Croix: of seventy-nine settlers, only forty survived. They

94 UNDER THE EDICT: ACADIA.

<small>Chap. I.
1606.</small>

were joined in the summer of 1606[1] by Marc Lescarbot, a Protestant lawyer and man of letters, who has left us a lively account of the infant colony in his History of New France. He found it without a religious teacher. The priest and the minister whom De Monts brought over with him, both died during the sickness that prevailed on the island of St. Croix. Lescarbot tells us that he did his best to supply the vacancy. "Being requested," he says, "by the Sieur de Poutrincourt,[2] our chief, to give some portion of my time to the Christian instruction

<small>Lay preaching at Port Royal.</small>

of our little community, in order that we might not live like the beasts, and that we might afford the savages an example of our way of living, I did so every Sunday, and also upon some extraordinary occasions, nearly all the time we were there. And it happened well that without anticipating this, I had brought with me my Bible and a few books; for else the duty would have wearied me greatly, and I might have been compelled to decline it. As it was, the labor was not without fruit; for several persons have testified to me that they had never heard so much said and well said concerning God, having been pre-

---

[1] Le Samedi veille de Pentecoste trezieme de May [1606] nous levames les ancres & fimes voiles en pleine mer tant que peu à peu nous perdimes de veüe les grosses tours & la ville de la Rochelle puis les isles de Rez & d'Oleron, disans Adieu à la France.—Lescarbot, Histoire de la Nouvelle France, pp. 523, 524.

[2] This nobleman, if nominally a Roman Catholic, appears to have been in full sympathy with his Huguenot associates, De Monts and Lescarbot. His hatred of the Jesuits was undisguised.

viously unacquainted with the principles of the Christian doctrine." "A condition," adds the Calvinist, "in which the mass of Christendom is living."¹

Great hopes were cherished among the Protestants of France for the success of this colony as a missionary expedition. The conversion of the heathen natives was indeed one of the chief of its avowed ends. At La Rochelle, where Lescarbot took ship for New France, he found the Huguenots praying for this object daily in their public assemblies. He intimates that a number of the savages were brought under religious instruction during the time of his stay in America, and professed their readiness to be baptized.² The Jesuit historians throw discredit

Chap. I.
1606.

Converts to Christianity.

---

¹ "Meme je ne seray point honteux de dire qu' ayant esté prié par le Sieur de Poutrincourt notre chef de doñer quelques heures de mon industrie à enseigner Chretiennement nôtre petit peuple, pour ne vivre en betes, & pour donner exemple à notre façon de vivre aux Sauvages, je l'ai fait en la necessité, & en etat requis, par chacun Dimanche, & quelque fois extraordinairement, presque tout le temps que nous y avons eté. Et bien me vint que j'avoy porté ma Bible & quelque livres, sans y penser : Car autrement une telle Charge m'eut fort fatigué & eust eté cause que ie m'en serois excusé. Or cela ne fut point sans fruit, plusieurs m'ayant rendu temoignage que jamais ils n' avoient tant ouï parler de Dieu en bonne part, & ne sachant auparavant aucun principe en ce qui est de la doctrine Chretienne."— Histoire de la Nouvelle France, par Marc Lescarbot. Livre iv., chap. v.

² "Le principal but de sa [de Poutrincourt] transmigration, qui estoit de procurer le salut de ces pauvres peuples sauvages et barbares. Lors que nous y estions nous leurs avions quelquefois donné en l'ame de bonnes impressions de la connoisance de Dieu, comme se peut voir par le dis-

Chap. I.
1604.

upon these early efforts to Christianize the Indians; and in fact they represent that the Huguenot De Monts was required, by the terms of his commission, as viceroy of Acadia, to propagate the Roman Catholic faith among them. This statement, for which the authority of Champlain himself is given, has hitherto passed unquestioned. But we have already seen that De Monts' commission contained no such stipulation. It differed in this respect very significantly from the commissions that had been given to previous applicants. The patent granted by Francis I. to Jacques Cartier speaks of "the augmentation of our Mother Holy

---

cours de notre voyage, & en mon Adieu à la Nouvelle France."—Lescarbot, Histoire de la Nouvelle France, p. 636.

> Adieu donc ie te dis, ile de beauté pleine,
> Et vous oiseaux aussi des eaux et des forets,
> Qui serez les témoins de mes tristes regrets.
> Car c'est à grand regret, et ie ne le puis taire,
> Que ie quitte ce lieu, quoy qu' assez solitaire.
> Car c'est à grand regret qu' ores ici ie voy
> Ebranlé le sujet d'y enter nôtre Foy,
> Et du grand Dieu le nom caché sous le silence,
> *Qui à ce peuple avoit touché la conscience.*
> *   *   *   *   *   *
> Temoins soient de ceci les propos veritables
> Que Poutrincourt tenoit avec ces miserables
> Quand il leur enseignoit nôtre Religion,
> Et souvent leur montroit l'ardente affection
> Qu'il avoit de les voir dedans la bergerie
> Que Christ a racheté par le pris de sa vie.
>
> Eux d' autre part emeus clairement temoignoient
> Et de bouche & de cœur le desir qu'ilz avoient
> D'estre plus amplement instruits en la doctrine
> En laquelle il convient qu' un fidele chemine.
>   —Lescarbot, Adieu à la Nouvelle France.

Church Catholic" (de notre mere Sainte Eglise Catholique). Henry IV. himself, in his commission to the Marquis de la Roche, a Roman Catholic nobleman, mentions the "aggrandizement of the Catholic faith" (la foy Catholique) as the aim in view. But the patent issued to the Huguenot De Monts was conceived in more general terms. It required that the heathen be converted "to Christianity," "to the knowledge of God, and to the light of the Christian faith and religion."[1] However this language might be understood by the zealots of Rome, it was not likely that Protestants would construe it as denoting the doctrines of the Papal system exclusively, nor indeed that the king, who, if not still a Protestant at heart, was far from being regardless of the rights of his Reformed subjects, could have so designed it. This significant omission, indeed, did not escape the notice of De Monts' enemies at the time.

Objections were raised to the expedition on the score of the religious belief of its leader. The Parliament of Rouen refused to register his commission, and sent one of its members to remonstrate with the king against the appointment of a heretic to be his lieutenant in Acadia. But before the envoy could reach Paris, a letter came from Henry, setting forth in very peremptory terms the royal pleasure. "We have been advised," said the king, "of the

---

[1] The correctness of Lescarbot's version of the patent granted to De Monts is attested by a contemporaneous translation, for which see the Appendix.

opposition that has been made to the execution of the powers we have given to the Sieur de Monts for the peopling and occupying of Acadia and other adjacent countries; and we have learned that you take chief exception to the pretended reformed religion, of which the said Sieur de Monts makes profession . . . Wherefore that you may be certified of our will and purpose, we let you know that we have given command that some ecclesiastics of good life, doctrine, and edification shall proceed to the said countries with the said Sieur de Monts, to counteract [prévenir] whatever of a contrary profession might be there sown and introduced.[1]"

Notwithstanding this assurance, the Parliament of Rouen still hesitated to confirm the commission. Manifestly, it was thought that no sufficient guarantee had been given for the

---

[1] "Nos amez et feaulx, nous avons esté adverty des oppositions formées à l'exécution du pouvoir que nous avons donné au Sieur de Monts pour le peuplement et l'habitation de la terre de l'Acadye et autres terres et provinces circonvoisines, selon qu'elles sont prescrites par ledit pouvoir et sceu que vous vous arrêtez principalement sur la religion prétendue réformée, dont ledict Sieur de Montz faict profession comme aussy sur l' interdiction que vous avons faicte à nos courts du Parlement de ce faict, des circonstances et dépendances et autres actions qui se pourroient mouvoir pour raison des ordonnances que nous avons faictes pour ce subject, ou, ce que l'on prétend de préjudice et intérêts en la liberté du commerce. Sur quoi afin que vous soyez assurez de notre vouloir et intention, nous vous dirons que nous avons donné ordre que quelques gens d'Eglise de bonne vie, doctrine et édification se transportent és dits pays et provinces avec le dict sieur de Montz pour prévenir ce que l'on pourroit y semer et introduire de contraire profession."
—Gosselin. (Nouvelles Glanes historiques normandes.)

spread of the true faith and the repression of heresy in New France. But the king deigned no further explanation; and all discussion of the subject was speedily cut off by a royal behest, which admitted of no further delay.

Champlain represents the heathen as greatly scandalized by the differences between the Catholics and the Protestants, which they witnessed from time to time. "One thing must be remarked," he observes, "to the disadvantage of this enterprise, namely, that two conflicting religions never produce any great results for the glory of God in the conversion of the unbelievers. I have seen the minister and our *curé* fighting with their fists, while discussing their religious differences. I do not know which one of the two may have been the braver, and may have dealt the better blow; but I do know that the minister used sometimes to complain to the Sieur De Monts that he had been beaten. Thus it was that they determined their points of controversy. I leave it to you to say whether this was a pleasant sight. The savages sided sometimes with the one party and sometimes with the other; and the French, mingling in the discussion according to their differing beliefs, vilified both religions, though the Sieur De Monts did his best to restore peace among them."

Port Royal was beginning to wear the aspect of a thrifty and prosperous settlement, when in the summer of the year 1607, tidings arrived from France that the privileges of trade granted to De Monts under his commission from the king were withdrawn. The merchants of St. Malo, in Bretagne, had long been foremost in the traffic pursued along the American coast. Great was their indignation when they learned that a rival company had obtained exclusive rights, shutting them out from the fisheries and the fur-trade which they prized so much. No efforts were spared to break down the odious monopoly ; and at length these efforts succeeded. De Monts was compelled to renounce his cherished plan. A good beginning had been made by the little band of colonists. Their cultivated lands gave promise of rich harvests. They had erected a small palisaded fort, a mill, store-houses and dwellings, and had undertaken the manufacture of tar. They had established friendly relations with the natives, and had met with some success in the effort to convert them to Christianity. But the experiment of colonization was costly, and, without the revenue to be derived from the monopoly granted them, could not be carried on. Port Royal was abandoned, at least for the present. The title to the lands upon which the settlement had been effected was still held, however, by De Monts' associate, De Poutrincourt, and two years later he returned and took possession of his grant, a confirmation of which he obtained from the king.

Meanwhile, baffled in the attempt to colonize Acadia, De Monts did not immediately renounce the scheme of a French settlement in the New World. Though he had lost his exclusive privileges of trade, the Huguenot leader still held his commission from Henry the Fourth, giving him vice-regal powers over the whole vast territory, which included not only the peninsula since known as Nova Scotia, but also Canada, and a great part of the continent to which it belongs. He was resolved to attempt a settlement in the interior; and in order to secure the means of accomplishing this purpose, he again petitioned the king, and obtained a renewal of the monopoly of trade with America, at first for a single year. Again he associated with himself the daring and enthusiastic Champlain. Two ships were equipped for the expedition; the one, to carry on the traffic in peltries from which the needed revenue for the enterprise was to be derived; the other, under the command of Champlain, to discover and to occupy a suitable site for the proposed colony.

<small>Chap. I.
1608.</small>

It was in the summer of the year 1608 that Champlain, acting under the authority of De Monts, landed on the bank of the St. Lawrence, upon the spot which was to be the site of the city of Quebec. The superb position must have impressed the great explorer, and perhaps, like Frontenac, at a later day, he too saw here "the future capital of a great empire."[1]

<small>Settlement at Quebec.</small>

For many years, however, the place was scarcely more than a trading-post. Little inducement was held out to settlers, and few came over with any design to remain and cultivate the soil. The attractions of commerce were stronger than those of colonization. De Monts'

---

[1] Frontenac and New France under Louis XIV. by Francis Parkman, p. 15.

company, holding nominally the exclusive right to trade with the New World, had been considerably enlarged. The sagacious and large-hearted Huguenot, more intent upon the success of his colony than upon his own personal interests, drew the rival houses of St. Malo into its service by admitting them as partners of the monopoly which they had endeavored to break down. But the company's ships were not alone in carrying on the traffic. Many merchants of Rochelle and other ports were actively engaged in it; and many a free-trader, besides, setting at defiance the restrictions placed upon commerce, sought the shores of New France, drove his own bargain with the savages, and sailed back to the French coast with rich cargoes of peltry.

Chap. I.
1608.

Religious liberty unrestricted.
As yet, there was no interference with religious liberty. Protestants and Romanists shared alike in the toils and the profits of trade, and often discussed the differences of their belief with a freedom that ran into license. Religious contentions were indeed among the chief troubles experienced by Champlain in the government of the colony, to which he had now been appointed. A few Franciscan friars were brought over in 1615, to undertake the spiritual care of the French, and the conversion of the Indians. But the Calvinist traders and sailors were proof against the persuasions of the zealous missionaries; and as yet, no harsher means than persuasion could be employed to subdue their heresy. On many of the company's vessels, as on most of the ships engaged in inde-

pendent trade, the crews were assembled daily for prayers, after the manner of Geneva; and even good Catholics, it was complained, were required by the Huguenot captains to join in the psalmody which formed so important a part of the Protestant worship,

But the Huguenots of France had now lost their royal protector. Henry the Fourth fell under the assassin's knife; and soon after, the honest and patriotic De Monts, relinquishing at length his cherished plan, surrendered the commission he still held as viceroy of New France. It was manifest that the infant colony needed a more powerful friend; and the Prince of Condé, a former chief of the Huguenot party, and still its recognized champion, was induced to lend his name to the enterprise. This headship, however, was only titular. The actual possessors of New France were no friends to Protestantism or to religious freedom. By a singular fatality, the proprietary rights which De Monts had parted with, were now, to all intents and purposes, lodged in the hands of the Jesuits. The ostensible purchaser was a woman. Antoinette de Pons, marquise de Guercheville, a lady of honor to the queen, was an intense devotee of the Church of Rome, and an enthusiastic admirer of the so-called Society of Jesus. The missions which that Society had been carrying on with wonderful energy for more than half a century in Asia and in South America, awakened her warmest interest. Plans for a similar work were now entertained with reference to the northern continent of the New World; and Madame de Guercheville readily gave her influence and her wealth for the furtherance of the scheme. Seeking out the Huguenot patentee of Acadia and Canada, she made him a tempting offer for the transfer of his rights in New France. She found De Monts in his native town of Pons, to the government of which he had lately been appointed. The moment was favorable to the success of the lady's plan. De Monts stood in pressing need of money for the defense of his town. Pons was one of the strong places secured to the Protestants by the Edict of Nantes, and great pains had been taken since the close of the civil war to repair its walls and fortifications. But Pons was poorly garrisoned; and its citizens, sharing in the uneasiness that pervaded the Reformed body ever since the tragic death of Henry the Fourth, were anxiously devising ways and means to augment the military force in command.[1] The bargain was made. The garrison of the little town—destined to be dismantled in a few years by the troops of Louis the Thirteenth—was strengthened; and the title to the proprietorship of half a continent passed from the hands of a Huguenot into those of a subservient tool of the Jesuits.

Acadia was the field chosen for the beginning of the missions of Rome in New France. On

---

[1] Histoire des églises réformées de Pons, Gemozac et Mortagne, en Saintonge. Par A. Crottet. Bordeaux, 1841. Pp. 101–107.

the twenty-sixth of January, 1611, a second expedition set forth from the French coast for the harbor of Port Royal. But this time, no Huguenot minister accompanied the colonists. Two Jesuit priests, the van-guard of the spiritual army of occupation that was to follow, were the chief passengers on board the well-freighted ship. They had been preceded, at Port Royal, by a small band of immigrants, under De Poutrincourt, who came in the spring of the year 1610 to resume possession of the place originally granted to him by De Monts. But the ill-success that attended the former settlement was awaiting the new enterprise. Bitter dissensions broke out among the colonists, which the presence of the Jesuit fathers did not contribute to allay. In 1613, another vessel came over, richly provisioned, and bearing a reënforcement of missionaries, to plant a second station on the American shore. A beginning was made, on the island of Mount Desert, off the coast of Maine. Both settlements, however, were speedily destroyed by an English freebooter. Cruising in these waters at the time of the arrival of the second colony from France, Samuel Argall, afterwards deputy-governor of Virginia, landed upon the island of Mount Desert, made prisoners of the French, took possession of their vessel, and then—guided, it has been said, by one of the Jesuit fathers, out of malice against the proprietor of Port Royal—proceeded to the older settlement of De Poutrincourt, and laid the place in ashes.

Chap. I.
1613-1621.

Acadia was now lost to the Jesuits; and some time must yet elapse before they could obtain possession of Canada. The commercial interests of France were still controlled largely, as they continued to be for many years, by Huguenot merchants; and in order to the prosecution of the important trade with the New World, the capital and enterprise of the great companies of La Rochelle, Rouen and Dieppe were indispensably needed. Hence, though the Prince of Condé was succeeded as viceroy of New France by the Duke of Montmorency, an open enemy of the Huguenots, no attempt was made as yet to exclude them from the colonies.

The Compagnie Montmorency.

In 1621, the duke, dissatisfied with the management of the trade with Canada, conferred the monopoly of that trade upon a body of merchants to be known as the Compagnie Montmorency. At the head of this company was Guillaume de Caen, sieur de la Mothe, a Huguenot of Dieppe.[1] De Caen was at once an enterprising merchant and an experienced navigator. Bred to the sea, he had already made many a trip, under his father's direction, to the banks of Newfoundland. His able administration soon raised the new company to a height of prosperity such as none of its predecessors had reached. Royal favors were showered upon it. Privilege after privilege was granted, in utter disregard of the rights previously conferred upon the older associations. A fleet was created for its

---

[1] Son of Guillaume de Caen and Marie Langlois his wife, (Gosselin: Nouvelles Glanes Historiques Normandes.)

service, with De Caen as its admiral, under the title of General of the Fleet of New France. Secure of government patronage, the company spent vast sums in building ships and storehouses, and in 1627 boasted of an annual revenue of one hundred thousand francs.

Among the conditions upon which the company held its monopoly, was that of transporting to Canada and there maintaining six friars of the order of St. Francis, for the religious instruction of the colonists and the natives. De Caen was faithful to this engagement, but he claimed for himself and for his fellow-religionists all the liberty which the Edict of Nantes secured to them, of conducting worship according to the Reformed rite. No great objection seems to have been made to this, until, five years later, three Jesuit fathers came to reënforce the band of Franciscans. De Caen and his fellow-traders gave them but a cold reception. True to their character, the new comers lost no time in stirring up strife with the hated heretics. Complaints were made to the viceroy that the Huguenot sailors at Quebec were regularly assembled by order of De Caen, for prayer, and the singing of psalms. It was represented that even Romanists in the company's employ, were forced to be present at these services. The most objectionable part of this heretical worship, was the singing. The followers of Loyola especially detested it. Their own rule exempted them from the chants and other choral services observed by religious orders in the Roman Catholic

Church. "They do not sing," said the enemies of the Jesuits; "birds of prey never do."[1] The governor of Quebec was instructed to forbid these disorderly practices. No public saying of prayers or singing of psalms was to be tolerated on the river St. Lawrence. But the company's men, and especially the crews of their vessels, refused to comply with these orders, and threatened mutiny. "At last," says Champlain, "it was agreed that they might meet to pray, but should not sing psalms. A bad bargain, yet it was the best we could do."

But the time was now drawing near, when the powerful Society of Jesus could carry its plans into effect, and Canada, closed against heresy, could be held as an exclusive field of missions for the Church of Rome. Another change in the vice-regency of New France took place; and Montmorency was succeeded by his nephew, the young Duke de Ventadour. At once, the new viceroy, who was a devoted friend of the Jesuits, sent over five members of the order. A few months later, the monopoly of trade was withdrawn from the Huguenot De Caen, and a company was formed, to be known as the Company of New France. At the head of this organization, upon which exclusive commercial and proprietary rights were conferred, was Cardinal Richelieu, the energetic and sagacious minister of Louis the Thirteenth. In return for the extraordinary privileges and powers granted to it, the com-

---

[1] Miscellanies, by William R. Williams. The Jesuits as a Missionary Order. New York: 1850. P. 175.

pany bound itself to transport emigrants to the New World, to give them lands, and to maintain them for three years after their arrival. But every emigrant must profess the Roman Catholic faith. From this vast region—the whole continent of North America, as claimed by France—heresy was to be rigidly and forever excluded.

<small>Chap. I. 1627.</small>

To the statesman and to the Jesuit alike, this exclusion appeared a master-stroke of policy. Richelieu, who had but lately taken his place in the royal council, was already maturing his plans for the depression of the Huguenot power in France. At this moment he was engaged in reducing La Rochelle, the political center of that power, with whose fall, a few months later, the hopes of the party were to be extinguished. The time had not yet come for a legalized and systematic persecution of the adherents of the Reformed faith. But meanwhile it was the object of the government to weaken and humiliate them. To throw open the colonies to the Calvinists, with their superior thrift and enterprise, would be to offer them enlarged opportunities of enrichment and advancement. On the other hand, their exclusion would increase the odium which it was for the interest of the king to connect with the Huguenot name.

The Jesuits, equally anxious to extirpate heresy at home, and to shut it out from their mission fields abroad, hailed this measure as a signal triumph. By a curious coincidence, their recall to power had followed closely upon the grant made to De Monts for the settlement of

<small>Triumph of the Jesuits.</small>

New France. They had viewed with an evil eye the broad provisions of that grant, which contained no discrimination in favor of the Roman Catholic religion, but admitted Huguenots to the privileges of trade and the ownership of land, upon the same footing with the sons of the true Church. The Jesuit historian Sagard deplores the spirit of toleration and indifference that was exhibited by the first settlers under De Monts' charter, and relates an incident that illustrates at once their rough pleasantry, and their freedom from religious animosity. "It happened in the course of those beginnings of the French in Acadia[1] that a priest and a minister died about the same time. The sailors who buried them laid them both in one grave, to see if they who could not agree whilst alive would dwell together in peace when dead. In short," he adds, "everything was made a matter of jest. The undevout Catholics readily accommodated themselves to the humor of the Huguenots; and these malicious heretics kept on, unrestrained, in their loose way of living."[2]

A better feeling had sprung up in France between the adherents of the two religions, at the close of the civil wars. The Edict of Nantes imposed some restraint upon the virulence of the Roman clergy; and the banishment of the Jesuits had already removed for the time the most zealous agents of religious agitation. An

---

[1] "En ces commencemens que les François furent vers l'Acadie."

[2] Sagard, Histoire du Canada, I., p. 26.

old writer, depicting the state of things then prevalent, tells us that at Caen, in Normandy, "Catholic and Huguenot lived side by side in a perfect understanding. They ate together, drank together, played together, enjoyed each other's society, and parted company without the slightest offense, the one to go to mass, the other to attend preaching."[1] The return of the fathers from their temporary exile broke up these amicable relations. Though in Caen, as in many other places, a strong opposition was made by Catholics and Protestants alike, to their admission, yet no sooner had this opposition been overcome, than the presence of the order was felt in sowing discord and fomenting strife. The reign of good feeling was at an end. Awaiting the time when severer means could be used to crush out heresy in the land, the Jesuits employed themselves in rousing the popular mind to suspicion, envy, and bitter resentment. Frequent infractions of the Edict of Nantes occurred. The government itself, whilst professing to maintain the Edict, winked at many violations of its provisions.

In the meantime, no compromise with heresy must be suffered, in that vast territory which the Jesuits now controlled in the New World. Canada was to be the patrimony of the Church of Rome. Its savage population must be won to the true faith, through the labors of an army of devoted missionaries, trained in the school of

---

[1] Essai sur l'histoire de l' Eglise réformée de Caen, par Sophronyme Beaujour. Caen ; 1877. P. 208.

<small>Chap. I.
1627.</small>   Ignatius Loyola. And the coming generations of its colonists must be shielded from the malign influences that had been at work in France, ever since the days of Calvin.

<small>England enters the lists.</small>   At the last moment, however, the prize seemed about to elude the hands that were stretched out to grasp it. Heretic England entered the lists for the acquisition of Canada. While Richelieu was organizing the Company of New France, a project was entertained at the British court, having in view the conquest of the French possessions in the western hemisphere. England still claimed the North American con-

<small>September 1621.</small>   tinent by right of discovery: and in 1621, James the First, acting upon this assumption, made over to one of his subjects, a Scottish gentleman, Sir William Alexander—afterward Earl of Stirling—the whole territory east of the St. Croix river, and south of the St. Lawrence. The grant included all Acadia; and the peninsula, with the lands conveyed on the main—now forming the province of New Brunswick—was to be known as Nova Scotia. For several years, however, little was done, either by the king or by the nobleman, to make good these pretensions to a region already held, and held with a clearer title certainly, by the French. France and England were at peace; and the question of proprietorship in a distant wilderness was not important enough to provoke a conflict. But in 1627 a sudden war—soon to terminate—broke out. Charles the First, declaring himself the protector of the persecuted Protestants of France, sent

a fleet under the command of his favorite the Duke of Buckingham, for the relief of La Rochelle, then blockaded by the troops of Louis XIII. The ill-contrived and ill-conducted expedition ended ignominiously. Buckingham was no match for Richelieu. The starving inhabitants of La Rochelle saw a second and a third fleet approach their city only to sail away after a few feeble demonstrations; and on the twenty-eighth day of October, 1628, La Rochelle was taken.

<small>Chap. I. 1627.</small>

Better success attended another enterprise of the English in the course of the same brief war. The patentee of Nova Scotia, Sir William Alexander, saw the opportunity to obtain possession of his grant; and under his auspices, a squadron was fitted out for the conquest of New France. It was easy to find good material for the expedition. England was now the refuge of many brave Huguenot seamen and soldiers, well qualified, and more than ready for such an adventure.

<small>Huguenots join the expedition.</small>

Among the refugees were three brothers, David, Louis, and Thomas Kirk, natives of Dieppe in Normandy. To David, as admiral, the command of the expedition was given, his brothers serving under him. The sailing master was one Jacques Michel, a "furious Calvinist," who had been in the employ of Guillaume de Caen, and was forward in promoting the present enterprise. Many other Huguenots joined it, all eager for the conquest of New France. Acadia fell an easy prey to the invaders. After taking pos-

Chap. I.
1628.

Quebec taken.

session of Port Royal, and capturing a French fleet on its way to Canada with supplies for Champlain's colony, Kirk returned to England with flying colors, and the next year sailed for the St. Lawrence. Anchoring with the body of his fleet at the port of Tadoussac, the commander sent his brother Louis up the river, with three ships, for the capture of Quebec. The little fort, held by a mere handful of soldiers under Champlain, and utterly without provisions, was in no condition to withstand an assault. On the twentieth day of July, 1629, Quebec surrendered. The Huguenot officer in command of the English force took possession of the place; and the Jesuit fathers, who had lately come to occupy the mission field which they hoped to secure against the intrusion of heresy, found themselves prisoners in the hands of the very men against whom they purposed to close Canada forever.

The war, however, was already over, and peace had been signed between France and England three months before the capture of Quebec. Canada must revert to its original proprietors; and after three years of negotiations, during which Louis Kirk remained in command, the English yielded Quebec to the French. The Huguenot governor won the respect and confidence of the inhabitants by his lenient course, and his courteous manners. He was, according to Champlain, a thorough Frenchman, though the son of a Scotchman who had married in Dieppe; and he did all in his power to induce the French families, whose company he preferred to that of the English, to remain in Quebec. He permitted the Jesuit fathers to say mass, and entertained them at his table, to the great displeasure of his sailing master Captain Michel, who could scarcely restrain himself from coming to blows with the members of the hated fraternity. The death of this stubborn heretic, which occurred a few days later, was regarded as a judgment, in view of his violent abuse of "the good fathers;" and dying in his pretended religion, I do not doubt, says Champlain, that his soul is now in hell.[1]

Singularly enough, the agent whom France now appointed to receive back her American province, was likewise a Huguenot. This agent was Emery de Caen, the son[2] of Guillaume, sieur de la Mothe. Emery had been associated with his father in the company holding the monopoly of the Canadian fur-trade; and to indemnify him for the losses he had sustained in the late war, he was permitted to enjoy the benefits of that monopoly during a single year. At the expiration of this term, the Company of New France entered upon the full possession of its rights.

It was on the twenty-third day of May, 1633, that Champlain, again appointed governor, took

---

[1] Voyage de Champlain, II., p. 313. "Deux ou trois jours apres ledit Jacques Michel estant saisi d'un grand assoupissement fut 35 heures sans parler, au bout duquel temps il mourut rendant l'ame, laquelle si on peut juger par les œuvres et actions qu'il a faites, et qu'il fit le jour auparavant; et mourant en sa religion pretendue, je ne doute point qu'elle ne soit aux enfers."

[2] The First English Conquest of Canada, with some account of the Earliest Settlements in Nova Scotia and Newfoundland. By Henry Kirk, M.A. London, 1871. P. 69.

Chap. I.
1633.
May 23.

from the hands of the Protestant De Caen, the keys of the fort of Quebec. Two Jesuit missionaries, who had come over with De Caen, were already in possession of their convent, built shortly before the capture of the place by Kirk.

From this time forth, Canada was formally closed to the Protestant colonist. The heretic trader continued to be tolerated, but he was jealously watched, and restricted in his intercourse with the inhabitants. The privilege of a permanent residence was granted to none but to Frenchmen professing the Roman Catholic faith.

The doom pronounced.

In this prohibition, religious intolerance pronounced the doom of the French colonial system in America. The exclusion of the Huguenots from New France, was one of the most stupendous blunders that history records. The repressive policy pursued by the French government for the next fifty years, culminating in the revocation of the Edict of Nantes, tended more and more to awaken and to strengthen among the Protestants a disposition to emigrate to foreign lands. Industrious and thrifty, and anxious at any sacrifice to enjoy the liberty of conscience denied them at home, they would have rejoiced to build up a French state in the New World. No other desirable class of the population of France was inclined for emigration. It was with great difficulty that from time to time the feeble colony could be recruited, at vast expense, and with inferior material. Meanwhile, hundreds of thousands of expatriated Huguenots carried into the Protestant countries of Northern Europe, and into the British colonies of America, the capital, the industrial skill, the intelligence, the moral worth, that might have enriched the French possessions, and secured to the Gallic race a vast domain upon the North American continent.[1]

There is reason to believe that in spite of

---

[1] The enlightened author of the *Histoire du Canada depuis sa Découverte jusqu' à nos Jours*, has fully recognized the greatness of this mistake. "Le dix-septième siècle fut pour la France l'époque la plus favorable pour coloniser, à cause des luttes religieuses du royaume, et du sort des vaincus, assez triste pour leur faire désirer d' abandonner une patrie qui ne leur présentait plus que l'image d' une persécution finissant souvent par l' échafaud ou le bûcher. Si Louis XIII. et son successeur eussent ouvert l' Amérique à cette nombreuse classe d'hommes, le Nouveau Monde compterait aujourd'hui un empire de plus, un empire français ! . . . . Richelieu fit donc une grande faute, lorsqu'il consentit à ce que les protestans fussent exclus de la Nouvelle-France ; s' il fallait expulser une des deux religions, il aurait mieux vallu, dans l' intérêt de la colonie, faire tomber cette exclusion sur les catholiques qui émigraient peu ; il portait un coup fatal au Canada en en fermant l' entrée aux Huguenots d' une manière formelle par l' acte d' établissement de la compagnie des cent associés. . . . . Le système colonial français eût eu un résultat bien différent, si on eût levé les entraves qu' on mettait pour éloigner ces sectaires du pays, et si on leur en eût laissé les portes ouvertes. . . . . Et pourtant c' était dans le temps même que les Huguenots sollicitaient comme une faveur la permission d' aller s' établir dans le Nouveau-Monde, où ils promettaient de vivre en paix à l' ombre du drapeau de leur patrie, qu'ils ne pouvaient cesser d' aimer ; c'était dans le temps, dis-je, qu' on leur refusait une prière dont la réalisation eût sauvé le Canada, et assuré pour toujours ce beau pays à la France. Mais Colbert avait perdu son influence à la cour, et était mourant. Tant que ce grand homme avait été au timon des affaires, il avait protégé les calvinistes qui ne troublaient plus la France, mais l' enrichissaient."—Histoire du Canada depuis sa Découverte jusqu' à nos Jours. Par F. X. Garneau. Québec: 1845. Tome I., pp. 155, 156, 157, 493.

Chap. I.
1633.

prohibitory laws and ecclesiastical vigilance, Huguenot settlers succeeded from time to time in establishing themselves in Canada. We may infer as much from the boasted success of the Jesuits in their efforts to convert heretics whose presence in the colony was detected.[1] Sixteen

---

[1] Tanguay, Dictionnaire Généalogique des Familles Canadiennes, depuis la fondation de la colonie jusqu' à nos jours, mentions the following instances of abjuration prior to the year 1700:

David Beaubattu, baptized 1668, son of Jean Beaubattu and Marie Champagne, of Lairac, [Layrac,] near Agen, [Lot-et-Garonne]. Soldier in the company of M. de Muy. Abjured Calvinism, Jan. 6, 1686, at Pointe-aux-Trembles, Quebec.

François Bibaud, baptized 1642, son of François Bibaud, of La Rochelle, [a Protestant: comp. La France Protestante, *s. v.*,] was living in Quebec in 1671.

Charles-Gabriel Chalifour, born in 1636 in La Rochelle, after spending some years in New England, went to Montreal, where he abjured Calvinism and was baptized Dec. 26, 1699.

Pierre Champout, son of André Champout and Marie Lavau, of St. Germain d' Hemet, in Périgord, diocese of Périgueux, abjured August 16, 1672, at Three Rivers.

Matthieu Doucet, miller, baptized in 1637, came from France in 1656. Made abjuration of heresy. Was buried March 25, 1657, at Three Rivers.

Daniel Fore, son of Isaac Fore and Anne Tibault, of St. Jean d' Angély, diocese of La Rochelle. Soldier, called Laprairie. Made abjuration in April, 1685.

François Freté, called Lamothe, baptized in 1668, of Lamotte St. Eloi, diocese of Poitiers, abjured Calvinism, June 29, 1699, in Montreal.

Isaac Le Comte, tailor, of Linctot, [Lintot,] diocese of Rouen; a Calvinist converted in Canada; buried March 9, 1635, at Three Rivers.

Daniel Pépie, called La Fleur, soldier in the company of M. Cahouac; son of Jacques Pépie and Isabelle Fore, of the diocese of Xaintes. Abjured Calvinism, March 4, 1685, in Montreal.

Jacques Poissant, called Laselline, soldier in the company

were discovered in a regiment of regular troops sent over by the government in 1665 ; and the royal intendant hastened to inform the king of their speedy conversion. About the same time, a number of the proscribed religionists were found among a body of emigrants who landed at Quebec. We read in the Jesuit " Relations " an edifying account of the miraculous change effected in one of these men, through the pious ingenuity of a hospital nun. " I cannot," writes Le Mercier to the Reverend Father Bordier, "omit the mention of a very wonderful act of grace, performed upon another heretic, one of the most stubborn of those whom we have seen here. He was entreated repeatedly, and with all possible urgency, in order that his heart might be touched, and that he might be made to see his wretched condition, but always in vain. And not only was he unwilling to listen to the holy and charitable solicitations that were addressed to him, thrusting them from him with indignation, but he even bound himself with fresh protestations to die sooner than to abandon the religion to which all his relatives were attached. Nevertheless, having fallen very grievously ill, he was carried, like others, to the hospital ; and there the good nuns, who are not less zealous for the salvation of the souls of their patients, than anxious for the health of their bodies, did everything in their power to win him over. One of

---

of M. De Noyan, son of Jacques Poissant and Isabelle Magos, of Bourg-Marennes, diocese of Xaintes. Made abjuration in April, 1685, at Pointe-aux-Trembles, Montreal.

them, who had frequently had occasion to prove the virtue of the relics of the deceased Father de Brebeuf, (who was burned some years ago very cruelly by the Iroquois in the country of the Hurons, while engaged in the endeavor to convert that barbarous people), bethought herself of mingling—unknown to this man—a small quantity of these relics, reduced to powder, in a potion which she was about to administer to him. Wonderful to relate, this man became a lamb; he asked that he might receive instruction. He admitted into his heart the impressions of our Faith; he publicly abjured heresy, and that with such fervor as even to astonish himself. And to crown the mercies of God bestowed upon him, he received health for the body as well as for the soul." [1]

---

[1] Relation de ce qui s'est passé en la Nouvelle France és années 1664 & 1665 ; envoyée au R. P. Provincial de la Province de France. A Paris, chez Sebastien Cramoisy, M. DC. LXXVI. Avec Privilege du Roy. Chapitre dernier. Pp. 124, 126. Au Rd. Pere Jacques Bordier. Dated à Kebec le 3, Novembre 1665.

"Je ne puis pas aussi omettre un coup de la grace, bien merveilleux, en la personne d' un autre Heretique, des plus opinionastres que nous ayons veus ici. On le sollicita à plusieurs reprises & avec toutes les instances possibles, pour lui toucher le cœur, & pour lui faire voir son mal-heureux estat : mais toujours en vain. Et non seulement il ne vouloit pas escouter les saintes & charitables instances qu'on luy faisoit, les rebutant avec indignation mais mesme il s'engageoit par de nouvelles protestations, à mourir plutost, que de quitter la Religion, dans laquelle estoient tous ses parens. Cependant estant tombé tres-griévement malade, & ayant esté porté à l' Hospital comme les autres, ces bonnes Religieuses, qui n'ont pas moins de zele pour le salut de l'ame de leurs malades, que d' affection pour la santé de leurs corps, faisoient de leur costé tout leur possi-

The commercial relations of the colony with La Rochelle increased the difficulty of excluding heresy from Canada. That ancient stronghold of the French Protestants had lost its military consequence: but it retained its maritime importance, and the chief part of its wealth and trade were still in the hands of Huguenot capitalists. Quebec depended upon them for its principal importations: and the yearly visits of the merchants concerned in the fur-trade must needs be endured. They were, however, forbidden to exercise their religion while in the colony; and their stay was strictly limited. Emigrants from La Rochelle were looked upon with special distrust. For a time they were admitted: but in 1664, the imperious bishop Laval, of Quebec, declared that he wanted no more colonists from that hot-bed of heresy.[1]

Scarcely less obnoxious to the clergy than the Protestant settler was the agent or factor representing in Canada some Huguenot firm in

---

bles pour le gagner. Une d' entre-elles ayant souvent experimenté la vertu des Reliques de feu Pere de Brebeuf, brûlé autrefois tres-cruellement par les Iroquois, dans le päis des Hurons, lors qu'il travailloit à la conversion de ces Barbares, s' advisa de mesler à son insceu, un peu de ces Reliques pulverisées dans un breuvage qu' elle luy fit prendre. Chose admirable! cét homme devint un agneau, il demande à se faire instruire et il reçoit dans son esprit et dans son cœur, les impressions de nostre Foy & fait publiquement abjuration de l' heresie, avec tant de ferveur, que luy-mesme en est estonné : & pour comble des graces de Dieu sur luy, il reçoit la santé du corps, avec celle de l' ame."

[1] The Old Régime in Canada. By Francis Parkman. P. 216.

Chap. I.
1670.
France. The bishop of Quebec complains in 1670 that these persons are still permitted to come into the province, though the evil effects of their presence have long been felt and made known to the government. These effects may be seen both as it regards religion and as it regards the state. On the side of religion it must be observed that these commercial agents use many enticing words, that they lend books, and sometimes hold meetings among themselves; and, moreover, to the bishop's knowledge, there are people who speak honorably of these men, and cannot be persuaded that they are in error. Nor is the matter less important as viewed on the side of the state. For every one knows that the Protestants are in general not so strongly attached to his Majesty as the Catholics. Quebec is not very far from Boston and from other English towns. To multiply Protestants in Canada would contribute at some future day to revolutions. Those who are here already have not appeared to take any very special interest in the success of his Majesty's arms. On the contrary, they have been seen spreading with some eagerness the intelligence of every slight mischance that has occurred. A sufficient remedy would be applied to this abuse if French merchants were forbidden to send over Protestant clerks.[1]

Dangerous proximity of Boston.

---

[1] " L'Eveque de Quebec represente que les commerçants de France envoyent des commis Protestans, que depuis longtems le clergé en a fait connoitre les inconveniens et par rapport à la religion et par rapport à l'Etat. A l'égard de la

The fact that the persecuted Huguenots of France were taking refuge, in large numbers, in the neighboring English colonies, greatly disturbed the Canadian government and clergy during the last quarter of the seventeenth century. Naturally enough, it was apprehended that in the event of an invasion of the province, on the part of New York and New England, these "renegades," as they were opprobriously styled, would be among the foremost assailants of the power that had oppressed them in the old world. Occasionally, the refugees in those colonies were joined by some Protestant compatriot from Montreal or Quebec. Strict laws were passed for the punishment of any Canadians who might attempt to leave the country for the purpose of removing to Orange or Manatte—as Albany and New York were still

---

religion, l'Eveque de Quebec assure qu'ils tiennent plusieurs discours séduisans, qu'ils pretent des livres et que quelquefois même ils se sont assemblés entr'eux ; qu'enfin il a connoissance que plusieurs personnes en parlent honorablement, et ne peuvent se persuader qu'ils soient dans l'erreur. En examinant la chose du costé de l'état, il paroit qu'elle n'est pas moins importante. Tout le monde sçait que les protestans en général ne sont pas si attachés à sa Majesté que les Catholiques. Quebec n'est pas bien loin de Boston et autres villes Anglois : multiplier les Protestans dans Canada, ce seroit donner occasion pour la suite à des revolutions. Ceux qui y sont n'ont pas paru prendre une part particulière au succès des armes de Sa Majesté : on les a vûs repandre avec un certain empressement tous les petits contretems arrivés. Une defense aux commerçans François d'envoyer des commis Protestans suffiroit pour remedier à l'abus."—Mémoire de l'Evêque de Quebec sur les Protestans, 1670. Massachusetts Archives : French Collections, vol. II., p. 233.

Chap. I.
1683.

called by the French. But in spite of royal edicts, and military surveillance, whole families sometimes succeeded in escaping to the English. The governor of Canada wrote home in 1683: "There are at present over sixty of those miserable French deserters at Orange, Manatte, and other Dutch places under English command."[1] Some years later, an agent of Massachusetts, who had been sent to Quebec for the purpose of effecting an exchange of prisoners with the Canadian government, found there "several French Protestant officers and soldiers," who had "a great desire for Protestant liberty," and "to be under the English protection." These men were only deterred from escaping to New York as "being the most nigh, and the way they are best acquainted with thither," by the fear of "the Maquas' cruelty, who have already murdered several in making their escape."[2]

Protestant soldiers in Canada.

Masters of the arts of intrigue, the Jesuits of

---

[1] Documents relative to the Colonial History of the State of New York. Vol. IX., p. 203.

[2] The Information of Mathew Carey received from severall ffrench Protestants officers and soldiers at Quebeck, Oct. 28, 1695.—Massachusetts Archives, A. 38. This information was communicated by Lieutenant-governor Stoughton, Nov. 25, 1695, to Governor Fletcher of New York.—English Manuscripts in the Office of the Secretary of State, Albany, N. Y., vol. XL., pp. 100, 101. Governor Fletcher, in acknowledging the communication, Dec. 3, 1695, writes, "It is the first time I heard there is any ffrench Protestants in Canada."—Mass. Archives, II., 409. In the margin of Carey's letter occurs the name, probably that of one of the officers referred to, "Monsr. Delarogtterie Cap. of a Marine detachmt." (Nicolas Lecompte de la Ragotterie, capi-

Canada had their agents among the Huguenot refugees in the English colonies; and one of these, it would seem, was Jean Baptiste de Poitiers, sieur Du Buisson, a prominent French resident of Harlem, New York, between the years 1676 and 1681. The accurate historian of Harlem mentions him as "evidently a person of character, and of standing and influence among the refugees," taking much interest in their affairs and rendering them many friendly services.[1] It is to be feared that the Sieur Du Buisson was a Canadian spy of the most accomplished type.[2] Lord Bellomont had him in mind, perhaps, when he reported to the British Board of Trade in 1698: "Some French that passed for Protestants in this province during the war, have since been discovered to be Papists; and one would suspect their business was to give intelligence to Canada."

Meanwhile the zeal of the Canadian clergy for the exclusion and suppression of heresy had

---

taine, était à Québec en 1695.—Tanguay, Dict. gén. des fam. Canadiennes, p. 362.)

[1] Harlem (city of New York): its Origin and Early Annals. By James Riker. P. 416.

[2] Jean Baptiste du Poitiers, sieur du Buisson, was the son of Pierre du Poitiers and Hélène de Belleau, of St. Martin d'Annecour, diocese of Amiens. In 1700 he made declaration, at the Seminary of St. Sulpice, that he had caused several of his children to be baptized in certain heretical countries near Menade [New York] by priests who were then in flight because of persecution. Meanwhile he was passing for a Protestant. It appears from the above declaration that he resided at various times in Flushing, on Staten Island, in Hotbridge [?], three leagues from Menade, and in Esopus, where his youngest child was baptized

Chap. I.
1686.

been stimulated by the Revocation of the Edict of Nantes. A letter of Louis XIV. to Governor de Denonville, in the spring following that event, informed him of the brilliant success of the measure, and expressed his Majesty's persuasion that the example of his subjects of the Pretended Reformed Religion in France, all of whom had now abjured their heresy, would determine those heretics who might still remain in Canada to do likewise. If, however, there should be found among them any stubborn persons unwilling to be instructed, the governor was authorized to quarter his troops in their houses, or to imprison them; being careful to accompany this rigorous treatment with the necessary provisions for their instruction, and to concert with the bishop for this purpose.[1]

Echoes of the Revocation.

(*ondoyé*) by a Protestant minister.—Tanguay, Dict. géneal. des fam. Canadiennes, *s. v.*—In 1693 he was sponsor at the baptism of two children of Pierre Montras, who had renounced the Roman Catholic faith. Riker, p. 416. Suspicions were entertained during his stay in Albany, in 1689, that Du Buisson was maintaining "a secret correspondence with the French" in Canada.—Riker, 416. These suspicions must have been allayed, since he remained several years longer in the province. But in the light of the facts given above, they seem to have been well founded.

[1] Mémoire du Roy à M. de Denonville, Versailles, le 31 May, 1686. * * * Quoyque Sa Majesté soit persuadée qu'il est à present informé de l'heureux succés que son zele pour la conversion de ses sujets de la R. P. R. a eu, elle est bien ayse de luy faire sçavoir qu'ayant reçu des advis de toutes les provinces de son Royaume dans les mois d'aoust et de Septembre dernier du Grand nombre de conversions qui s'y faisoient des villes toutes entieres dont presque tous les marchands faisoient profession de la d. Religion l'ayant abjurée ; cela obligea Sa Majesté à faire publier un edit au

No occasion was found to use the severities thus permitted. The governor speedily wrote to his royal master, assuring him that there was not a heretic in Canada.[1]

One of the effects of the Revocation, was the exclusion of the Huguenot merchants who had so long been tolerated in the province for the sake of its commercial interests. Henceforth the Protestant trader could remain in Quebec only upon condition of a change of religion. The principal French merchant in Canada at this time was one Bernon, who had done great service to the colony. "It is a pity," wrote Denonville, "that he cannot be converted. As he is a Huguenot, the bishop wants me to order him home this autumn, which I have done, though he carries on a large business, and *a great deal of money remains due to him here.*"[2]

---

mois d' Octobre dernier pour revoquer celuy de Nantes. Depuis ce tems, Dieu benissant les pieux desseins de Sa Majesté, tous ses sujets qui restoient encore dans l'heresie en ont fait abjuration de sort que Sa Majesté a à present la satisfaction non seulement de ne voir plus aucun exercise de cette Religion dans ses états, mais meme de voir tous ses sujets faire profession de la religion Catholique. Elle est persuadée que cet exemple determinera les heretiques qui peuvent estre en Canada à faire la même chose, et elle espere que le dit Sr. de Denonville y travaillera avec succes ; cependant si dans ce nombre il s'en rencontrait quelques uns d'opiniatres que refusassent de s'instruire, il peut se servir des soldats pour mettre garnison chez eux, ou les faire mettre en prison, en joignant à cette rigeur le soin necessaire pour les instruire, en quoy il doit agir de concert avec l'Evesque.—Massachusetts Archives, French Collections, vol. III., 183.

[1] Documents relative to the Colonial History of the State of New York. Vol. IX., Page 312.
[2] The Old Régime in Canada. By Francis Parkman. Pp.

Forbidden to land on the shores of the St. Lawrence, the Huguenot could not so well be shut out from the waters of that great Bay of Fundy which had first been visited by the Protestant, De Monts. For while Canada remained during a century and a half, almost uninterruptedly, in the possession of France and of the Jesuits, Acadia, more accessible to commerce, and more exposed to the fortunes of war, was passing from hand to hand between rival claimants, French and English. Five times within the century that followed Poutrincourt's second settlement at Port Royal, the peninsula was seized by the English;[1] each time to be ceded

Chap. I.
1603–1713.

Changing owners.

291, 292.—This was probably Gabriel Bernon, of La Rochelle, who afterwards settled in Boston. His brother Samuel, a zealous Romanist, as we shall see in another chapter, continued to be engaged in trade with Canada, and is spoken of by La Hontan, (Nouveaux Voyages, p. 66), as the merchant who carried on the most extensive business there. (Le Sieur Samuel Bernon de la Rochelle est celui qui fait le plus grand commerce de ce païs-là.) Gabriel's accounts, drawn up in 1686, before his flight from France, mention a sum due to him "en Canada;" and after his coming to Boston he maintained relations with several prominent French officials in that country.

[1] Acadia was feebly held by the French after the destruction of Port Royal by Argall in 1613, and that place was rebuilt, and was occupied until the year 1627, when Sir David Kirk took possession of it. By the treaty of St. Germain-en-Laye, March 29, 1632, Acadia was ceded back to France. In 1654, Port Royal was seized by a British fleet. Negotiations for the restoration of the province to France were opened the next year, but it was not until the year 1667 that England, by the treaty of Breda, surrendered her acquisition. In 1690 an expedition from New England under Sir William Phips captured Port Royal. The French recovered it in the course of the same year. Another New England force, under General Nicholson, conquered Acadia in 1710;

back after a few years' occupation to its original proprietors; until in 1713 by the treaty of Utrecht, "all Nova Scotia or Acadia" was finally secured to the crown of England.

Under such conditions, heresy could not be excluded from the country, even during those periods when it formed a part of the territory of New France. The strict surveillance maintained at Quebec over the traders from La Rochelle and Dieppe, was out of the question at Port Royal and La Hève. Maine and Massachusetts were near neighbors to Acadia. A brisk run of twenty-four hours before the wind brought the Acadian coaster to Casco Bay or to Boston.[1] And with the free intercourse which neither civil nor ecclesiastical police could prevent, kindly feelings were engendered, and social relations were constituted. Even the Church of Rome relaxed its severe features, and moderated its harsh tone, under the softening influences of these associations. Far removed from the scrutiny of the bishop of Quebec, and the espionage of the Jesuits, the parish priest of Acadia tolerated the presence of the Huguenot settler, and sometimes condescended to engage in trade for himself, with the Puritans of New England.

For several years after the destruction of Port Royal by Captain Argall, in 1613, Acadia attracted little attention. The claim which

---

and three years later, by the treaty of Utrecht, April 11, 1713, the province was finally secured to Great Britain.

[1] The distance from Annapolis to Boston is two hundred and fifty miles.

130   UNDER THE EDICT: ACADIA.

Chap. I. had been violently asserted for England in that
1614.   piratical act, was not pressed. The French continued in possession of Port Royal, and kept up their fisheries and their trade in peltries. Poutrincourt remained in the province, consorting with the friendly Indians, and awaiting more favorable times for his unfortunate colony. About this time, it is related, a French Protestant, engaged in a fishing expedition in these waters, was driven by stress of weather into Massachusetts Bay, and was cast ashore. He found the coast inhabited by numerous tribes of savages, who received him kindly, and among whom he lived for two years. Pitying the dense ignorance of these heathen, whom he took to be worshipers of the devil, the zealous Huguenot used his utmost efforts to persuade them to embrace Christianity, but all to no purpose. At length, discouraged, the missionary turned prophet, and warned his hearers that for
1617-   their obduracy God would destroy them. Not
1620.   long after, they were visited by an epidemic that continued for three years, and swept away almost the entire Indian population for sixty miles along the coast.[1] This was the "wonder-

---

[1] Narrative concerning the settlement of New England, 1630. Papers in the State Paper Department of the British Public Record Office. Vol. V. 77. (Calendar of State Papers. Colonial, 1574–1660. P. 111).

"About 16 yeares past an other ffrench man being nere the Massachusetts upon a ffishing voyage, and to discover the Bey, was cast away, one old man escaped to shoare, whom the Indians pserved alive, and after a yeare or 2, he having obteyned some knowledge in their languadge pceiving how they worshipped the Devill, he used all the meanes

ful plague," of which the Pilgrim Fathers of New England heard, upon their arrival a few years later at Plymouth, and which they devoutly regarded as a providential preparation "to make room for the settlement of the English."¹

The feeble remnant of Poutrincourt's party that continued in Acadia, was reënforced, in the year 1633, by forty families brought over from France. These families settled at La Hève, on the coast, and engaged in fishery and in the cultivation of the soil. The greater number of them removed, after a few years, to Port Royal, where they were joined, in 1638, by twenty families more. Still another body of settlers, consisting of some sixty individuals, came over in the year 1671. All these colonists were from La Rochelle and its vicinity.² And inasmuch

---

he could to pswade them from this horrible Idolotrye, to the wop : [worship] of the trew God, whereupon the Sagamore called all his people to him, to know if they would follow the advise and councell of this good old man, but all answeared with one consent that thei would not change their God, and mocked and laughed at the ffrenchman and his God, then said he I feare that God in his anger will destroy you, then said the Sagamore yor God hath not thus manie people neither is he able to destroy us, whereupon the ffrenchman said that he did verily feare his God would destroy them and plant a better people in the land, but they contynewed still mocking him and his God until the plague cam wh was the yeare following, & continewed for 3 yeares until yt God swept almost all the people out of that country, for about 60 miles togeather upon the sea coast."

¹ Palfrey, History of New England, vol. I., p. 177, *note*.

² The History of Acadia, from its first Discovery to its Surrender to England by the Treaty of Paris. By James Hannay. St John, N. B., 1879, pp. 128, 141, 282, 290, 291.

as the population of Aunis, and the adjoining provinces, was at that time largely Protestant, and the Protestants of France were emphatically the emigrating class, it is likely that many, if not most of the emigrants, previous to the Revocation, may have been of the same faith with De Monts, the founder of the colony. This would seem the more probable, in view of the fact that a considerable proportion of the names of Acadian families, believed to have come over at this period, are names of Protestant families of Aunis, Saintonge, and Poitou.[1]

There was one of these Acadian families, about whose Protestant antecedents there can be no question, and which was destined to take a prominent part in the history of the colony. Its founder was Claude de St. Etienne, sieur de la Tour. He is said to have been allied to the noble house of Bouillon.[2] About the year 1609 he came, a widower, with his son Charles, then a boy of fourteen, to Port Royal, for purposes of trade, having lost the greater part of his estates in the civil wars. When that settlement was broken up, in 1613, La Tour removed to the

---

[1] Such as Alain, Barillot, Beaumont, Blanchard, Bobin, Bobinot, Boisseau, Briand, Cadet, Chauvet, Clemenceau, Commeau, Cormié, D'Amboise, D'Amours, Duguast, Goujon, Gourdeau, Landry, La Tour, Lourion, La Parière, Morin, Petiteau, Petitpas, Robichon, Robin, Roy, Sibilleau. (Lièvre, Histoire des Protestants du Poitou, *passim*. La France Protestante, *passim*. Crottet, Histoire des Eglises réformées de Pons, Gémozac et Mortagne, en Saintonge, *passim*. Archives Nationales, TT. Compare Hannay, History of Acadia, pp. 284–290.—Mass. Archives, II., p. 540.

[2] Hannay, History of Acadia, p. 114.

coast of Maine, and built a fort and trading house at the mouth of the Penobscot river, which was claimed by the French as within the limits of Acadia. Here he continued for a number of years, until finally dispossessed by the English of Plymouth.

Meanwhile, Charles de la Tour, now a bold and active youth, had formed a close friendship with young Biencourt, the son of Poutrincourt, the proprietor of Port Royal. Biencourt had remained in Acadia after the destruction of the settlement, at first seeking a home among the Indians, and then engaging, with a few companions, in the attempt to rebuild the trading post whose beginnings had been so unfortunate. The two friends, nearly of the same age, became inseparable; and when in the year 1623, Biencourt died, he appointed Charles his successor in the government of the colony, bequeathing to him all his rights in Port Royal.

From this time forth, La Tour led a life of extraordinary vicissitude, in the course of which he displayed immense energy, and a singular ability to win the confidence and secure the cooperation of his associates. Having fortified himself in a stronghold which he built among the rocks near Cape Sable, and gained the friendship of the neighboring savages, he aspired to something more than the position of a petty chieftain; and in 1627 he petitioned Louis XIII. to be placed in command of the province of Acadia. The elder La Tour undertook the voyage to France, for the purpose of presenting his son's request and of urging his suit. The mission proved successful, and Claude was on his way back to Acadia, when he was taken prisoner by an English man-of-war, and carried to London. Through the influence of some of the Protestant refugees, however, he was soon released. His rank as a Huguenot nobleman brought him into notice at the court of Charles I., who showed him marked favor. He married one of the maids of honor of Queen Henrietta Maria: and in 1630 he returned to Acadia a baronet, with a grant of a large tract of land from Sir William Alexander, the patentee of Nova Scotia, who was now about to renew the attempt to effect a settlement in that country. Equal honors and benefits were to be conferred upon Charles, if like his father he would own allegiance to the crown of England. But this he utterly refused to do. Arriving with two armed vessels at Cape Sable, Claude de la Tour visited his son, and urged him to surrender his fort, promising him that he should continue to hold it under the English government, and setting forth all the advantages that would accrue to him by this exchange of masters. Young La Tour replied, professing his gratitude to the king of England for the favor he was disposed to show him, but declaring that he could not betray the trust committed to him by his royal master the king of France. In this determination he remained firm, in spite of the remonstrances and the threats of his father, who at length, in his desperation, undertook, with the aid of the soldiers and armed seamen at his command, to seize the fort by assault. Charles met force with force, and succeeded in repelling his assailants, who retired after a fierce struggle, in which a number of the English were killed and wounded. Compelled to renounce his plans for his son's advantage as well as for his own, La Tour withdrew in deep mortification to Port Royal, where a colony of Scotch families had been planted some time before under Sir William Alexander's patent. The next year, however, his son induced him to come and take up his abode near the fort, where a comfortable house was provided for him.[1] Soon after, by the treaty of St. Germain-en-Laye, Acadia was ceded back to France, and Charles de la Tour was permitted to hold the office of lieutenant-general, to which, in recognition of his loyalty and courage, Louis XIII. had appointed him. A few years later he received a grant of a large tract of country on the river St. John, and he removed thither, establishing himself in a fort at the entrance of the harbor.

La Tour did not find it easy to retain the post that he had coveted, and that he deserved by his fidelity. A rival soon appeared, and an implacable enemy, in the person of Charles de Menou d'Aulnay, better known by his title as Sieur de Charnisé. Charnisé had acquired possession of a part of Acadia, including the lands around Port

---

[1] Description Géographique et Historique des Costes de l'Amérique Septentrionale. Par M. Denys. Paris: MDCLXXII. Pp. 68–71.

Royal. He held a commission similar to that of La Tour, as lieutenant-general for the king. Both were largely engaged in the fur-trade and in the fisheries of the province. Their interests conflicted at every point: and Charnisé, a man of unscrupulous ambition and unyielding purpose, bent all his energies to the work of supplanting and ruining his opponent. For the next fifteen years the struggle was maintained, Charnisé persistently seeking by intrigue at the court of France to procure the displacement and arrest of his rival, and to obtain the means for enforcing the orders issued to that effect; and La Tour appealing at one time to his co-religionists in La Rochelle, and at another time to his good neighbors in New England, for assistance in defending his rights.

Charles de la Tour had married, about the year 1625, a lady of his own Huguenot faith. Nothing is known of her origin; but it would seem probable that she may have belonged to some Protestant family transplanted at an early day from La Rochelle or its vicinity to Acadia. Madame de la Tour was a woman of heroic character. Sharing her husband's privations and perils, she was often his most trusty agent as well as his wisest counselor. At a time when he was in great straits, she crossed the ocean to La Rochelle, hoping to obtain for him the assistance of his Huguenot friends. Charnisé was then in France, and hearing of her arrival, procured an order for her arrest, but she succeeded in making her escape to England.

There she freighted a ship with provisions and munitions of war for her husband's relief, and set out for Acadia, narrowly escaping capture by one of Charnisé's vessels on the homeward voyage. At another time, Madame de la Tour was left in charge of the fort at the mouth of the river St. John, during her husband's absence, when his enemy's ship entered the harbor, and summoned the feeble garrison to surrender. The heroic woman inspired the few soldiers at her disposal with her own dauntless courage. For answer to the summons, the guns of the fort opened an effective fire upon the besiegers. Twenty were killed and thirteen wounded, and the ship itself was so shattered that it was with difficulty withdrawn to a place of shelter. Two months later, however, Charnisé renewed the attack. This time the approach was made on the side of the land. La Tour had not yet returned, and again his brave wife assumed the command. For three days the assailants were kept at bay. The fourth day was Easter Sunday, and while the garrison were at prayers, the besiegers, through the treachery of a sentinel, were admitted within the palisades. They were scaling the walls of the fort, when Madame de la Tour, apprised of the assault, rushed forth at the head of the little band of defenders, who succeeded in driving back the enemy with great loss. Charnisé now offered terms of capitulation. But no sooner did he obtain possession of the fort, than he sentenced the whole garrison to be hanged. Madame de la Tour was

Chap. I.
1643–1645.

April 13.

compelled to witness the execution of her brave soldiers, with a rope around her own neck. The barbarous Charnisé spared her life, but she did not long survive the indignity and the humiliation thus endured. Within three weeks from the time of the capture, this noble woman was laid to rest on the bank of the St. John river.[1] Her memory has long been held dear in the land of her adoption; and the story of her courage and her constancy certainly deserves to have a place in the record of Huguenot endurance and achievement.[2]

The death of his devoted wife, and the loss of his fort and his lands on the St. John, were strokes of misfortune under which even so strong a nature as that of Charles de la Tour could with difficulty bear up. His rival, Charnisé, was now triumphant, and for the next five years the dispossessed *seigneur* of Acadia was a wanderer in Massachusetts, Newfoundland and Canada. But in the height of his ambitious career, Charnisé suddenly died; and the indomitable La Tour, hastening to Paris, obtained

---

[1] Description Géographique et Historique des Costes de l'Amerique Septentrionale. Par M. Denys. P. 40.

[2] The enemies of Charles de la Tour, in the charges which they brought against him at the court of France, did not fail to make use of the fact that his wife was a staunch Protestant. He himself appears to have been more pliant in his religious professions, and sometimes conformed to the Church of Rome, when he deemed it politic to do so. He continued, however, to appeal to Boston for aid, on the score of his Protestant faith (Palfrey, History of New England, II., 144); and his Huguenot brethren in La Rochelle retained their warm regard for him to the last.

from the queen a renewal of the commission which the late king, Louis XIII., had given him, as governor and lieutenant-general in Acadia. Soon, however, by another change of masters, the province reverted to England. La Tour surrendered his fort to the vessels of Oliver Cromwell; but again his ready wit and his extraordinary powers of persuasion served him, and loss was converted into advantage. Betaking himself to England, he sought an interview with Cromwell, and pleading the grant that had been made by the English government twenty-five years before to his father and himself, under Sir William Alexander's patent, he obtained from the Protector the cession of a vast territory, including the whole coast of the Bay of Fundy on both sides, and extending one hundred leagues inland. The next year, La Tour sold his rights to a portion of this territory, and withdrew from public life. His long and changeful career terminated peacefully in the year 1666, when he died at the age of seventy-two.[1]

---

[1] By his second marriage, Charles de la Tour had two sons and three daughters. The elder son, Jacques de St. Etienne, born in 1661, married Anne Melançon, and lived at Cape Sable. He died before 1688, leaving four children. The younger son, Charles, born in 1664, lived at Port Royal, and was not married. In 1696, we find him engaged with young Gabriel Bernon, son of the refugee, in trade between Boston, Portsmouth and Port Royal. He was arrested in November or December of that year, when about to proceed from Portsmouth to Acadia, or Nova Scotia—just then under British rule—and his sloop was condemned as a lawful prize, under charge of having violated one of the provisions of the oppressive Navigation Laws, as well as a

Chap. I.
1711–
1760.

In the century following, under British rule, Acadia, or Nova Scotia, as it was now called, saw another Huguenot occupying the chief office in the province. This was John Paul Mascarene, a native of Castres in Languedoc: of whose parentage and early life an account will be given in a subsequent chapter. Coming to England in his boyhood, a refugee from persecution in France, Mascarene was naturalized in the year 1706, and received a lieutenant's commission in the British army. In 1711 he was sent to Nova Scotia in command of a body

---

recent enactment of the colonial legislature of Massachusetts, that prohibited all commerce between that colony and Nova Scotia. This enactment, which had been inspired by the suspicion that the French—then at war with England—obtained supplies at Port Royal, bore very heavily on the Acadians, who depended so greatly for subsistence upon their dealings with New England. Bernon, and other French refugees in Boston, who were interested in the trade with Acadia, especially resented it, and several of them left Massachusetts soon after, in consequence, it would appear, of this interference with that trade. "You can well see," wrote young Bernon to his father, then in England, "from the manner in which these people treat us, that it will be impossible for us to live any longer among them, without strong recommendations to the governor who is expected soon. They commit the greatest possible injustice toward the inhabitants of Acadia; for whilst they assume to take them under their protection, they pass laws that condemn them to perish with cold and hunger; and if they do any thing contrary to the interests of the English, they punish them as subjects of the king of England."—(Bernon Papers.)

Charles de la Tour went to France, and died before the year 1732; and the only son of Jacques, his elder brother, removed also from Nova Scotia. The descendants of two of the three sisters, Anne and Marguerite de la Tour, are numerous in that province.—(Hannay, History of Acadia: pp. 206, 287, 324. Mass. Archives, French Collections, vol. III., p. 331.)

JOHN PAUL MASCARENE. 141

of troops. He rose to the rank of lieutenant-colonel, and became a member of the provincial council; and in 1740 he was appointed lieutenant-governor of Nova Scotia. His administration of affairs in the province was eminently wise and able. Succeeding an injudicious and incompetent governor, he pursued a course so conciliatory, and at the same time so firm, that he won the entire respect and confidence of both the French and the English. When a strong French force besieged Annapolis, in 1744, the Acadians refused to take part with the besiegers against the British, declaring that they " lived under a mild and tranquil government, and had all reason to be faithful to it."[1] Mascarene's moderation, characteristic of his Huguenot race, was sometimes an occasion of perplexity to the French authorities in Quebec and in Versailles. The Indians, friendly to the English, having burned down the church at Port Royal or Annapolis, he ordered it to be rebuilt. He encouraged the Acadian villagers in their efforts to obtain missionaries, and protected the priests when peaceable and loyal to the English government. The governor of Canada writes home that he cannot perceive the motives for this policy, "unless Mr. Mascarene calculates that mild measures will be more effectual than any other to detach the affections of the Acadians from France."[2] Unlike the career of the adven-

Chap. I.
1740–1760.

October 28, 1745.

---

[1] Hannay, History of Acadia. P. 336.
[2] Documents relative to the Colonial History of the State of New York. Vol. X., p. 17.

turous La Tour in so many respects, that of John Paul Mascarene resembled it in two particulars. His relations with New England were always intimate. Massachusetts shared his affections with Nova Scotia, and he had fast friends among its leading citizens. Like La Tour also, he spent his last years in honorable retirement, dying in Boston on the fifteenth day of January, 1760, at the age of seventy-five.

But we must go back to the seventeenth century. For a number of years preceding and following the period of the Revocation of the Edict of Nantes, Acadia was a possession of the French crown: and insecurely as he held it, Louis XIV. did not overlook this province, in taking measures for the extirpation of heresy, in the colonies of France as well as at home. Occasionally, his faithful clergy saw fit to remind him of the duty. The bishop of Quebec, and his grand vicar, always keen to detect heresy, represent to the king the danger of its spread in this remote part of their large diocese, and urge upon him the importance of crushing it at once. They learn with alarm that a stationary fishery is about to be established in Acadia, by a number of Huguenots, who will bring over a minister with them. The king is reminded that these people have been forbidden to settle in Canada, and it is especially important that they be not tolerated in Acadia.[1] The governor of Canada

---

[1] Résumé d' une lettre de M. Douyt, Grand Vicaire de l'Evesque de Quebec. (1681). A appris qu'on se prepare a faire un etablissement en l' Acadie pour une pesche seden-

concurs in these representations, but writes more cautiously, and as if aware of the difficulties of the situation. It would be unwise, he thinks, to permit French Huguenots to come and form an establishment so near to the English in New England, who are likewise of the religion called Reformed, and in a country to which no vessels from France come for purposes of commerce, and which subsists only through intercourse with the inhabitants of Boston. It would indeed be dangerous to set up any new claims there, inasmuch as the king has neither an armed force nor a governor of his own in that territory, and hence there would be the risk of losing it in a single day.[1]

The enterprise viewed with so much anxiety by the Canadian authorities, clerical and lay, was conducted by one Bergier,[2] an intelligent

---

taire, que M. le Sr. Berger et ceux qui passent avec luy sont tous Huguenots, et menent un ministre.—*Massachusetts Archives, French Collections*, III., 23.

M. l' Evesque de Quebec, 19 Novembre, 1682. Il est important de ne point donner d' atteint a l' Edit qui deffand aux Huguenots de s'establir en Canada, et surtout de ne les point souffrir dans l' Accadie.—*Id.*, III., 45.

[1] *Rapport de M. de la Barre au Ministre.* A Quebec le 4 Novembre 1683. * * * Il est important, Monseigneur, de ne pas permettre que des Huguenots François viennent former un etablissement si proche des Anglois de la Nouvelle Angleterre, qui sont aussi de la religion qu'on appelle Reformée et en un pays ou il ne vient point de navires de France pour y faire le commerce, et qui ne subsiste que par celuy qu'il fait avec les Bostonnais. Il est mesme dangereux d' y establir aucuns droits nouveaux, parceque le Roy n' ayant ny force ny Gouverneur en son nom au dt pays, l' on courreroit risque de le perdre en un jour. *Id.*, III., 93.

[2] The family of Bergier was prominently represented in

and energetic merchant of La Rochelle, and "a most obstinate Huguenot," who had associated with himself three Protestant citizens of Paris, the Sieurs Gautier, Boucher, and De Mantes, for the purpose of engaging in the shore fishery in Acadia. This important business had been, of late, greatly interfered with by the fishermen of New England, who were permitted by the acting commandant of Acadia, De la Vallière, to follow their craft freely in the waters of the province, upon payment of a certain toll. Bergier, who had visited Acadia, succeeded in obtaining from the government of Louis XIV. the right to establish a stationary or coast fishery, and to build a fort for its protection. The great Colbert was still in power, though that power was waning:[1] and it was doubtless due to his urgency that Bergier and his associates were permitted to carry out their plans, in spite of the remonstrances from Quebec.[2] In 1684, the king appointed Bergier his lieutenant for the

---

the municipality of La Rochelle during the sixteenth and seventeenth centuries. The Acadian trader may have been one of the numerous sons of Isaac Bergier, who was "capitaine de la ville," in 1651.—La France Protestante, deuxième edition, s. v.

[1] He died September 6, 1683.

[2] Memoire sur l'Acadie, Mass. Archives, French Collections, III., 49. It appears that Bergier went by Colbert's orders in 1682 to Acadia to effect the establishment, and came back in December in the same year to make his report to the minister. A second visit was made in the spring of 1683 by command of Colbert, who died before Bergier's return.

coast and country of Acadia, for the following three years.[1]

East of Nova Scotia and the adjoining island of Cape Breton, the French had planted a colony, some years before, in the bay of Placentia, on the southern coast of Newfoundland. The Sieur Parat, governor of Placentia, reports to Louis XIV., in 1686, that in consequence of the measures he has taken, there remains but a solitary Huguenot family in the place. Several have renounced heresy, as will be seen by the inclosed certificates of abjuration. The surgeon of the port being a Huguenot, he has sent him home upon a ship sailing for Marseilles.[2] One is tempted to suspect that a vein of irony can be discovered in the governor's communication, as

---

[1] Provision de Lieutenant de Roy pour le Sr. Bergier. Mass. Archives, French Collections, III., 113.

[2] Mémoire du Sieur Parat: Plaisance, 1686. Mass. Archives, French Collections, III., 321.

In another case of expulsion, which occurred the following year, M. Parat failed to gain the approval of his superiors. From the minister's letter to him, November 9, 1687, it appears that the person expelled was named Basset, that he had lived in Boston for fourteen years, and that Parat was indebted to him for a considerable sum of money. Investigation showed that very probably the governor had been prompted by a desire to avoid payment, and to take possession of his creditor's goods. He is roundly berated by the minister, and ordered to make instant restitution.—Mass. Archives, French Collections, III., 279. The subject of this treatment was undoubtedly David Basset, mariner, whose petition for denization had been granted by Governor Andros the year before. The letter of denization states that he "hath been a Resident and Inhabitant with his famyley in ye Towne of Boston for the space of fourteene Yeares Last past."—Mass. Archives, CXXVI., 373.

he proceeds to ask whether he ought to arrest the French of the Pretended Reformed Religion who are on board English vessels, and if so, whether the requirement extends to the case of those who have been naturalized as Englishmen. If such be his Majesty's intention, he adds demurely, a force will be needed to enable him to execute it. The king's reply is equally demure. The governor may very properly cause such seamen to be arrested and sent to France, but let him be careful not to undertake anything in this regard without being sure of success.[1]

Both the king and his servant knew that France held the little settlement of Placentia by a very feeble tenure. Six years later, the place was destroyed by the English. Meanwhile the governor could enforce upon the few defenseless Huguenots of his colony the penalties of the Edict of Revocation, without fear of rebuke from his royal master. How faithfully he did so we learn by a letter of the minister Louvois to the Sieur Parat in 1689. "The king has approved of the course you have taken in the case of the daughter of the Sieur Pasteur,[2] in sending her to the nuns of Quebec, and his Majesty gives you liberty to compel the new converts whose conduct is not sufficiently exact, to send their

---

[1] Documents relative to the Colonial History of the State of New York, Vol. IX., 318.

[2] "M. Pastour" writes from Placentia, January 1, 1691, to the French minister of marine, informing him that the island of St. Peter, in Acadia, has been pillaged by a party of Englishmen.—Documents, etc., IX., 922.

daughters thither, in order that they may be taught the duties of religion, and may be kept there until an opportunity may be found to marry them to good Catholics. You will, however, be careful to proceed cautiously in this matter, lest these efforts should alarm the new converts, and drive them to the resort of escaping to the English."[1]

---

[1] Lettre du Ministre au Sieur Parat. A Versailles, le 7 Juin, 1689. Le Roy a approuvé la conduite que vous avez tenu pour la fille du Sieur Pasteur, en l'envoyant aux Religieuses de Quebec, et Sa Majesté vous laisse la liberté d'obliger les nouveaux convertis dont la conduitte n'est pas assez exacte, a y envoyer leurs filles, pour leur apprendre les devoirs de la religion et y etre gardées jusqu' a ce qu' on trouve a les marier a des bons catholiques. Vous observerez cependant d' y aporter quelque menagement, en sorte qui ce soin n'effarouche point les nouveaux convertis, et ne les oblige point a prendre le party de passer aux Anglois.— Mass. Archives, French Collections, III., 357.

CHAPTER II.

NEW NETHERLAND.

1623—1664.

Chap. II.
March 1, 1562.
August 8, 1570.

Eight years of strife and bloodshed in France, beginning with the massacre of Vassy, were terminated by the peace of Saint Germain, at the close of the third civil war. The treaty that announced to the distracted country a cessation of hostilities between Protestant and Romanist, secured to the former a certain measure of religious liberty. "For the first time in their history, the relations of the Huguenots of France to the state were settled by an edict which was expressly stated to be perpetual and irrevocable."[1] Not many months elapsed, however, before the insincerity and the ineffectiveness of the Edict of Pacification became apparent; and scarcely two years had passed when the massacre of Saint Bartholomew's day realized the worst fears of the Protestant party. The satanic scheme that aimed at the extermination of the hated sect, failed of accomplishing its end; but France was deluged in blood; and among the thousands who were butchered in cold blood, or in the

August 24, 1572.

---

[1] History of the Rise of the Huguenots of France, by Henry M. Baird. Vol. II., p. 366.

frenzy of fanatical zeal, many of the noblest and purest of her sons perished.

Immediately after the massacre of St. Bartholomew's day, large numbers of the inhabitants of Bretagne, Normandy, and Picardy fled to the English islands of Jersey and Guernsey, as well as to Great Britain itself; and larger numbers emigrated, both to England and to Holland, from the Walloon country, on the north-eastern border of France. The Walloons were the inhabitants of the region now comprised by the French département du Nord, and the south-western provinces of Belgium. They were a people of French extraction, and spoke the French language. Zealous missionaries had preached the doctrines of the Reformation among the Walloons, about the middle of the sixteenth century; and although the mass of the people remained attached to the Roman religion, multitudes embraced the new faith. In spite of the measures employed by the Spanish government for the repression of the movement, secret assemblies of Protestant worshipers were held. In all the principal towns of the region—at Lisle, at Arras, at Douay, Valenciennes, Tournay, Mons, Oudenarde, Ghent, Antwerp and Mechlin—congregations were organized; and in 1563 the Synod of the Walloon Churches in the provinces of Artois, Flanders, Brabant, and Hainault was formed.

The introduction of the Spanish Inquisition into the Netherlands had already driven thousands of Walloon families into exile. Of these,

Chap. II.
1572.

1544.

1561.

many established themselves in England, taking with them the industries and the commercial enterprise that brought new prosperity to that country. The manufacture of woolen, linen and silk fabrics, introduced by Protestant workmen from the Belgian and Flemish provinces, spread from London and Sandwich, where the refugees first settled, to many other places, and was carried on with singular success. Exposed sometimes to annoyance and injury, as their skill and thrift excited the jealousy of native artisans, the strangers enjoyed for the most part the favor of the people among whom they had come to dwell, and found England a sanctuary both for their temporal interests and for their religion. Walloon churches were founded more than a century before the revocation of the Edict of Nantes, in London, Canterbury, Norwich, Southampton and other principal towns of the kingdom. The Walloons in Canterbury, as early as the year 1561, were granted the use of the under-croft or crypt of the cathedral, as a place of worship.

Another and a larger emigration took place a few years later, setting toward the Protestant state of Holland. The Walloon provinces of Artois, and Hainault, with a part of French Flanders refused to join Holland and Zealand in forming the commonwealth of the United Netherlands, preferring a reconciliation with Spain. The Protestants who still remained in these provinces, now removed by thousands into Holland. Here they were welcomed, as well by the government as by their co-religionists, and were admitted with characteristic liberality to the enjoyment of equal rights, social, political and religious. Walloon colonies were formed, and Walloon churches were organized, in all the principal cities of the Dutch republic. These communities, while they acquired the language of their adopted country, retained their own; and the Walloon families, though not unfrequently allied by intermarriage with those of their hosts, preserved for several generations a character distinctly French. From time to time they were recruited by accessions from the persecuted Huguenots of France. Eminent Frenchmen came to occupy the pulpits and to fill the chairs to which they were welcomed in the universities of the land. The Walloon churches, while retaining their own ritual and mode of government, became incorporated with the ecclesiastical establishment of the nation. The contribution thus made to the industrial, the intellectual, and the religious strength of the people was of incalculable worth.

Early in the seventeenth century, not a few families, French and Walloon, that afterwards took root in America, were living in these hospitable towns of Holland. Among the leading names that may be mentioned, were those of Bayard, De Forest, De la Montagne. Nicolas Bayard, a French Protestant clergyman, had taken refuge in the Netherlands after the massacre of St. Bartholomew's day. His name appears among the earliest signatures attached

Chap. II.
1580.

to the articles of the Walloon Synod. Tradition reports that he had been a professor of theology in Paris, and connects him with the family represented by the famous knight "sans peur et sans reproche." In the next generation, Lazare[1]

1608.

Bayard, perhaps a son of Nicolas, was enrolled among the Walloon clergy in Holland. It was this Huguenot pastor, we are led to believe, whose daughter Judith married Peter Stuyvesant, the last of the Dutch governors of New Netherland; and whose son, Samuel, was the father of Nicolas, Balthazar, and Peter Bayard, from whom the American branches of this family descend. Amsterdam was the adopted home of the Bayards, and of several other families that eventually removed to New Netherland.

1584.

No city of Holland drew to itself greater numbers of the Walloons and French, than Leyden; and no other is invested with so much interest for the student of American history. For it was here that the Puritan founders of Plymouth colony sojourned during almost the

Leyden.

whole period of their stay in the Netherlands. Here they conceived and matured the plan of removing to the New World, and of laying the foundations of a state, in which, while free to worship God according to their own consciences, they might live under the protection of England,

---

[1] The traditional name is Balthazar Bayard. It is probable that he bore both names; for his daughter Judith, who married Governor Stuyvesant, named her eldest son (baptized in the Dutch Church, New Amsterdam, October 13, 1647,) "Balthazar Lazarus."

and enlarge her dominions. And it was here that a body of Protestant Walloons and Frenchmen, influenced no doubt by the example of their Puritan neighbors, entertained a similar project, and engaged in an enterprise that led to the colonization of New York.

"Fair and beautiful"[1] Leyden had regained its eminence among the flourishing cities of Holland, since the memorable siege of 1574. It was now the principal manufacturing town in the Netherlands; and its great university, founded as a memorial of the heroism of its inhabitants during that siege, held the foremost place among the universities of Europe. Attracted doubtless both by the educational and by the industrial advantages of the place, many of the French Protestants had chosen this town as their home. A Walloon church was founded in Leyden as early as the year 1584. Some of its members were of noble rank; a few were scholars; but most of them were artisans, who met with encouragement in this busy and populous city to ply their several crafts. Almost every branch of industry was represented among them; but the principal employments were those of the wool-carder,[2] the weaver, the clothier, and the dyer.

The Walloons and French in Leyden composed a considerable colony, when in 1609 they

---

[1] Bradford.

[2] It was among the humble workmen who pursued these crafts that the Reformation in France won some of its earliest adherents: as Jean Leclerc, "the wool-carder of Meaux."

saw a company of English refugees arrive in that city. The strangers were simple farmers from Nottinghamshire, who, learning that religious freedom could be enjoyed in the Low Countries, had come with John Robinson their teacher to seek an asylum there. The Brownists, as they were opprobriously called, had first designed to make Amsterdam their home; but after a few months' stay, they determined to remove to Leyden, a place recommended to them by its "sweet situation." They soon "fell to such trades and employments as they best could, and at length came to raise a competent and comfortable living, but with hard and continual labor."[1] Their relations with the Dutch, and with their French and Walloon neighbors, are known to have been most friendly. Some of the English became weavers; Bradford, one of their number, "served a Frenchman at the working of silks."[2] It is not unlikely that others were similarly associated. Religious interests drew them still more closely together. The magistrates of Leyden had granted the use of the same church to the French and the English strangers. St. Catharine Gasthuis was the building thus occupied from 1609[3] till 1622. In the course of time,

---

[1] Bradford, History of Plymouth Plantation, 17.
[2] Mather, Magnalia, II., chap. I., §4.
[3] History of the Scottish Church, Rotterdam. Notices of the British Churches in the Netherlands. By the Rev. William Steven. Edinburgh, 1832, p. 314. Mr. George Sumner has questioned the statement, so far as it concerns the Brownists.—(Contributions to the History of the Pilgrim Fathers.)

some of the French in Leyden, as well as several members of the Dutch churches,[1] embraced the distinctive religious views of the English Separatists, and were admitted into their communion.

But the Puritans were not long content to remain in Holland. Their children were exposed to many temptations in a large city; the laxity with which the Sabbath was observed by the Dutch distressed them sorely; they could not bear the thought of losing "their language and their name of English;" and besides, they longed that God might be pleased "to discover some place unto them, though in America, where they might live and comfortably subsist," and at the same time "keep their name and nation."[2]

Projects of American colonization had long been entertained in England. From time to time, British merchants and adventurers had embarked in the enterprise, and the government had encouraged it by ample charters. But the attempts of the Virginia Company to plant settlements at various points along the coast, from Cape Fear to Nova Scotia, had failed, with a

---

[1] "Divers of their members [members of the Dutch churches] . . . betook themselves to the communion of our church, went with us to New England. . . . One Samuel Terry was received from the French church there into communion with us. . . . There is also one Philip Delanoy, born of French parents, came to us from Leyden."— Winslow, Brief Narration, 95, 96; Palfrey, History of New England, I., 161.

[2] Winslow, Brief Narration, 81 ; Palfrey, History of New England, I., 147.

single exception. The colony founded at Jamestown in 1607, after years of struggle and weakness, was now well established: and the eyes of England were directed with hope and satisfaction to this rising state, which was ultimately to enjoy the name heretofore applied indefinitely to the whole seaboard south of Acadia—the name of Virginia.

The Leyden Puritans at length determined to remove, under the favor of the Virginia Company, to America. Their design was to plant a colony "in the northern parts of Virginia":—south of the territory then claimed by the Dutch, but north of Virginia proper. Negotiations were opened with the Company, and with merchants in London friendly to the undertaking, for the purpose of procuring a patent, and of obtaining the money needed for the expenses of the voyage and the settlement. These negotiations lasted through two or three years. Various difficulties were raised in the way of the expedition. The king was reluctant to encourage a colony of Separatists. Severe terms were proposed by the London merchants, to whom the Puritans looked for pecuniary aid. The Virginia Company delayed to grant a patent.

Meantime the plans of their English guests had come to the knowledge of the Dutch. Robinson himself, discouraged by the ill-success of the efforts made in England, was inclined to seek aid from capitalists in Amsterdam, and to plant a colony near the Hudson river, under the protection of the States-General of Holland. The Dutch merchants entered heartily into the project. They made "large offers" of assistance, engaging to transport the English families to America, free of expense, and to furnish them abundantly with cattle. It was for the government, however, to sanction the expedition, to give the lands, and to pledge its protection. The States-General of Holland were not prepared to do this. At the very moment when the application of the Puritans was made, the scheme of a Dutch West India Company was engaging the attention of that body. But the plan was not yet mature: and when a memorial was addressed to the Prince of Orange, asking that the English families might be sent to New Netherland as colonists, it was, after much consideration, refused.[1]

At length, however, the original application of the Puritans to England proved successful: a patent came from the Virginia Company; the Brownists,—those at least of the number who were to go as pioneers for the rest,—sold their little property; and leaving "that good and pleasant city" of Leyden, "which had been their resting place near twelve years," the Pilgrim Fathers of New England sailed from Delft-Haven, fourteen miles from that city. Among the passengers on the Speedwell were several of the French, who had

Chap. II.
1620.

April 11.

July 21.

August 5.

---

[1] Documents relative to the Colonial History of the State of New York. Vol. I. Holland Documents. Pp. 22-24.

Chap. II.
1620.

decided to cast in their lot with these English brethren. William Molines and his daughter Priscilla, afterwards the wife of John Alden; and Philip Delanoy,[1] born in Leyden of French parents, were of the number. Others followed, the next year, in the Fortune.

Meanwhile, the Walloons of Leyden had planned to follow the example of their Puritan neighbors,—with whom they had doubtless consulted freely on the subject,—and were prepared to remove, in a considerable body, to America. Less than a year[2] after the sailing of the Speedwell, the British ambassador at the Hague, Sir Dudley Carleton, was approached by a delegate from this band. "Here hath been with me of late," wrote the minister, "a certaine Walon, an

July 19, 1621.

inhabitant of Leyden, in the name of divers families, men of all trades and occupations, who desire to goe into Virginia, and there to live in the same condition as others of his Maties subjects." The messenger brought a petition, signed by fifty-six heads of families, Walloon and French, all of the Reformed Religion. He in-

---

[1] Others of this name remained in Leyden. Jaques de la Noy, perhaps a brother of the emigrant to New England, presented his son Philippe for baptism in Leyden, June 1, 1625. Guillaume de Lannoy and Geertje Barthelemi were married September 19, 1633. A daughter was baptized July 23, 1634: Marie de Lannoy and Jeanne de Lannoy, witnesses.

[2] Mr. Brodhead, History of the State of New York, vol. I., p. 146, has by mistake placed this interview a year later—in 1622. The letter of Sir Dudley Carleton to Secretary Sir George Calvert, which fixes the time, is dated July 19, 1621.—(State Papers, Holland, Bundle 141 (folio 308), in Public Record Office, London.)

formed the ambassador further that if the proposition should find favor with his Majesty, the petitioners would send over one of their number to England, to treat with the Virginia Company. Carleton himself strongly seconded their request, judging that the colonists "may surely be of singular use to our Company," if some equitable terms might be agreed upon for their transportation to America.

The spokesman, and undoubtedly the leader of the Leyden band of Walloons, was Jesse de Forest. The petition which he presented to the ambassador was signed by him, in the name of the rest. It read thus:

"His lordship the ambassador of the most serene king of Great Britain is very humbly entreated to advise and answer us in regard to the articles which follow.

"I. Whether it would please his Majesty to permit fifty to sixty families, as well Walloons as French, all of the Reformed religion, to go and settle in Virginia, a country under his obedience, and whether it would please him to undertake their protection and defense from and against all, and to maintain them in their religion.

"II. And whereas, in the said families there might be found nearly three hundred persons; and inasmuch as they would wish to carry with them a quantity of cattle, as well for purposes of husbandry as for their support, and for these reasons they would require that they should have more than one ship; whether his Majesty would not accommodate them with one, equipped and furnished with cannon and other arms, on board of which—together with the ship which they may be able to provide for themselves—they could accomplish their voyage, and which might return and obtain commodities to be conveyed to the places that may be granted by his Majesty, as well as carry back the products of that country.

"III. Whether he would permit them, upon their arrival in the said country, to choose a spot convenient for their abode, among the places not yet cultivated by those whom it has pleased his Majesty to send thither already.

"IV. Whether, having reached the said spot, they might be allowed to build a town for their security, and furnish it with the requisite fortifications; where they might elect a governor and magistrates, for the administration of police as well as of justice, under those fundamental laws which it has pleased his said Majesty to establish in the said territories.

"V. Whether his said Majesty would give them cannon and munitions for the maintenance of the said place, and would grant them, in case of necessity, the privilege of manufacturing powder, making bullets and casting cannon, under the arms and escutcheon of his said Majesty.

"VI. Whether he would grant them a township or territory, in a radius of eight English miles or say, sixteen miles in diameter, which they might improve as fields, meadows, vineyards, and for other uses; which territory, whether conjointly or severally, they would hold from his Majesty upon fealty and homage; no others being allowed to dwell within the bounds of the said lands, unless they shall have taken letters of citizenship; in which territory they would reserve to themselves inferior manorial rights; and whether it might be permitted to those of their number who are entitled to maintain the rank of noblemen, to declare themselves such.

"VII. Whether they would be permitted in the said lands to hunt all game, whether furred or feathered, to fish in the sea and the rivers, to cut heavy timber, as well for shipbuilding as for commerce, at their own will; in a word, whether they could make use of all things, either above or beneath the ground, at their pleasure and will, the royal rights reserved; and whether they could dispose of all things in trade with such persons as may be permitted them.

"Which provisions would extend only to the said families and those belonging to them, without admitting those who might come afterwards to the said territory to avail themselves of the same, except so far as they might of their own power grant this to them, and not beyond, unless his said Majesty should make a new grant to them.

"And whereas, they have learned that his said Majesty has established in London a public warehouse at which all merchandises from those countries must be unloaded, and not elsewhere; and considering that it is more than reasonable that those who by their toil and industry have procured to the public the enjoyment of that country, should be the first to enjoy the fruits thereof: They will submit to the ordinances which have been established there to this effect, which will for their better observance be communicated to them.

Promises of fealty. " Under which conditions and privileges, they would promise fealty and obedience as would become faithful and obedient subjects to their king and sovereign lord, submitting themselves to the laws generally established in the said countries, to the utmost of their ability.

"Upon that which precedes, his lordship the ambassador, will, if he please, give his advice; as also, if such be his pleasure, to have the said privilege forwarded in due form as early as possible, in view of the shortness of the time that remains from this to the month of March (the season favorable for the embarkation), in order to give due attention to all that may be required. So doing he will lay his servants under obligation to pray God for the accomplishment of His holy purposes, and for his health and long life."

This petition was accompanied by a paper containing the signatures of all the petitioners, attached to a contract or covenant in the following terms:

"We promise his lordship, the ambassador of the most serene king of Great Britain, that we will go to settle in Virginia, a part of his Majesty's dominions, at the earliest time practicable, and this under the conditions set forth in the

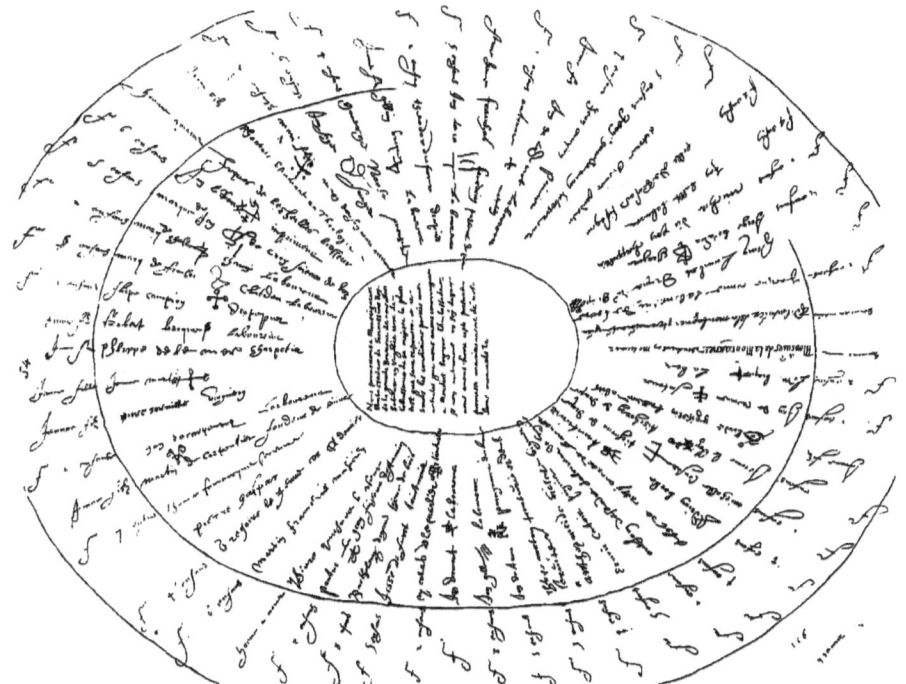

THE COMPANY'S ANSWER.

articles which we have communicated to his said lordship, the ambassador, and not otherwise."[1]

Sir Dudley Carleton favored the project of the Leyden Walloons.[2] Some of their demands he deemed "extravagant" in certain points, but thought that if his Majesty should approve the expedition, these features might be modified. The Lords in Council referred the application to the Virginia Company. The Company's answer was not altogether adverse. They did "not conceive it any inconvenience at present to suffer sixty families of Walloons and Frenchmen not exceeding the number of three hundred persons to go and inhabit in Virginia; the said persons resolving and taking oath to become his Majesty's faithful and obedient subjects: and being willing as they make profession to agree in points of faith, so likewise to be conformable

---

[1] British State Papers: Holland. 1622, Jan.—March. Bundle No. 145. Indorsed: "Supplication of certaine Wallons and French who are desirous to goe into Verginia. 1622." The date should be 1621, since the petition was inclosed in Sir Dudley Carleton's letter of July 21, 1621 (see above). "I required of him his demands in writing, with the signatures of such as were to bear part therein, both which I send your Honor herewith."

The error is repeated in Documents relative to the Colonial History of New York, Vol. III., p. 9, where a translation of this petition is given. For the original French, see the Appendix to the present volume.

[2] He refers to it again, February 5, 1621 [1622, n. s.]: "Within these few months divers inhabitants of this country to a considerable number of familyes have been suters unto me, to procure them a place of habitation amongst his Maties subjects in those parts."—Documents relative to the Colonial History of the State of New York, Vol. III., p. 7.

to the form of government now established in the Church of England." But the Company gave no encouragement to the expectation of material help for the emigration. They deem it "so royal a favor in his Majesty, and so singular a benefit" to those Walloons and Frenchmen, to be admitted to live in that fruitful land, under the protection and government of so mighty and pious a monarch, that they ought not to expect of his sacred Majesty any aid of shipping "or other chargeable favor." As for themselves, "their stock is so utterly exhausted by these three last years' supplies," that "they are not able to give them any help, other than their advice and counsel as to tne cheapest transportation of themselves and their goods, and the most frugal and profitable management of their affairs." The request of the emigrants that they might be allowed to live in a distinct body by themselves, was also thought inadmissible. The Company "conceive that for the prosperity and principally the securing of the plantation in his Majesty's obedience, it is not expedient that the said families should set down in one gross and entire body, which the demands specified, but that they should rather be placed by convenient numbers in the principal cities, boroughs and corporations in Virginia, as themselves shall choose: there being given them such proportion of land, and all other privileges and benefits whatsoever, in as ample manner as to the natural English." This course the Company "out of their own experience do conceive likely to prove better, and more comfortable to the said Walloons and Frenchmen, than that other which they desire."[1]

The correspondence between the Walloons of Leyden and the Council for Virginia went no further.[2] Its discontinuance can be easily ex-

---

[1] The humble answere of His Maties Councell for Virginia concerning certaine Articles put up by some Walloons and Frenchemen desirous to goe to Virginia. See the Appendix to this volume.

[2] Eight years later, a similar application was made to the English government, in behalf of a body of French Protestants, asking for encouragement to settle in Virginia. In 1629, Antoine de Ridouet, Baron de Sancé, addressed the following letter to the Secretary of State:

MONSEIGNEUR :
Le désir que j'ay de servir Sa Majesté et me retirer en ce pays issy avec ma famille et tout ce qui j'ay en France aussy pour faire habituer des franssois protestans en Virginie pour y planter des vignes, olives, faire des soyes, et du sel me fait vous suplier tres-humblement d' obtenir de Sa Majesté quil luy plaise m'honorer de letres de gentilhomme de sa chambre privée. Avec letres de Denison pour moy et mon fils. Et quil luy plaise donner ordre à Monseigneur l'Ambassadeur qui ira en France d'obtenir comme ayant l'honneur d'estre son domestique, liberté et sureté pour moy avec la jouissence de mon bien afin que par ce moyen et soubs la faveur de sa Majesté je puisse issy faire transporter ma famille et mon bien pour estre plus prest à servir sa Majesté et vous aussy mon seigneur.   SANCÉ.
(State Papers, Colonial Series, Vol. V., No. 14. Public Record Office, London.)

The Baron de Sancé was a devoted follower of the Duke of Soubise, with whom, after the siege of La Rochelle, he took refuge in England. His proposal to form a colony of French Protestants in America was favorably entertained by the government. Elaborate plans for the voyage and the settlement were drawn up by the leader in consultation with the attorney-general; and after many delays the refugees embarked. Their destination was Carolina; but they were landed in Virginia. Of this colony, which maintained a languid existence for a few years, particulars will be given in a subsequent volume.

plained. The project of a Dutch West India Company had long been agitated, and it was now about to be carried into effect. While Jesse de Forest was in communication with the British ambassador at the Hague, the States-General of the United Provinces, sitting in the old palace of the Binnenhof, in the same city, were preparing a patent for such a company, and conferring upon it vast powers and privileges. The final organization, however, was delayed for two years more. Meanwhile the government became aware of the designs of the Walloons and French in Leyden. Jesse de Forest, the intelligent and capable leader of the proposed movement, had not desisted from the effort to bring it to a successful consummation. Before the West India Company had actually commenced its operations, he submitted his cherished plan of emigration to the Provincial States of Holland. That body referred it to the directors of the new Company, who reported most favorably. "They have examined the paper relative to the families to be conveyed to the West Indies, and are of opinion that it is very advantageous for the Company, and therefore that an effort ought to be made to promote it, with a promise that they shall be employed." It was suggested, however, that action upon the subject be postponed until the Board of Directors be formed. The assembly, after due consideration, resolved that such promise should be given, with the knowledge of the magistracy.[1]

---

[1] Documents relative to the Colonial History of the State of New York, Vol. I., p. 28.

A mind disposed to observe the events of history as ordered by a divine Providence, may notice with interest the circumstances by which the course of these two important migrations was determined. The English exiles purposed to seek a home near the Hudson river. Discouraged in their application to England for aid, they turned to Holland; but the Dutch were debarred at that moment from accepting them as colonists, and they went to Massachusetts. Following their example, the Walloons sought first the patronage of the Virginia Company, having in view perhaps the very same region for their settlement; but yielding to the solicitations of Holland, now ready to welcome their services, they found a home in New Netherland, at the mouth of the Hudson river. Thus, like Ephraim and Manasseh, in patriarchal story, each band received, as from hands "guided wittingly," the appropriate and intended blessing.

The enterprising Walloon lost no time in urging his request before the States-General of the United Netherlands. On the twenty-seventh of August, the councilors of the States of Holland reported to that august body upon a petition which had been submitted to them for their consideration. It appears from that report that Jesse de Forest has applied to the States-General for their permission to enroll families or individual colonists professing the Reformed religion, who may be inclined to undertake the voyage to the West Indies,[1] for the advancement and promo-

---
[1] By the West Indies, it was common at that day, to desig-

tion of the West India Company. The report favors the granting of the request: and Jesse de Forest is permitted to enroll all families having the required qualifications, to be transported to the West Indies, there to be serviceable to the country: on condition that the said DeForest shall do this with the knowledge and concurrence of the several cities in which he shall make this enrollment: and that he shall be held to make return of the same to the States of Holland.[1]

---

nate the whole continent of America. Jean de Laet, one of the directors of the West India Company, wrote a "Description of the West Indies," the third chapter of which, entitled "Virginia," included an account of New Netherland. Baudartius speaks of "divers families," most of whom were English Brownists, as going in 1624 and earlier "from Holland to *Virginia in the West Indies.*"—Doc. Hist. of N. Y., IV., 131. In 1632, the ambassadors of the States-General at the English court, speak of the Mauritius. [Hudson] river "*in the West Indies;*" and in 1665, they mention "*New Netherland in the West Indies.*"—Doc. rel. to Col. Hist. of N. Y., I., p. 56; II., pp. 341–343.

[1] La requête, présentée par Jesse des Forest aux hauts et puissants les Etats généraux des Provinces Unies, a été renvoyée le 16ᵉ d'Août dernier aux Etats de Hollande qui l'ont mis entre les mains de leurs conseillers. Il résulte de leur examen, que Jesse des Forest désirerait obtenir la permission d'enrôler des familles ou colonistes de la religion réformée, inclinés à faire le voyage aux Indes occidentales pour l'avancement et le progrès de la Compagnie des Indes Occidentales—et disposant à la requête du dit Jesse des Forest lui accordent d'enrôler toutes les familles ayant la qualité requise afin d'être transportées aux Indes occidentales pour être utiles au service du pays, sous condition que le dit des Forest le fasse avec connaissance et correspondance mutuelles des villes respectives où il fera le dit enrôlement et qu'il sera tenu d'en faire rapport aux Etats de Hollande.

Ainsi fait à la Haye le 27 d'Août 1622 par ordonnance des Conseillers. (Signé) Van der Wolf.—Copie des actes

The six months that followed were doubtless occupied in preparations for the long-contemplated emigration ; and early in March, 1623, the ship New Netherland sailed from the Texel, having on board a company of thirty families, "mostly Walloons."[1] The emigrants were bound for the site of the settlement now projected by the Dutch West India Company, at the mouth of the Hudson river. Nearly a hundred years had passed since the Florentine explorer Verazzano, sailing under the flag of France, had entered the Narrows, and discovered that "most beautiful bay," which now invites and shelters the commerce of the world. The intervening century had been one of restless adventure. Many a daring navigator had searched the Atlantic coast, seeking for a passage to the Indies, or hoping to discover the fabled country abounding in gold and precious stones. But the "great river of the North" had remained hidden, until visited in 1609 by Henry Hudson. And now, fourteen years later, the first permanent settlement was to be effected upon its banks by colonists from Protestant Holland.

The little ship—of two hundred and sixty tons—took a southerly course, by the Canary Islands. The vessel was new and staunch, and

Chap. II.
1623.
March.

March or April, 1524.

échevinaux de Leide, 27 Août, 1622. (Communicated by Dr. W. N. du Rieu, bibliothécaire de la bibliothèque Wallonne à Leide.)

[1] Documentary History of the State of New York, vol. III., p. 35.—Documents relative to the Colonial History of the State of New York, vol. I., pp. 149, 181, 283.

its commander, Cornelis Jacobsen May, was an experienced seaman. Favorable winds were encountered, off the coast of Guiana, and early in the month of May the "New Netherland" reached the mouth of the Mauritius, or Hudson river. It was a short trip for those days, and the season was a pleasant one; but the discomforts of the passengers—numbering perhaps one hundred and fifty persons—were likely to be considerable, in the crowded cabin. Great must have been their joy, when that "sweet and cheerful prospect," of which travelers have spoken ever since, greeted their eyes:—the wooded shores rising on either side of the Narrows, and receding to encircle the broad harbor; the beautiful expanse of the bay, over whose waters, teeming with fish, flocks of birds were seen darting in search of their prey. But an unexpected sight awaited the voyagers, as they approached the land. A French ship lay in the harbor. Her errand was to take possession of the country discovered by Verazzano in the preceding century, and now claimed by France in virtue of that discovery. The captain was about to set up the standard of the French king upon the soil of New Netherland. The company of peaceable emigrants could scarcely have diverted him from his purpose: but happily there chanced to be a Dutch vessel of several guns, lying a short distance above: and the remonstrances of the colonists, seconded by a show of force from the "Mackerel," were effectual. The unwelcome visitor soon disappeared in the offing, and our Walloons were free to land upon Manhattan Island.

The settlers found a few huts standing near the southern end of the island. A trading-post had been maintained here for several years by the merchants of Amsterdam; and here Adriaen Block, a mariner in their employ, passed the winter of the year 1613, building a ship to replace his vessel, which had been burned. The first European child born in this region, Jean Vigné, of Huguenot parents, here saw the light, in 1614. But the permanent occupation of the site of the city of New York, dates from the arrival of the ship " New Netherland," in May, 1623.

The little company of passengers soon dispersed. Eight of them were landed at Manhattan, there to take possession for the West India Company. Two families went to the eastward, to seek a home near the Fresh or Connecticut river. Four couples, who had been married at sea, were sent by the first opportunity to form a settlement on the South river, or Delaware, about four miles below the present city of Philadelphia. Eighteen families remained on the ship, which now proceeded up the North river. Landing near the spot where the city of Albany now stands, the settlers built a fort which they called Orange. Around this fort huts of bark were hastily constructed. Soon the friendly natives came with presents of peltry, and a brisk trade was opened with the Mohawks and other tribes.

A ship that reached Holland in the following August, carried letters from New Netherland, making a cheerful report of the settlement.

Chap. II.
1623.
August.

"We were much gratified," wrote the colonists, "on arriving in this country. Here we found beautiful rivers, bubbling fountains flowing down into the valleys; basins of running waters in the flatlands; agreeable fruits in the woods, such as strawberries, walnuts, and wild grapes. The woods abound with venison. There is considerable fish in the rivers; good tillage land; here is, especially, free coming and going, without fear of the naked natives of the country. Had we cows, hogs, and other cattle fit for food—which we daily expect in the first ships—we would not wish to return to Holland."

1628.

By the autumn of the year 1628, the village of New Amsterdam, lying close to the fort on the southern point of Manhattan Island, numbered two hundred and seventy souls. Nearly all the settlers who sought to establish themselves at the South and Fresh rivers had returned. Troubles with the Indians had broken up the settlement commenced so hopefully at Orange, and all but a few men left for a garrison had removed to Manhattan. Among others came George de Rapalie, and his wife Catalina Trico, with their daughter Sarah, born at Orange on the ninth day of June, 1625.

The names of George de Rapalie and Catalina Trico are the only names of the Walloon or French colonists brought over by the New Netherland, in 1623, that have been known hitherto. No list of the first settlers of New Amsterdam has come down to us: and no records of the colony, for the first fifteen years of its existence, have been preserved. The earliest council minutes, and other historical documents in the possession of the State of New York, date only as far back as the year 1638; while the registers of the most ancient ecclesiastical body in the state, the Reformed Protestant Dutch Church of New York, commence in 1639.

In the absence of other sources of knowledge, the list of Walloons and Frenchmen presented in July, 1621, to Sir Dudley Carleton, assumes a special interest. Among the sixty names of families desiring to emigrate to America, it would seem highly probable that the names of some, at least, of the thirty families that emigrated to New Netherland less than two years after, might occur. The presumption is strengthened by the evidence that has been given above, showing that meanwhile the project was not abandoned; that the leader of the company that applied to the English government for permission to go to Virginia, afterwards sought the approval of the States-General of Holland: and that within six months of the time when the "New Netherland" sailed for Manhattan, he was engaged in obtaining recruits for the intended colony.

That Jesse de Forest came to America with the band of emigrants he had organized, can scarcely be doubted. In January following the departure of the Walloons for New Netherland, Gerard de Forest, dyer, petitioned the burgomasters of Leyden, representing that his brother, Jesse de Forest, had lately left for the

West Indies, and asking that he might be allowed to take his place in the practice of his trade.[1]

The Walloon leader brought with him his wife, Marie du Cloux, and her five children.[2] A young Huguenot student of medicine accompanied the De Forest family. He was, perhaps, already betrothed to the only daughter of the house. Jean Mousnier de la Montagne was a native of the town of Saintes, in the province of Saintonge, in France, and had come to the

---

[1] Requête de Gérard des Forest, teinturier, demeurant à Leide, où il dit que son frère Jesse des Forest est recemment parti pour les Indes Occidentales et à qui le Magistrat avait jadis permis de colorer des serges et des camelots, il demande maintenant de remplacer son frère qui est absent, pour exercer le même métier. Accordé en Janvier, 1624. —Copie des actes du 24 Janvier, 1624. (Communicated by Dr. W. N. du Rieu.)

The conjecture that Jesse de Forest may have joined the naval expedition against Brazil, that left Holland in the latter part of December, 1623, and perished in the course of that ill-starred enterprise (History of Harlem, N. Y., pp. 93, 94), is certainly unwarranted. His disappearance from Leyden, at the very time when the scheme of emigration which he had long sought to promote, reached its fulfillment, can be better accounted for by the presumption that he emigrated with the body of colonists who sailed in that year for New Netherland.

[2] The children of Jesse des Forest (du Forest, or de Forest) and Marie du Cloux, were Jean, Henri (born in 1606), Rachel, Jesse (born in Leyden, March 1, 1615), Isaac (born in Leyden, July 7, 1616), Israel (born in Leyden, and baptized October 7, 1617), and Philippe, born in Leyden, and baptized September 13, 1620. (Records of the Walloon Church, and Archives of the City of Leyden.) Two of these doubtless died young.

For an account of the De Forest family in America, descended from Isaac de Forest, son of Jesse, see the invaluable History of Harlem, N. Y., by Mr. James Riker, pp. 571-574.

city of Leyden a few years before the emigration, to attend the University.

There were other signers of the Leyden petition, whose names may be recognized more or less readily, in spite of the Batavian disguises in which they appear, beyond the gap of fifteen or twenty years in the records of New Amsterdam. Such are the names of De la Mot, Du Four, Le Rou, Le Roy, Du Pon, Ghiselin, Cornille, De Trou, De Crenne, Damont, Campion, De Carpentier, Gille, Catoir, de Croy, Maton, Lambert, Martin, Gaspar, and others.

Within three years from the time when these colonists reached New Netherland, their leader died. The widow of Jesse de Forest soon returned with her family to Holland, accompanied by the young medical student, Jean de la Montagne, whose marriage to Rachel de Forest took place in Leyden on the twenty-seventh day of November, 1626. Ten years later, Doctor de la Montagne, now known as a "learned Huguenot physician," went back to New Netherland, with his wife and children, and at once took a leading place in the colony,

Meanwhile, New Amsterdam had become the home of other French-speaking immigrants. Peter Minuit, the second director, was himself a Walloon. His family, during the persecutions in the southern provinces, half a century before, had taken refuge in Wesel, where Minuit was a deacon of the Walloon Church the time of his appointment as director.

It was during his term of office that New

Chap. II.
1628.
April 7.

Amsterdam was visited for the first time by a minister of religion. Jonas Michaëlius, a clergyman of the Reformed Church of Holland, came over in the year 1628. It is not known how long he remained; but a congregation was gathered, and public worship was instituted, both for the French and for the Dutch inhabitants. Two elders were chosen, the one of whom was "the honorable director" himself. "We have had," writes the worthy pastor, "at the first administration of the Lord's Supper, full fifty communicants, Walloons and Dutch: not without great joy and comfort for so many. Of these, a portion made their first confession of faith before us, and others exhibited their church certificates. Some had forgotten to bring their certificates with them, not thinking that a church would be formed and established here; and some, who had brought them, had lost them unfortunately in a general conflagration; but they were admitted upon the satisfactory testimony of others to whom they were known, and also upon their daily good deportment. We administer the Holy Sacrament of the Lord once in four months, provisionally, until a larger number of people shall otherwise require. The Walloons and French have no service on Sundays, other than that in the Dutch language, of which they understand very little. A portion of the Walloons are going back to Fatherland, either because their years here are expired, or also because some are not very serviceable to the Company. Some of them

August 11.

live far away, and could not come on account of the heavy rains and storms, so that it was neither advisable, nor was it possible, to appoint any special service for so small a number with so much uncertainty. Nevertheless, the Lord's Supper was administered to them in the French language, and according to the French mode, with a preceding discourse, which I had before me in writing, as I could not trust myself extemporaneously."[1]

Chap. II.
1628.

At an early day, settlements were commenced by some of the Walloons and French, on the neighboring shores, and at the upper end of Manhattan Island. Of this fact we have an intimation in the letter just quoted; from which it would appear that already, in 1628, a number of these colonists were living at some distance from New Amsterdam. The scanty records of these ancient times, however, afford us no more definite information on the subject. In 1636, William Adrianse Bennet and Jacques Bentyn purchased a tract of land at Gowanus; and in the following year, George de Rapalie bought the farm that long remained in the possession of his descendants, on a bay opposite to Corlear's Hook, which became known as the Waal-bocht, or Wallabout. Both of these localities are now within the limits of the city of Brooklyn. Tradition assigns a much earlier date to the settlement at Wallabout: and the

Bay of the Walloons.

---

[1] Documents relative to the Colonial History of the State of New York. Vol. II., pp. 764–765.

language of Michaëlius certainly favors the supposition that some of the first colonists had found a home on the "bay of the Walloons." Others established themselves on Staten Island. At a later day—in 1658—the village of New Harlem was laid out, on the northern end of Manhattan Island; and of thirty-two male inhabitants of adult age in 1661, nearly one-half were Frenchmen and Walloons.

The appointment of Petrus Stuyvesant to be director-general of the colony, marked an important epoch in the social as well as in the political life of the settlement on Manhattan Island. Stuyvesant, we have seen, had married in Holland Judith Bayard, the daughter of a French Protestant clergyman : and he was accompanied to America by his widowed sister, who had married Samuel Bayard, the son of the refugee. This two-fold alliance with a Huguenot family of high position, must have brought the new governor into close relations with the Walloons and French who had preceded him to New Amsterdam; while it doubtless contributed not a little to strengthen the interest that he felt, as his correspondence shows, in the exiles for conscience' sake who sought a home in the province during his long administration.

For several years after Governor Stuyvesant's arrival, the ships of the Dutch West India Company continued to bring over to New Amsterdam small bodies of French colonists, who had probably found a temporary home in Holland. The greater number of these emigrants came from the northern provinces of France. Isaac Bethlo, a native of Calais, in Picardy, arrived in 1652, and gave his name to the island in the harbor of New York, known as Bedloe's Island. The three brothers De la Grange, who came from Amsterdam in 1656, were natives of Normandy. Of the same province was Jean Perie, noted as the first trader that sent out a ship from New Amsterdam with a cargo for Canada. The first settlers of Bushwick, on Long Island— Toussaint Briell, François Grion la Capelle, Jean Casjou, Claude Barbier, and Antoine Jeroe, arrived about the same time, and originated probably in the same part of France.

But a fresh outbreak of religious persecution was now at hand in France, the consequences of which would soon be seen in a much more considerable emigration to America. During the early years of the reign of Louis XIV., the Protestants of France had enjoyed comparative tranquillity. In the political troubles that introduced that reign, they had given such proof of their loyalty to the crown as to call forth the thanks of the young king and his minister, Cardinal Mazarin. In recognition of these services, Louis had confirmed the Edict of Nantes, and all other edicts and regulations in favor of his subjects of the Reformed religion. Various infractions of those laws, which had been permitted to occur, were redressed; places of worship were re-opened; Protestants were admitted to public offices from which they had been excluded; religious liberty prevailed to a greater

Chap. II.

1647–1664

Growth of persecution.

degree than at any time since the reign of Henry IV. But the tolerant course adopted by the government was watched with growing displeasure by the clergy of the Church of Rome: and soon the king, yielding to their persuasions, entered upon a reactionary course which was to culminate in the revocation of the Edict of Nantes, and in the suppression of the Protestant faith in France. One by one, the rights conceded to the religionists were withdrawn. Among the first of these repressive measures,

December 16, 1656.

was a decree depriving pastors of the privilege of preaching in the *annexes*, or out-stations, connected with their charges. Other decrees, rapidly succeeding, enjoined upon the Protestants the observance of the fasts and feasts of the

1657.
1659.

Roman Catholic Church; prohibited the singing of psalms in private houses, in such a manner as to be overheard in the streets; and required Protestants to kneel, like the Roman Catholics, when the host was carried in public procession. The clergy, encouraged by the attitude which the government was now assuming toward the heretics, inflicted upon them various forms of persecution not yet legalized. The sick and dying were beset by the monks and priests with persuasions and threats, to induce them to abjure their faith. Children were enticed or carried off from their homes, to be educated as Roman Catholics. Judicial rights which had been secured to the Protestants by the Edict of Nantes were withdrawn. The complaints addressed to the court, in view of these abuses, were coldly received or

CONDITION OF FRENCH PROTESTANTS. 181

unheeded. At length the government proceeded to break up the ecclesiastical organization of the French churches, by interdicting the Colloquies and the national Synods, the last of which was held in November, 1659.

Chap. II.
1659.

The Protestants of France had grown in numbers and in wealth during the period of comparative repose that lasted through the early years of the reign of Louis XIV. They no longer formed a political party in the land, and were now devoting themselves chiefly to enterprises of commerce and manufacture. At least one-third of the tradesmen in the country were of the Reformed religion. In every sea-port there were to be found wealthy Protestant merchants, who by their ability and integrity commanded the confidence even of the Roman Catholics, and who were the trusted agents and correspondents of foreign houses. Many important branches of industry were controlled almost entirely by Protestant artisans. Acquainting themselves with the methods of business pursued in Protestant England, Germany, and Holland, they adopted very generally the system of combined labor, which enabled them to secure the best workmen, and to carry on extensive business enterprises. The northern provinces of the kingdom possessed a large share of this commercial and industrial wealth. The linen manufactures of Picardy, Normandy, Maine, and Bretagne, gave employment to thousands of families in the villages of those provinces, and enriched many a powerful commercial house,

Emigration from the northern provinces.

like that of Crommelin, a branch of which at a later day came to New York.

The increasing harshness of the government toward its Protestant subjects, at this period, led many of them to remove from the kingdom. As in the case of the earlier emigrations, the greater number of these refugees made their way to Holland; and from Holland not a few, between the years 1657 and 1663, crossed over to America. For the most part, they were natives of the northern provinces. Marc du Soisson, Philippe Casier, François Dupuis, David de Marest, Daniel Tourneur, Jean Mesurole, Martin Renard, Pierre Pia, David Usilie, were from Picardy. Jean le Conseiller, Robert de la Main, Pierre Pra, Jean Levelin, Pierre de Marc, were from Normandy. Arnout du Tois, of Lisle, Jean le Clercq and Adrien Fournie, of Valenciennes, Simon Drune, Bastien Clement, and Adrien Vincent, of Tournay, Juste Kockuyt, of Bruges, Meynard Journeay, Jean Gervon, Walraven Luten, and Juste Houpleine, were from Flanders. A few are mentioned as natives of other parts of France. Jean Lequier and Pierre Richard came from Paris; and Jacques Cousseau, Etienne Gaineau, Paul Richard, Jean Guenon, and Etienne Genejoy, came from La Rochelle.

Other French colonists, whose places of birth are not recorded, emigrated about this time to New Amsterdam, by way of Holland. We have the names of Charles Fonteyn, Simon Bouché, Amadée Fougie, Jacques Reneau,

Jacques Monier, Pierre Monier, Matthieu Savariau, Pierre Grissaut, Simon Cormie, Gédéon Merlet, Louis Louhman, Jacques Cossart, Jean Paul de Rues, Jacques de Beauvois, François Bon, Louis Lackeman, François Rombouts, Paul Turck, Alexandre Cochivier, Jean Apre, François Breteau, Claude Charie, Guillaume de Honeur, Jacob Kolver, Jean Couverts, Antoine du Chaine, Laurent de Camp, Nicolas de la Plaine, Jean de la Warde. Though the fact is not expressly stated, it may be presumed that the greater number of these immigrants, like those previously named, originated in the provinces of Picardy, Normandy, and Bretagne.

The spring of the year 1657 witnessed the arrival of a band of colonists from the valleys of Piedmont, a portion of the persecuted people known as Waldenses. This ancient race, hidden among the Cottian Alps, between Italy and France, had preserved, according to their own traditions, the Christian faith in its simplicity from a very early age. Unnoticed and unmolested in their mountain retreats for twelve centuries, it was not until these valleys came into the possession of the dukes of Savoy, that efforts were made to convert or exterminate them as heretics in the eyes of the Church of Rome. Between the year 1487 and the close of the seventeenth century, the historians of the Waldenses count thirty-three distinct crusades waged against this innocent and unresisting people. One of the most dreadful of these assaults occurred in April, 1655, when by the order of the duke of Savoy

Chap. II.
1655.
April.

The Waldenses in Holland.

an army of fifteen thousand men entered the valleys, and commenced a massacre, which for horrors of cruelty is scarcely paralleled in the history of civilized men. The sickening details of this deed of blood, amply authenticated, were published throughout Europe, and called forth indignant remonstrances from all the Protestant powers. Cromwell was foremost in stimulating those powers to action, and hastened to offer the Waldenses a home in Ireland; while Milton, his secretary for foreign tongues, wrote upon this occasion his famous "Sonnet on the late massacre in Piedmont."

The States-General of Holland united in the effort to arrest the course of persecution. They too offered the fugitive Waldenses a refuge. Several hundreds came to the city of Amsterdam, where they were well received and liberally provided for. Just then the Dutch were considering a plan for the occupation and settlement of the land on the South or Delaware river. Excellent material for the projected colony presented itself in this body of exiles; and it was hoped that large numbers of their countrymen, when apprised of the opportunity, would flock thither as to an asylum. In December, 1656, the directors wrote to Governor Stuyvesant, informing him that the colony would soon, they hoped, receive an important accession, "since according to all appearances many of the exiled Waldenses would desire to go" to New Netherland in the following spring; and they instructed him to take immediate steps for the purchase of the land lying between the North river and the South river, or Delaware, before this could be done by any other nation, with a view to the settlement of these people, whose presence would be an advantage to both parties.[1]

The embarkation took place earlier than the time announced by the directors. On Christmas day, 1656, one hundred and sixty-seven colonists sailed for New Amsterdam, in three ships sent out by the West India Company, the Prince Maurice, the Bear, and the Flower of Guelder. They were accompanied by a schoolmaster, who was also authorized to act as a "comforter of the sick," until the arrival of a minister. "A storm separated the squadron: and, after a long voyage, the Prince Maurice, with most of the emigrants on board, struck about midnight on the south coast of Long Island, near Fire Island Inlet. The next morning, the crew and passengers escaped through the ice to a barren shore, 'without weeds, grass, or timber of any sort to make a fire.' The shipwrecked emigrants were visited before long by

---

[1] Naer alle apparentie menichte van de Verdrevene Vaudoisen (die des gewaerschout sullen werden) hun daerwaerts sullen comen te begeven.—New York Colonial Manuscripts, vol. XII., fol. 45, p. 8. That the persons thus designated were Waldenses, and not Walloons, appears further from a subsequent reference in the same correspondence, vol. XV., fol. 12, p. 3. The directors wrote to Stuyvesant, April 16, 1663, correcting an impression which he had received that another body of "the oppressed inhabitants of Piedmont" had made request to be brought over to New Netherland. (Dat de verdruckte pimontoisen op nieuios aensocok soude hebben gedaen omme nae nieuo nederlandt te mogen werden getransporteert.)

Chap. II.
1657.

some of the neighboring Indians, by whom they sent a letter to Stuyvesant, imploring help. Yachts were immediately despatched from New Amsterdam, and the director went in person to the scene of the disaster. The emigrants, and most of the cargo, were brought in safety to New Amsterdam, where the other vessels had arrived meanwhile."[1] A few weeks later, they proceeded on their way to the South river. We shall not at present follow the history of this Waldensian colony, but will reserve for another volume the account of the settlement in Delaware. It is not unlikely that some of the colonists may have remained in New Amsterdam, instead of re-embarking for the place of their original destination. Certain it is, that in the course of the next few years, a number of Waldensian families came over from Holland, several of whom established themselves on Staten Island. Pierre Martin, Gerard Ive, and Juste Grand, arrived in August, 1662, on the ship Fox; and Jerome Bovie, Pierre Noue, and Pierre Parmentier—all from " Walslant "—arrived in April, 1663, on the Spotted Cow. The imperfect lists of emigration that we possess afford us no further particulars concerning this interesting episode in the history of New Netherland. But it is believed that others of the first settlers of Staten Island, besides those that have been named, were Waldenses.[2] Such, we conjecture, may have been

Waldenses on Staten Island.

---

[1] History of the State of New York, by John Romeyn Brodhead, Vol. I., pp. 631, 632.

[2] Brodhead, History of the State of New York, vol. I., p. 692.

the origin of the families of Martinou, Crucheron, Poillion, Martiline, Gannepaine, Regrenier, Casée, Perrin and Canon; all of whom appear at an early day in the history of that settlement.

<small>Chap. II. 1660.</small>

Among the Walloons that came to New Netherland, in the last days of the Dutch occupation, was Louis du Bois, founder of the Huguenot settlement of New Paltz, in Ulster county, New York.

Louis was the son of Chrétien du Bois, an inhabitant of Wicres, a hamlet in the district of La Barrée, near Lille, in Flanders, where he was born on the twenty-seventh day of October, in the year 1627. The province of Flanders was at that time a dependency of Spain; and when, twenty years later, the rights of conscience were secured by the treaty of Westphalia to the Protestants of Germany, the benefits of that treaty did not extend to the Spanish dominions. It was perhaps on this account, and in quest of religious freedom, that Louis left his native province, in early manhood, and removed, as numbers of his countrymen were doing, to the lower Palatinate. This Calvinistic state, which had taken the lead among the Protestant powers of Germany, from the outbreak of the Thirty Years' War, now offered a refuge to the oppressed Huguenots, and to the Waldenses, driven from their Alpine valleys by the fierce soldiery of Savoy. Long before this, indeed, a little colony of Walloons, flying before the troops of Alva, had come to settle within the hospitable territory of the Palatinate, at Frankenthal, only

<small>1648, October 14.</small>

<small>1601.</small>

a few miles from Mannheim, its capital. Mannheim itself now became the home of many French refugees, and among them we recognize several families that afterwards removed to America. Here David de Marest, Frederic de Vaux, Abraham Hasbroucq, Chrétien Duyou, Mathèse Blanchan, Meynard Journeay, Thonnet Terrin, Pierre Parmentier, Antoine Crispel, David Usilie, Philippe Casier, Bourgeon Broucard, Simon Le Febre, Juste Durié, and others, enjoyed for several years the kindness of their German co-religionists and the protection of the good Elector Palatine. Hither Louis du Bois came, and here, on the tenth day of October, 1655, he married Catharine, daughter of Mathèse Blanchan, who, like himself, was from French Flanders. Two sons, Abraham and Isaac, were born of this marriage in Mannheim.

The refugees found much, doubtless, to bind them to the country of their adoption. They were encouraged in the free exercise of their religion. The people and their prince were Calvinists, like themselves. Openings for employment, if not for enrichment in trade, were afforded in the prosperous city, where, a century later, Huguenot merchants and manufacturers were enabled to amass large fortunes. How pleasantly and fondly they remembered the goodly Rhine-land, in after days, we may gather from the fact that the emigrants to America named their home in the wilderness, not from their native province in France, but from the place of their refuge in Germany, calling it

"The New Palatinate." In spite, however, of all inducements to remain, Louis du Bois and certain of his fellow-refugees determined to remove to the New World; influenced, it may be, by a feeling of insecurity in a country lying upon the border of France, and liable to foreign invasion at any moment.

Chap. II. 1660.

The Dutch ship Gilded Otter, in the spring of the year 1660, brought over several of these families. Others followed, in the course of the same year. The little town of New Amsterdam, nestled upon the lower end of Manhattan island, presented a curious appearance to the strangers. Inclosed within the limits of Wall street and Broadway, "two hundred poorly-constructed houses gave partial comfort to some fourteen hundred people. The fort loomed up broadly in front, partially hiding within it the governor's residence, and the Dutch church. The flag of the States-General, and a wind-mill on the western bastion, were notable indications of Holland rule."

Arrival in New Amsterdam.

Our colonists did not linger long in New Amsterdam. Taking counsel doubtless of their Walloon countrymen, and obtaining permission from the governor and his council, they soon decided upon a place of settlement: and by the end of the year, Matthew Blanchan and Anthony Crispel, with their families, had established themselves in Esopus; where, before the following October, they were joined by Louis du Bois and his wife and sons.

The country lying south of the Catskill mountains, and north of the Highlands, on the west side of the North or Hudson river, was known to the Dutch from the earliest times as Esopus. Thither, even before the settlement of New Amsterdam, the Dutch traders went to traffic with the friendly Indians; and here, in 1623, the ship New Netherland, after landing some of her passengers on Manhattan island, stopped on her way up the river, to lighten her cargo. This picturesque region — now included within the bounds of Ulster county —lay midway between the two rising towns of New Amsterdam and Beverwyck. Broken by mountain ranges, the Catskills in the north, and the Shawungunk in the south; watered by numerous streams, and extensively improved by the rude husbandry of its savage occupants, the pleasant land must have attracted the longing view of the Dutch immigrants as they sailed up the Hudson to the patroon's colony at Fort Orange. But though a Dutch fort was built here—at Rondout, now a part of Kingston—as early as the year 1614, it does not appear that any settlement was effected before the year 1652. Thomas Chambers, an Englishman by birth, was the first purchaser and patentee of Esopus. He had been engaged with several others in an attempt to obtain lands near the site of the present city of Troy; but being dispossessed by the patroon, whose patent covered the locality chosen for their settlement, the associates removed to this region, and bought from the Indians a tract of land, comprising seventy-six acres, on Esopus creek, where the city of Kingston now stands. But in 1655 the Indian tribes along the Hudson river joined in attacking the Dutch settlements; and in the consternation that prevailed, the farmers at Esopus fled, leaving their homes and fields to the depredation of the savages. On the conclusion of peace, in the autumn of the same year, they returned. Neglecting, however, to form a village, suitably protected by stockades and by a fort or blockhouse, as they were urged by the government to do, the settlers were again disturbed in 1658, and implored the Director Stuyvesant to come to their relief. By his advice they now laid out a town-spot, the site of Wiltwyck, the future city of Kingston. The colonists, sixty or seventy in number, went to work with a will, under the personal supervision of the determined governor; and in less than three weeks, the place that he had chosen for the village was surrounded with palisades, a guard-house was built, and the dwellings of the settlers were moved into the space inclosed. Pleased at his own success, and delighted with the beautiful land of the Esopus, the director sailed back to New Amsterdam, " praising the Lord for His mercy on all concerned," and cautioning the Indian chiefs to leave the white men alone, inasmuch as "he could come again as easily as he went."

Wiltwyck, however, did not long enjoy repose under shelter of its new defenses. Another outbreak of Indian ferocity—stimulated by the white man's "fire-water," and provoked by the brutality of some of the Dutch themselves—occurred in the following year, when a band of several hundred Indian warriors invested the little town for three weeks. Again Director Stuyvesant came to the rescue. Partly by force of arms, and partly through the mediation of other Indian tribes, he succeeded in bringing the savages to terms; and on the fifteenth day of July, 1660, peace was concluded.

It was at this juncture that Louis du Bois and his companions arrived in New Amsterdam. The great "Esopus war," which, for many months past, had convulsed all the settlements, from Long Island to Fort Orange, with fear, was now over. The prospects of the little colony at Wiltwyck were brightening; and the beautiful region which Governor Stuyvesant had found so fruitful, and "capable of making yet fifty farms," was open to the new immigrants. Lands in the rich valleys of the Rondout and the Esopus were to be had for the asking. Provision was made for the religious instruction of the colonists. Hermanus Blom, a clergyman of the Reformed Church of Holland, sent over expressly to minister at Esopus, had been, for several weeks, awaiting in New Amsterdam the result of the negotiations for peace. These, not improbably, were the considerations that led our Walloons to fix upon Esopus as their future home. Early in the autumn of the year 1660, they took their departure from New Amsterdam. The Company's yacht, which carried Dominie Blom to the place of his labors, may have had on board some of their number. Certain it is, that among the persons admitted to the Lord's Supper, upon the occasion of its first celebration in Esopus, on the seventh day of December in that year, were Matthew Blanchan, with Madeleine Jorisse, his wife, and Anthony Crispel, with Maria Blanchan, his wife.

The spot where, after many wanderings, our refugees at length had found a home, was happily chosen. It lay but a short distance from that noble river, whose majestic course and varied scenery must have vividly recalled to them the Rhine. The plateau upon which the village of Wiltwyck stood was skirted by Esopus creek. From the banks along which the palisades protecting it had been constructed, the settlers overlooked the fertile lands occupied by the farms of the white men, and by the patches upon which the Indian women still raised their crops of maize and beans. The beautiful valley of the Wallkill opened toward the southwest. On the north, the wooded slopes of the Catskill mountains were visible.

Blanchan and Crispel were soon joined at Wiltwyck by Louis du Bois, and shortly after by a fourth Walloon family, that of Rachel de la Montagne, daughter of Jean de la Montagne of New Amsterdam, and now wife of Gysbert Imborch. Meantime, another settlement had been commenced in the Esopus country. The "New Village," afterwards known as Hurley, was founded about a mile to the west of Wiltwyck. Taught by experience, the settlers took pains to protect their homes against the attacks of the savages. The houses and barns were built within a fortified inclosure, where fifteen families formed a compact community. Blanchan and his two sons-in-law were among those who removed from Wiltwyck to the New Village. A summer passed by, and the colonists remained undisturbed. They were, however, by no means safe from molestation. Stuyvesant's severity in sending some of his Indian prisoners, at the close of the Esopus war, to the island of Curaçoa, had left a lasting impression of resentment in the minds of the savages. The building of the "New Village," upon land to which they still laid claim, was an additional grievance. Underrating either the courage or the strength of their wild neighbors, the settlers took no suitable precautions against attack, but on the contrary, with strange infatuation, sold to them freely the rum that took away their reason and intensified their worst passions. The time came for an uprising. Stuyvesant had sent word to the Indian chiefs, through the magistrates of Wiltwyck, that he would shortly visit them, to make them presents, and to renew the peace concluded the year before. The message was received with professions of friendliness. Two days after, about noon, on the seventh of June, a concerted attack was made by parties of Indians upon both the settlements. The destruction of the "New Village" was complete. Every dwelling was burned. The greater number of

ATTACK ON THE SETTLEMENTS. 195

the adult inhabitants had gone forth that day as usual to their field work upon the outlying farms, leaving some of the women, with the little children, at home. Three of the men, who had doubtless returned to protect them, were killed; and eight women, with twenty-six children, were taken prisoners. Among these were the families of our Walloons: the wife and three children of Louis du Bois, the two children of Matthew Blanchan, and Anthony Crispel's wife and child. The rest of the people, those at work in the fields, and those who could escape from the village, fled to the neighboring woods, and in the course of the afternoon made their way to Wiltwyck, or to the redoubt at the mouth of Esopus creek.

Meanwhile, the attack at Wiltwyck had been less successful. Parties of Indians had entered the village in the morning, carrying maize and beans to sell, and under this pretense, had distributed themselves in the different houses; when suddenly a number of men on horseback came dashing through the mill-gate, shouting, "The Indians have destroyed the New Village!" At once, the savages already within the place began their work of havoc. Twelve houses were burned, and but for a timely change of wind the entire settlement would have been consumed. Some of the Indians, seizing the women and children, hastened away with them into the forest: whilst others, stationed near the gates, despatched those of the men who attempted to enter the town. As at the New Village, most

Chap. II.
1663.

Brave defense of Wiltwyck.

of the inhabitants were away, at their employments in the neighboring fields. A few brave men, however, chanced to be at home. These, though without guns or side arms, soon rallied, and resolutely facing the assailants, succeeded in driving them out. By nightfall, Dominie Blom and his companions were joined by the people from the farms, and by straggling fugitives from the New Village. No time could be spent in lamentation over their losses. The palisades surrounding the place had been destroyed by the fire. All night long the colonists toiled to replace them, or kept watch along the exposed borders. Day dawned upon a scene of woe and desolation. Seventy of the inhabitants were missing. Of these, twenty-four had been ruthlessly murdered; while forty-five, women and children, had been hurried away into captivity. The sight of the burned and mutilated bodies, lying amid the ruins of the dwellings and in the streets, was scarcely more affecting than the thought of the living, in the hands of the merciless savages. Among these were Rachel de la Montagne, and the wife and child of Dominie Blom.

The tidings of this disaster spread consternation throughout the Dutch settlements. Director Stuyvesant, always energetic, and ready for severe measures, was the more disposed to act promptly and resolutely in the present case, because of the loss incurred by his trusty councilor in the capture of his daughter. With some difficulty, a force was raised for the defense of

The Library, University of Toronto, CANADA

TO.

Wiltwyck, and for the rescue of the prisoners in the hands of the Esopus Indians. Nearly a month elapsed, however, before two sloops, carrying supplies to the destitute inhabitants, and having on board a company of Dutch and English soldiers, and of friendly Indian braves, entered Esopus creek. They were joined at Wiltwyck by a band of five Mohawks, sent down from Fort Orange, for the purpose of endeavoring to secure the release of the captives through mediation. In the meantime, Rachel de la Montagne had made her escape from the savages, and was ready to conduct the rescuing party to the Indian fort, thirty miles to the south-west of Wiltwyck, whither the prisoners had been conveyed. The expedition set forth, under the command of the fearless Captain Krygier, on the twenty-sixth of July, and on the next day reached the fort, but found it deserted. The Indians had retreated with their captives to a more distant fastness in the Shawungunk mountains. Krygier pursued them, but without success, and after setting fire to the fort, and destroying large quantities of corn which they found stored away in pits, or growing in the fields, the party returned to Wiltwyck without the loss of a man. Another month passed before a second attempt could be made. Information came through friendly savages that the Esopus Indians were building another fort. So soon as the weather permitted, and a supply of horses could be obtained, Krygier set forth again. This time, the enemy was taken by surprise. A fierce combat ensued; many of the

Chap. II.
1663.

savages were taken, and twenty-three of the captives were recovered, and brought back in triumph to the settlement. Their absence had lasted just three months. Tradition represents the pious Walloons as cheering the tedious hours of their bondage with Marot's psalms. When rescued by their friends, just as the savages were about to slaughter them, they were entertaining their captors, and obtaining a momentary reprieve, by singing the one hundred and thirty-seventh psalm: "By the rivers of Babylon, there we sat down, yea, we wept, when we remembered Zion. . . For there they that carried us away captive required of us a song."[1]

The rescue.

The worthy Dutch pastor of Wiltwyck gives a touching account of the grief and anxiety that reigned in the desolate homes from which the captives had been taken. Every evening the little congregation gathered, on the four points of the fort, under the blue sky, and offered up their fervent prayers.

To Louis du Bois, whose entire family were

---

[1] The words were those of Marot's version:

" Estans assis aux rives aquatiques
De Babylon, plorions melancholiques,
Nous souvenans du pays de Sion,
Et au milieu de l'habitation,
Où de regrets tant de pleurs espandismes,
Aux saules verds nos harpes nous pendismes.

Lors ceux qui là captifs nous emmenerent,
De les sonner fort nous importunerent,
Et de Sion les chansons reciter.
Las ! dismes-nous, qui pourroit inciter
Nos tristes cœurs à chanter la louange
De nostre Dieu en une terre estrange ?"

in the hands of the savages, this season of suspense must have been peculiarly trying. Tradition states that he was one of the foremost members of the rescuing party. An instance of his vigor and presence of mind, given by Captain Krygier in his journal after the return of the expedition, may lead us to credit this statement. "Louis, the Walloon, went to-day to fetch his oxen, which had gone back of Juriaen Westphaelen's land. As he was about to drive home the oxen, three Indians, who lay in the bush and intended to seize him, leaped forth. When one of these shot at him with an arrow, but only slightly wounded him, Louis, having a piece of a palisade in his hand, struck the Indian on the breast with it so that he staggered back, and Louis escaped through the kill, and came thence, and brought the news into the fort."

These troubles over, the settlement enjoyed security from savage molestation. The Esopus tribe, in the course of the contest with the white man, was almost exterminated. The Walloons were free to extend their plantations further into the rich lands that were now without an owner. Some years later, Louis du Bois, with several associates, removed from Wiltwyck to a spot which they had discovered during their pursuit of the Indians. Here, in the beautiful Wallkill valley, they built their homes, near the base of the Shawungunk mountains. The settlers had not forgotten the Rhine, and the days of their exile in Mannheim, and they named their village "le nouveau Palatinat," or New Paltz.

Chap. II.
1664.
September 6.

But meanwhile, New Netherland had become an English possession. On the sixth day of September, in the year 1664, articles of capitulation were signed, by commissioners representing the States-General of Holland and the king of England: and the Dutch city and province received the name of the city and province of New York.

DAVID PROVOST, the founder of an important family of New Amsterdam and New York, arrived from Holland as early as the year 1639. He is said to have been the descendant of one Guillaume Provost, a Huguenot, who was a resident of Paris at the time of the massacre of St. Bartholomew's day, and who succeeded in escaping to Holland. (The New York Geneaological and Biographical Record. Vol. VI., pp. 1–24.)

The family of DE PEYSTER, originating, it is believed, in France, was likewise driven from that country, according to tradition, at the time of the massacre, and took refuge in Holland. Johannes de Peyster, born in Haarlem early in the seventeenth century, came to America, and about the year 1652, established himself in New Amsterdam, where he became a leading merchant. He died previous to the year 1686, leaving four sons, the eldest of whom, Colonel Abraham de Peyster, took a distinguished part in public affairs. (Manual of the Corporation of the City of New York for 1861. Pp. 556–576.)

It is possible that Rouen, in Normandy, may have been the birthplace of this family. Two facts would indicate this. (1.) A sister of the refugee who fled to Holland, "returned to settle at Rouen, where, in the succeeding century, she lived a widow, in the possession of an ample fortune." (Manual, etc., p. 556.) (2.) In a "mémoire" of persons conspicuous in the town of Rouen, in 1689, for their zeal in behalf of their religion, I find the name of "Le sieur Depeister, Hollandois, depuis longtemps establi à Rouen. C'est un marchand naturalisé." (Le protestantisme in Normandie, par M. Francis Waddington. P. 25.) Perhaps a descendant of the refugee, this merchant may have gone back, like the sister mentioned above, to the ancient home.

PART OF THE
LESSER ANTILLES

CHAPTER III.

THE ANTILLES.

1625–1686.

Early in the seventeenth century, the archipelago that lies between the two American continents became the resort of French commerce : and here, particularly in the islands of St. Christopher, Guadeloupe and Martinique, the Protestants of France found a comparatively safe retreat during the fifty years preceding the Revocation of the Edict of Nantes. This fact, singularly enough, has escaped the attention of the writers who have traced the wanderings of the Huguenot exiles.[1] Yet we shall see that it has had an important bearing upon the history of their emigration to North America.

---

[1] The invaluable work of M. Charles Weiss (Histoire des Réfugiés Protestants Français) contains no allusion to this emigration, nor to the subsequent deportation of French Protestants to the Antilles.

For a clue to this episode in the history of the Refuge, I am indebted to a casual mention, made in the correspondence of the Marquis de Denonville, governor of Canada, 16 Nov., 1686, with the Ministry of the Colonies, of the arrival of fifty or sixty Huguenots at Manat [New York] *from the islands of St. Christopher and Martinique.* (Documents relative to the Colonial History of the State of New York. Vol. IX., p. 309.)

Chap. III.
1625.

Caribbean Islands.

French geographers limit the name *Antilles*[1] to the Caribbean Islands, or the group that stretches in a curved line between the Greater Antilles and the coast of South America, forming the eastern boundary of the Caribbean Sea. These islands, twenty-eight in number, had been passed by as insignificant, since their discovery by Columbus in the year 1493. But in 1625, two navigators, landing on the same day upon opposite sides of the island of St. Christopher, took possession in the name of their respective sovereigns, the kings of France and England. Both nations had the same objects in view. These were to secure safe anchorage and convenient victualing stations for their merchant ships engaged in the South American trade, and to strengthen themselves against their common enemy, the Spaniard. No time was lost by either commander in carrying out this design. A company was organized in each country, under a royal grant, with privileges and powers for the occupying and settling of St. Christopher, as well as of the neighboring islands.[2]

---

[1] Histoire naturelle et morale des Iles Antilles de l' Amérique. A Roterdam, M. DC. LVIII. [By Charles de Rochefort.] P. 1.—De Rochefort considers that the islands are so named, "parce qu'elles sont comme une barriere au devant des grandes Iles."
Manuel de la Navigation dans la Mer des Antilles et dans le Golfe du Mexique, par Ch. Ph. de Kerhallet. Paris, 1853, I. 19.

[2] Histoire nat. et mor. des Iles Antilles, pp. 268, 269.—The History, civil and commercial, of the British Colonies in the West Indies. By Bryan Edwards, Esq.—London, M. DCC. XCIII. Vol. I., p. 422.

The lesser Antilles, like the greater, are of volcanic origin, and present similar features of beauty and grandeur, in their rich tropical vegetation, and in their bold outlines of bluff and mountain. St. Christopher, though not the largest of the French islands, was first in importance among them, as the place of earliest settlement, and for a long time the seat of the colonial government. Its highest peak, Mount Misery, rises nearly four thousand feet above the level of the sea, and is visible at a distance of fifty miles. The island is twenty-one miles long, with an average breadth of five miles for about two-thirds of its length. The remaining part is less than a mile wide, except at the extreme south-east, where it expands to a breadth of about three miles. A Huguenot pastor gives a pleasing description of the island, as he saw it about the middle of the seventeenth century. The interior, he tells us, is occupied by a range of mountains, intersected with rocky precipices almost impassable, and abounding in hot springs. At the base of these mountains, the land slopes gently down to the coast, here and there broken by spurs or ridges that stretch out to the sea. The grounds under cultivation, reaching up to the steeper acclivities, are for the most part disposed in natural terraces, one above another. Upon these terraces, the gardens and fields of the plantations are seen, the pale green of the tobacco plant contrasting with the yellow sugar cane, and the dark green leaves of the ginger and the sweet potato. Amid these terraced plantations, the houses of the planters appear, built generally of wood, and roofed with red tiles, and completing the picture which to the enthusiastic Frenchman seemed one of rare beauty. On the south-western shore of the island, near the shipping, stood the pleasant little town of Basse-terre, the residence of the merchants and other leading inhabitants.

From the first, these islands extended a welcome to the Protestant colonist. No religious qualification was imposed upon the settlers. The commission given in 1626 by Cardinal Richelieu to the leaders of the enterprise, required them " to instruct the inhabitants of those islands in the Catholic, Apostolic, and Roman Religion, and to plant the Christian Faith among them," but omitted any reference to their own religious belief.[1] Twelve years later, in renewing the Company's charter, the government stipulated that none but persons professing the Roman Catholic religion should be sent over as colonists. If by mistake any of a different faith should come, they were to be sent back immediately upon the discovery of the fact.[2] But the

---

[1] Commission donnée par le cardinal de Richelieu aux sieurs d' Enambuc et de Rossey, pour établir une Colonie dans les Antilles de l' Amérique. Du 31 octobre, 1626. (Loix et Constitutions des Colonies Françoises de l' Amérique sous le Vent. Paris. [Without year of publication. Approbation dated 1784.] Tome I., pp. 20–22.)

[2] Contrat de Rétablissement de la Compagnie des Isles de l' Amérique. Du 12 Fevrier, 1635. (Loix et Constitutions, etc., vol. I., pp. 29–33.) " Ils ne feront passer esdites Isles, Colonies et Habitations, aucun qui ne soit naturel Fran-

Basse-Terre, St. Kitts; and the Island of Nevis.

order remained unobserved. The interests of trade and of colonization forbade any such discrimination. "At all times," complained a friar of St. Francis, a missionary to the Antilles, "the governors here have suffered heretics."[1]

The period of toleration continued for half a century. Meanwhile, the Protestants came to be very numerous and very wealthy, exceeding, indeed, the Roman Catholic population in influence, if not in numbers.[2] They were not allowed the public exercise of their religion. But throughout the French islands, meetings were held statedly for worship in private houses, with the tacit permission of the governors. Protestant pastors administered the rite of baptism, and performed marriages under government

---

çois et ne fasse profession de la Religion Catholique, Apostolique, et Romaine ; et si quelqu' un d' autre condition y passoit par surprise, on l' en fera sortir aussi-tôt qu'il sera venu à la connoissance de celui qui commandera dans la dite Isle."

[1] Histoire Générale des Antilles habitées par les François. Par le R. P. du Tertre, de l' Ordre des F.F. Prescheurs de la Congrégation de S. Louis, Missionnaire Apostolique dans les Antilles. Paris, MDCLXVII. Vols. I.—IV. "Bien que suivant les pieuses intentions du feu Roy Louis XIII. de triomphante mémoire, qui permit l' Etablissement des Colonies Françoises dans l' Amérique, il n'y deust passer personne qui ne fist profession de la Religion Catholique, Apostolique et Romaine. . . . Neantmoins les Gouverneurs y ont souffert de tout [temps] des Hérétiques." Vol. II., pp. 421. 422. "L' on permet indifferemment à toutes sortes de personnes de quelque Religion qu'elles soient, de s'établir dans les Isles en qualité d' Habitans." Vol. III., p. 312.

[2] "Dans toutes les Isles il y a un tres-grand nombre de gens de la Religion plus puissans en fond de terre et en Esclaves, que les Catholiques Romains."—(Du Tertre, Hist. Gén. des Antilles, etc , Vol. III., p. 312.)

sanction.[1] On board the Company's ships, the greater number of which were commanded by Huguenot masters, the Reformed service was celebrated with all publicity, both in port and at sea. Calvin's prayers were said in the forecastle, and Marot's psalms were sung, the loud voices of the sailors drowning the chant of the priest, as he said mass in another part of the ship, for the Roman Catholic portion of the crew. In some of the French islands, there were Huguenot congregations, duly organized, though without "temples" or houses of worship. The governor and council of Massachusetts received certificates in 1680 from "the French Protestant Church at St. Christopher's," attesting the character of two of its members.[2] These congregations were supplied with pastors by the Synod

---

[1] "Ces Messieurs de la Religion commencent d' exercer presque leur fausse religion, puis qu' ils font des mariages autorizés par quelques Gouverneurs, qu' ils baptisent leurs enfans dans leurs maisons .... qu' ils s' assemblent tous les Dimanches dans quelques maisons pour y faire leurs prières et autres exercises ; que dans les navires de la Compagnie, ils chantent à haute voix leurs Pseaumes, ce qui ne leur est pas permis dans les vaisseaux du Roy, et ils estouffent la voix du Prestre qui dit la Messe, et interrompent les prières des Catholiques."—(Du Tertre, Hist. Gén. des Antilles, etc., III., 312.)

[2] "Certificates from the ffrench Protestant Church att S^t. Christopher's on the behalfe of M^r. Poncet Stell called the Larier and Frances Guichard, two French Gentlemen, that they have renounced the Romish Religion in which they were born and bred, and have Imbraced the true faith and protestant Religion."—(Orders, Warrants, etc., XXXII., p. 16 ; in Office of Secretary of State, Albany, N. Y.) As these men had in 1680 been for some time residents here, the date of the certificates may have been earlier by several years.

of the Walloon Churches of Holland.[1] But when destitute of such ministrations, the Huguenot islander could readily obtain the benefits of religious instruction and consolation, by visiting the neighboring islands of the Dutch and English.[2] The English quarter of St. Christopher was well provided with churches. At St. Eustatius, the Dutch pastor preached in French

---

[1] Charles de Rochefort, the presumed author of the "Histoire Naturelle et Morale des Iles Antilles" already cited, was at the time of its publication pastor of the Walloon church in Rotterdam. In 1650, he is named as "ci-devant Ministre du St. Evangile en Amerique."—(Signatures des Pasteurs, etc.; Confession de Foy des Églises Réformées des País-bas. Leyden, 1769.) From various indications it would seem probable that the author of the "Histoire" had exercised his ministry in the islands of Martinique and St. Christopher.

[2] "The English have built as many as five handsome churches in this island [St. Christopher]. The first, which is met upon leaving the French quarter, is at the *pointe des Palmistes*. The second stands near the great bay (*la grande rade*), below the Governor's residence. The third is at the *pointe de Sable*, and the other two are in the quarter of Cayonne. The first three are structures of pleasing appearance, after the fashion of the country; the interior being adorned with fine pulpits and chairs of valuable kinds of wood. The clergymen who perform Divine Service were formerly sent hither by the Archbishop of Canterbury, whose vicar was Doctor Fiatley, chaplain to the late King of England, and pastor of the church at the *pointe des Palmistes*. But at present [1658] they receive their ordination from the Synods, which possess the episcopal authority."—(De Rochefort, Hist. Nat. et Morale des Iles Antilles, etc., p. 40.)

Besides these five churches, there were three on the island of Nevis, which is separated from St. Christopher by a channel only two miles in width.—(Ibid. p. 29.)

The facilities which the French Protestant inhabitants of St. Christopher enjoyed for attending these English services —"d'aller au prêche chez les Anglois"—are noticed in a government order in 1686. See below.

Chap. III.
1650.

"for the edification of the French inhabitants," as well as in Flemish.¹ On the island of St. Martin, which was occupied by both nationalities, a Walloon minister officiated in both tongues.² And on the island of Tobago, then belonging to the United Provinces, a French church existed in the year 1660.³

The virtues of the Huguenots received, in these distant colonies of France, the same recognition as in the mother country. "Whosoever knows the merchants of the Pretended Reformed Religion," writes a historian of the Antilles, "knows that commerce has no better and more faithful agents."⁴ A large proportion of the Company's employes, as well as many of the most prosperous merchants in the islands, were Protestants.⁵ The zealous missionary who

Protestant Merchants.

---

¹ De Rochefort, Hist. des Iles Antilles, etc., p. 42.—M. de Graaf, "at present pastor of the church of Trevers, in the island of Walcheren," was succeeded by M. de Mey, "a celebrated preacher of the church of Middelburg."

² "The French and the Dutch have their particular churches, in the quarters of which they have jurisdiction. M. des Camps, who is at present pastor of the Dutch church, was sent out in this capacity in September, 1655, by the Synod of the Walloon Churches of the United Provinces, which has this colony under its spiritual care."—(De Rochefort, Hist. des Iles Antilles, etc., p. 44.)

³ " F. Chaillon, Pasteur de l'Eglise de Tabago," signed the Articles of the Synod of Dort in 1660.—(Confession de Foy des Egl. Réf. des Païs-bas.)

⁴ Histoire Générale des Antilles, par M. Adrien Dessalles. Paris : 1847. In five volumes. T. III., p. 215.

⁵ " Ils sont élevez aux Charges publiques, tant de la milice, que du négoce ; ce sont eux qui commandent les deux tiers vaisseaux de la Compagnie, et ont en leurs mains les meilleurs commissions pour la distribution des marchandises."—(Du Tertre, Hist. Gén. des Antilles, etc., vol. III., p. 312.)

reports these facts, explains them with remarkable ingenuity. "These gentlemen of the Company," says he, "have no other end in view than traffic and gain. Hence they seek for such only as they esteem best fitted to carry their enterprise to a successful issue. And since all our sea-ports teem with Huguenot captains, pilots, and merchants, whose souls are wholly buried in trade and navigation, and who consequently become more skilled in these matters than the Catholics, it is not to be wondered at that they should make use of this sort of people to fill the places at their disposal." [1]

It was among these islands of the French West Indies [2], that many of the Huguenot families that came at a later day to Massachusetts,

---

[1] "Comme tous nos ports de mer sont remplis de Capitaines, de Pilotes, et de Marchands huguenots qui ayant l'ame toute ensevelie dans la navigation et dans le négoce, s'y rendent plus parfait que les Catholiques ; ils ne se faut pas estonner s'ils se sont servi des ces sortes de gens, pour remplir les charges et les commissions qu'ils avoient à donner."—(Du Tertre, Hist. Gén. des Antilles, etc., III., p. 316.)

[2] Some French Protestants went to the islands of other nationalities. A Count Crequi—according to the tradition of the Markoe family—left France with a number of followers, shortly before the Revocation, and sailed for the West Indies. Several of the vessels that carried them were destroyed by a hurricane ; but two, on board of which were Crequi himself and his friend Marcou—said to have been a native of Montbéliard, in Franche-Comté—finally reached Santa Cruz, where, with their fellow-passengers, they settled, and became subjects of Denmark. They had large plantations, and lived as a distinct community, intermarrying for several generations. About the middle of the last century, Abraham Marcou came to Philadelphia, and established himself in that city. He took a

Chap. III.
1667.

New York, and South Carolina, found homes, before the Revocation of the Edict of Nantes. The greater number of them resided upon the islands of St. Christopher, Guadeloupe and Martinique. The Protestant population of Guadeloupe was at that time very considerable. "There is a quarter of the island," complained the apostolic missionary, Du Tertre, in 1667, "which is quite thickly inhabited, but in which there are neither priests nor churches. This fact hinders the Catholics from settling there, but the Huguenots establish themselves in that part of the island all the more willingly, because they find greater freedom for the exercise of their religion."[1]

Larger numbers settled on the island of St. Christopher. Here, as early as the year 1670, were the Allaires, the Pintards, the Marions, the Le Contes, the L'Hommedieus, and many others, whose names have become familiar to American ears, or have suffered changes that make them difficult to recognize. Some of these families appear to have remained in the French islands for more than a single generation.[2] In the lists

---

prominent part in the Revolution, and in 1774 formed the first company of volunteer cavalry organized in Pennsylvania. (Communicated by his descendant, William Camac, M.D., of Philadelphia.)

[1] Du Tertre, Hist. Gén. des Antilles, *u. s.*

[2] Histoire Générale des Antilles, par M. Adrien Dessalles. Tome II., pp. 417-437. Role Général des Habitants de Saint Christophe. Extrait des cartons non datés, de cette colonie, conservés aux Archives de la marine. Although without date, this list may be presumed to be of the same period with similar lists of the inhabitants of Martinique —(Ibid. vol.

particularly of families that settled at New Rochelle, near the city of New York, mention is made of several children that were born on the island of St. Christopher. Here, too, lived the first pastor of New Rochelle, David de Bonrepos.

But the time was approaching, when these remote islands were to be visited by the storm that burst upon the Protestants in France. The policy of Richelieu and Mazarin had now been abandoned; and the government, bent upon the extirpation of the Huguenots at home, sought to inflict the same severities upon

---

I., pp. 562-572), and Guadeloupe (vol. II., pp. 438-453), both of which bear the date 1671.

The "role des habitants de Saint Christophe" embraces some twelve hundred names. Among them are the following which re-appear among the Huguenot families in America:

Jacques Allaire, Jean Baton, Elie Baudry, Elie Bonrepos, François Bellereau, Antoine Bocquet, Jean Boyer, François Bourdeaux, Pierre Bureau, Jean Buretel, Isaac Caillaud, Jean and Pierre Campion, Aymé [Ami] Canche, Charles Carrelet, Pierre Chevalier, Jean David, François Deschamps, Louis Desveaux, Louis and Pierre Dubois, Daniel Duchemin, Pierre Durand, Christophe Duteil, Gabriel, Jean, Michel, Noël and Robert Duval, Jacques and Pierre Le Tellier, Pierre Fleuriau, Jean Gaillard, Noël Gendron, Antoine Gosselin, Jean Grignon, René Guerineau, François Guichard, Jean Hastier, Antoine Jollin, Pierre Jouneau, Jean de Lafont, Louis and Pierre Le Breton, Jean Le Comte, Jean Le Maistre, Pierre Le Lieure, Pierre and Jacques Le Roux, Josias Le Vilain, Benjamin L'Hommedieu, Étienne Maho [Mahault], Antoine Marion, François and Pierre Martin, François, Louis and Jean Massé, Thomas Maurice, François Mesnard, Jacques Mesureur, Jean Morin, Jean Noël, Pierre Nollo, Jean Nos [Neau], Elie and Gabriel Papin, Antoine Pintard, Philippe Poirier, Jean Poulain, François Ravaux, Pierre and François Renard, Nicolas Requier, Jean Roze,

Chap. III.
1664.

them in the colonies. Edicts came across the water, ordering the enforcement of the decrees published for the suppression of the Protestant worship, and the proscription of the Protestant name. In 1664, the religionists were cautioned not to exceed the privileges which had until then been permitted them, and which they had thus far enjoyed, of assembling themselves in private houses to make their prayers; and they were particularly admonished to avoid being present in places where the host was carried, or other religious processions were passing,

---

Elie Rousseau, Jean Rulland, Joseph Sauvage, Nicolas Thevenin, René Tongrelou.

It is not to be supposed that the above list contains the names of all the French Protestant families transported from the Antilles to America. Many Huguenots doubtless emigrated from France to those islands after the presumed date of this list (1671) and before the date of the Revocation of the Edict of Nantes (1685). Neither does the list contain the names of those unfortunate victims of persecution who, as we shall see further on, were transported to the French West Indies *after* the Revocation. To the former class belong the names of Guillaume Le Conte, Jacques Lasty, Jean Thauvet, Gerard Douens, Alexandre Allaire, of whose residence in St. Christopher, previous to the Revocation, we have evidence from other sources.

Among the inhabitants of Guadeloupe in 1671, we recognize the following American names :

Jean and Pierre Allaire, Thomas Colin, Michel Cotonneau, Elie Coudret, Jean Dallé, Delanoe, Jean Gombault, Paul Guionneau, Elie Gosselin, Jean Hamel, Abraham Hulin, François Le Blond, Jean Lespinard, Jean Le Comte, Jamain, Edouard Machet, Thomas and Vincent Mahau, Jacques Potel, Daniel Roberdeau. Among the inhabitants of Martinique in 1671 were Antoine Bonneau, Jean and Thomas Chevalier, Mathurin Coudray, Etienne Joullin, François Massé, François Monnel, Jean Neuville, Jean le Vilain, Jean, Martin, Michel, Nicolas le Roux.

unless willing to show the usual marks of respect.¹ Another law in the same year took from Protestants the right to sell their estates in the islands.² A third prohibited them from engaging in conversation upon the mysteries of the faith.³ Still another decree forbade the public singing of psalms, upon vessels commanded by Huguenot captains, whether at sea or in harbor.⁴

These were the echoes of a legislation that was being rigidly executed, as we shall see, in France: but with reference to the colonies, it seems to have been as yet ineffectual. The governors of the islands, from the first, had shown an utter indifference to the religious concerns of the inhabitants.⁵ One of them, at least, Levasseur,

---

¹ Loix et Constitutions des Colonies Françoises de l'Amérique sous le Vent. Tome I., p. 118.
² Ibid. p. 131.
³ Ibid.
⁴ Ibid. p. 180. The government of Louis XIV. had commenced the forced "conversion" of the officers and seamen in the public service. The greater number of these were Protestants. In 1680, the king announced his intention to remove by degrees from the navy all those who should continue to profess the Pretended Reformed Religion. A few months later, it was ordered that inquiry be made whether the mass was celebrated, and other exercises of the Catholic religion were observed, publicly and aloud, and in the poop, on board the king's ships, at the appointed times; whether the captains in any way hindered the performance of these duties; and also as to the manner in which the prayers of those of the Pretended Reformed Religion were observed, whether in the foreship or between decks; and whether they took care to say them in a low voice, and in such a way as not to be overheard.—(Bulletin de la société de l'histoire du protestantisme français, tome II., pp. 335, 336.)
⁵ "Il est vray que long-temps auparavant que la Com-

for twelve years governor of the island of Tortuga, was himself an avowed Protestant.[1] The apostolic missionary Du Tertre complained in 1671 that the governor of Guadeloupe had raised a Huguenot gentleman to the most important posts in that island.[2] The heretics were practicing the rites of their religion with growing audacity. Nothing but the remonstrances of the vigilant friars and priests deterred the authorities from permitting the open and public celebration of the Reformed worship in the islands.[3]

As the violence of persecution increased in France, other Huguenots sought refuge in the Antilles. Among these, in 1679, came Elie Neau, afterwards the heroic confessor of the

---

pagnie feust en possession de ces Isles, il y avoit des Heretiques tolerez par toutes les Iles : mais en très-petit nombre ; lesquels s'estant accreus *par la connivance de quelques Gouverneurs*, ont toûjours tenté," etc.—(Du Tertre, Hist. Gén. des Antilles, etc., T. III., p. 317.)

[1] Dessalles, Hist. Gén. des Antilles, T. I., p. 87.

[2] Le sieur Potel. (Du Tertre, Hist. Gén. des Antilles, etc., T. II., p. 422.)—Rochefort mentions Monsieur Postel among "les principaus Officiers, et les plus honorables Habitans" of Guadeloupe, 1658.—(Hist. des Antilles, etc., p. 26.) Jacques Potell is named among the habitants of Guadeloupe in 1671.—(Dessalles, Hist. Gén. des Antilles, T. II., p. 447.)

[3] "Il est vray que le zele des Religieux Missionaires a empesché qu'ils n'ayent fait en public l'exercice de leur Religion, et ils en ont porté de si frequentes plaintes aux Gouverneurs, qu'on a tousiours puni par des Amendes pecuniaires, ceux qui se sont assemblez pour en faire les fonctions, de sorte que jusqu'à présent il ne s'est fait dans les Iles aucun exercice public, que de la Religion Catholique, Apostolique et Romaine."—(Du Tertre, Hist. Gén des Antilles, etc., T. II., p. 422.)

faith in the French galleys, and the devoted teacher of negro slaves in New York. Bred to a sea-faring life, Neau had left his home in the principality of Soubise, in Saintonge, at the age of eighteen, apprehending the troubles that began in that province under the administration of Marillac and Demuin. He spent several years in the Dutch and French islands of the West Indies, and would have settled in one of the latter, but for the prospect that the freedom of conscience enjoyed by the colonists would soon be invaded. Neau, at a later stage of his life, dated the commencement of his own profound experience of the power of religion, from the period of his sojourn among the French islands. Alluding to a severe affliction that befell him about this time, he says: "It was there that God began to speak to my heart, and granted me His love. My ignorance, however, made me to be like the blind man, who saw men as trees walking, the first time that the Lord touched his eyes. For I did indeed love God: but I did not know Him well enough to be constrained to live only for Him."[1]

Chap. III.
1679.

Instances of interference with the rights of conscience had indeed occurred in the French islands, before the catastrophe of the Revocation. In 1664, a school-book containing verses deemed to be contrary to the Roman religion and the mass, having been found in the possession of a child of tender years, he was sentenced

June 16, 1664.

---

[1] Histoire abbregée des Souffrances du sieur Elie Neau, sur les galeres, et dans les Cachots de Marseille.—A Rotterdam, chez Abraham Acher. M.DCC.I. P. 99.

to be beaten at the church door by his father; the parents were subjected to a heavy fine, and the schoolmaster was held for trial.[1] About the same time, it was decreed that persons who should speak in public against the doctrines and ceremonies of the Roman Religion, should be punished by having the lips slit, and the tongue pierced by a hot iron, and by perpetual banishment from the islands.[2] In the year 1678, the Council of Martinique, rendering judgment against Jean Boutilier, merchant, prohibited all persons of "the Religion" from assembling in any wise for the purpose of saying their prayers, whether aloud or in a low voice.[3] But the reluctance of the colonial government to proceed to such extremities, appears from the increasing strictness of the orders sent from France for the enforcement of the royal decrees. In 1683, the Council of Martinique registered the following order from the king: "As for the pretended Reformed, you shall not suffer them to practice any public exercise of their religion, nor permit any of them to be employed in the [public] charges. You shall not even allow any inhabitant of that religion to settle in the islands, with the purpose of acquiring lands, unless by express order. Concerning those who may frequent the islands for the purposes of trade, they may be

---

[1] Loix et Constitutions des Colonies Françoises de l'Amerique sous le Vent. Paris. [1784.] Tome I., Page 116.
[2] Ibid. P. 117.
[3] Histoire Générale des Antilles, par M. Adrien Dessalles. T. III. P. 213.

tolerated, but without any exercise whatsoever of their religion."[1]

Another chapter of Huguenot history in the Antilles—and a sadder one—begins with the Revocation of the Edict of Nantes. The voluntary emigration of French Protestants to these colonies, and their quiet establishment among them, during a time of comparative freedom from persecution, was now followed, in 1686, and the two succeeding years, by the compulsory transportation of persons sentenced to penal servitude, on account of their religion.

This method of intimidation, and of punishment, was employed for a while with great effect by the government of Louis XIV. It was a refinement upon the *dragonnades*, and other measures for the enforced conversion of his Majesty's Reformed subjects. No other fate was so dreaded. Even the galley-slave viewed the sentence of transportation to the islands of America, as a doom far more terrible than his own. The populations, especially, of the inland provinces of France, were made to believe that the condition of persons sent to the French islands would be one of utter misery and degradation. They were to be held as slaves, and subjected by the planters to the same treatment with their negroes and their cattle. America was pictured to them as a country where they would be not only friendless, but reduced to a hopeless and cruel captivity.

---

[1] Ibid., III., 214.

Chap. III.
1686.

These apprehensions were far from groundless. A system of peonage, attended with many of the worst features of slavery, prevailed in the French islands. Introduced by the "boucaniers," or sea-rovers, who infested the Antilles at an early day, it had been adopted by their successors, the planters. The "*engagés*," as they were called, were generally Frenchmen, who had sold themselves to serve for three years in the colonies. They were employed in severe field labors, under the burning sun of the tropics: and they were wholly at the mercy of masters often inhuman, and always irresponsible. It was said that one of these masters boasted openly that he had killed three hundred "engagés" with his own hand.[1] Stories like the following, which had come down from the times of the buccaneers, were doubtless known in France, and were heard with horror by the Sabbath-keeping Huguenot:—An "engagé," not improbably a Protestant, whose master was accustomed to send him every Sunday to the sea-shore, to carry the skins of cattle that had been slaughtered during the week, ventured to remind him of the divine command: Six days shalt thou labor, and do all thy work: but the seventh day is the Sabbath of the Lord thy God: in it thou shalt not do any work. "And I," answered the fierce freebooter, "I tell thee, Six days shalt thou slaughter bullocks, and skin

The 'engages.'

---

[1] Histoire des Aventuriers qui se sont signalés dans les mers des Indes. Par Alex. Oexmelin, Paris: 1713.—Quoted in Routier des Iles Antilles. Paris: 1824. P. 20.

them; and the seventh day thou shalt carry their hides to the sea-shore": and, as Raynal says, the command was enforced with blows, compelling the violation of the law of heaven.[1]

It is not to be supposed, however, that the French government seriously contemplated, at any time, the transportation of large numbers of the Huguenots, to serve as slaves in the colonies. It was undoubtedly for the purpose chiefly of intimidation that the measure was announced. All conceivable pains were taken to intensify the impression of horror which that announcement produced. Those who had withstood every other effort to shake their firmness, were now driven by hundreds to the sea-ports. The miseries of the journey were aggravated in every possible way. Parents and children, husbands and wives, neighbors and friends, were carefully separated from one another. Companies of soldiers escorted the wretched travelers, not so

---

[1] Un de ces malheureux, [les engagés,] à qui son avilissement avait laissé assez de religion pour qu'il se ressouvînt, que le dimanche est un jour de repos, osa représenter à son maître, qui chaque semaine choisissait ce jour pour se mettre en route, que Dieu avait proscrit un tel usage, quand il avait dit : *Tu travailleras six jours, et le septième tu te reposeras : Et moi*, reprit le féroce boucanier, *et moi je dis! six jours tu tueras des taureaux pour les écorcher, et le septième tu en porteras les peaux au bord de la mer:* et ce commandement fut accompagné de coups de bâtons qui, dit l'abbé Raynal, [Histoire philosophique et politique des etablissements et du commerce des Européens dans les deux Indes, t. V. p. 213,] tantôt font observer, et tantôt font violer les commandements de Dieu.—Histoire politique et statistique de l' Ile d'Hayti, Saint Domingue. Paris: 1826. P. 61.

much to prevent their escape, as to degrade them, by giving to the procession the aspect of a gang of criminals. Some were carried in carts, bound in such a manner as to increase their discomfort at every motion: while others walked, tied two by two, like convicts on their way to prison. Most of them were conducted to the sea-port of Marseilles. Many sickened and died on the way. Others perished in the famous Tour de Constance, while waiting for the vessels that were to transport them to the islands. But many thousands, after resisting every effort to overcome their faithfulness, and bearing the hardships of this shameful journey, yielded in the end. At the sight of the ships, that were to carry them far from their native land into slavery, their hearts failed them.[1] Those who persevered, were the wonder and admiration of their brethren. To them, this kind of persecution was, as one expressed it, "a terrible temptation. So long as one is in the kingdom, one flatters one's self, one hopes, one receives a little comfort from one's friends and relations. The Church, whose eyes are upon us, the edification of our brethren, and all things conduce to animate and encourage us to the conflict. But to see one's self deprived of all those powerful motives at once—to go into a new world, there to be buried as it were, separated from the rest of mankind, in a state worse than that of a slave,

---

[1] Histoire de l'Edit de Nantes [par Elie Benoist]. A Delft, chez Adrien Beman, MDCXCV. Tome troisième, seconde partie. Pp. 973–975.

abandoned to the discretion of a man who goes to the end of the world in quest of riches, and who, without any regard to humanity, treats his slaves in proportion to their labor, and the profit which he reaps thereby—good God!—what an Egypt is this, to those faithful martyrs who are transported thither!"[1]

The numbers actually shipped for the French islands were considerable.[2] Between the month of September, 1686, and the beginning of the year 1688, as many as ten vessels sailed from Marseilles, most of them bound for Martinique, and carrying over one thousand Huguenots, men and women.[3] Our accounts of this forced

---

[1] A Specimen of *Papal* and *French Persecution.* As also, Of the Faith and Patience of the late *French* Confessors and Martyrs. Exhibited in the Cruel Sufferings, and most Exemplary Behaviour of that Eminent Confessor and Martyr, Mr. *Lewis de Marolles.—Done newly out of French.—London.* Printed by S. Holt, 1712. Pp. 69, 70.

[2] Benoist, whose work appeared in 1693 and 1695, speaks of "plusieurs centaines de personnes;" but from information that has been published in our own day, and that fully confirms the accounts given by the author of the History of the Edict of Nantes, it would seem that the number must have exceeded his estimate.

[3] A decree of the Council of State, Sept. 24, 1688, exempting religionists and new converts sent to the islands from the payment of a poll-tax for one year, alludes to them as having been thus transported "since the month of January of last year."—(Loix et Constitutions, etc., I., 474.) The first arrivals, then, occurred in January, 1687, and the ship that brought the first detachment may have been the one referred to by Louis de Marolles, who writes in September, 1686: "It is designed next week to embark 150 invalid galley slaves for America." (P. 69). De Marolles mentions a second ship as about to sail, in January, 1687, (P. 92.) This vessel may have carried about the same num-

emigration, however, are in complete. It is probable that the whole number was much greater.

There were some of these unfortunates, whose courage gave out just at the last. On the eve of their embarkation, overcome with fear, they recanted. This weakness did not save them from an irrevocable fate. The "new converts," as they were called, were shipped with the rest, and fared no better than their more resolute brethren.

The miserable fate of these exiles awakened a profound sympathy among the Protestants throughout France, and in all Europe. To the refugees in Germany, Switzerland, and Great Britain, the name America—destined to be the synonym of freedom—meant slavery; a lot infinitely more pitiable than their own. This sympathy found expression in many touching ways. The French pastors gathered in the city of Zurich testified their compassion "for those who are now weeping under the iron yoke of the

---

ber of passengers. The ship Notre Dame de bonne espérance, with another vessel, left Marseilles March 12, 1687, the two having on board two hundred and twenty-four persons. (Benoist, V., 976.—Bulletin de la société de l' histoire du protestantisme français, XII., 74-79.) Two ships that left Marseilles a little later, carried one hundred and sixty persons. (Bulletin, *u. s.*) On the 18th of September, 1687, the pink *La Marie*, with seventy-nine, and the ship *La Concorde*, with ninety passengers, sailed from the same port. (Mémoires de Samuel de Pechels. Toulouse: 1878, p. 50.) Two vessels that reached the islands in the beginning of the year 1688, had on board one hundred and eighty persons. (Bulletin, *u. s.*) Thus the transportations of which we have positive knowledge amount to at least a thousand.

heathen in Africa, and those who in America groan under the rod of wickedness."[1] Jean Olry, of Metz, sentenced with ten others to transportation for their religious faith, relates that on reaching the city of La Rochelle, where they were to embark for the West Indies, the prisoners found on board the vessel three ladies, who had been awaiting their arrival for several days, to offer them, in behalf of their brethren in that city, gifts of money and clothing, and of provisions, including wine and other delicacies, for their comfort on the voyage.[2] One of the ships that left Marseilles in the spring of the year 1687, carrying a large company of banished Huguenots, was forced by stress of weather to anchor in the port of Cadiz. The governor of that city had the curiosity to visit them, and was so touched by the condition of the women, that he sent them a present of fruit. Among other persons attracted by this strange arrival, was a French officer who chanced to be in the harbor. On the deck of the ship, he saw several young women, whose faces wore a deathlike pallor. I inquired of them, he says, how it happened that they were going to America. They replied in tones of heroic firmness, Because we will not worship the beast, nor fall down before images. This, they added, is our crime. The officer went below, and found in the ship's cabin eighty women and girls, lying upon mattresses, in the

---

[1] Bulletin de la soc. de l' hist. du prot. franç., VII., 57.
[2] Ibid., VI., 309.

most pitiable condition. My lips were closed, he writes; I had not a word of comfort to speak to them. But instead of my consoling them, it was they who consoled me, in language the most affecting; and as I continued speechless, they said, We entreat you to remember us in your prayers. Ask that God would give us grace to persevere to the end, that we may have part in the crown of life. As for us, we lay our hands upon our mouths, and we say that all things come from Him who is the King of kings. It is in Him that we put our trust.'

Two ships that sailed from Marseilles in September, 1687, only reached St. Domingo in February of the following year. The *Concorde* carried ninety Protestant captives; the *Marie*, seventy-nine. Of these prisoners, the greater number were from lower Languedoc and the Cevennes. Their sufferings during the long voyage of five months were extremely great. The vessels were small and overcrowded, and the supply of food and water was insufficient. On the *Marie*, fifty-nine persons were huddled together in a compartment not large enough to accommodate twenty. In an adjoining cabin, seventy worn-out galley-slaves, on their way to the islands to be sold to the planters, were confined, heavily chained, in a space equally contracted. Both classes of prisoners were devoured with vermin. Shut up, much of the time, in

---

' Bulletin de la soc. de l' hist. du prot. franç., XI., 156. Comp. Benoist, Hist. de l' Edit de Nantes, V., 976.

these wretched quarters, where the unfortunate occupant could neither stand erect, nor stretch himself on the floor, without incommoding another, the stifling heat, the consuming thirst, the pangs of hunger, to which the sufferers were exposed, were aggravated by the cruelty of their keepers. As often as they happened to see us engaged in prayer, or in singing psalms—writes one of the passengers—they would fall upon us with blows, or deluge us with sea-water. Their constant talk was of the miseries that awaited us in America. They told us that, when we should reach the islands, the men would be hung, and the women would be given up to the savages, should they refuse to attend mass. But far from being terrified by these threats, to which we had now become accustomed, many of us felt a secret joy at the thought that it had pleased God to call us to suffer even unto death for His holy name. Our resolution was unshaken by the abuse we experienced every day. As for myself, all this seemed to me as nothing, and as not worthy to be compared to the glory that should follow. Blessed are they which suffer for righteousness' sake, for theirs is the kingdom of Heaven.'

In this forced emigration, not a few perished at sea, through sickness, exposure, privation, or by shipwreck. From the accounts that have come down to us, it appears that at least one-

---

' Mémoires de Samuel de Pechels. Publiés par Raoul de Cazenove. Toulouse: 1878. Pp. 50–56.

fourth of the number embarked, died during the voyage. The *Espérance*, which left Marseilles on the twelfth of March, 1687, with a company of seventy men and thirty women, was wrecked, on the nineteenth of May, upon the rocks near the island of Martinique. Thirty-seven of the number perished. The survivors were hospitably received by the Caribs, who met them upon the shore, lighted fires to warm them, and brought them supplies of *cassava*, the native substitute for bread. Among the French, they were treated with similar kindness. Guiraud, of Nismes, after spending five months on that island, escaped to the English quarter of St. Christopher, where he found a home with a French planter, a naturalized subject of England, who treated him as his own son.[1]

Martinique, the principal destination of the transport-ships, was at this time one of the most populous and important of the French Antilles. As the Huguenots approached it, their impressions of gloom and dread must have been deepened by the aspect of the lofty island. Its broken outline, bearing with remarkable distinctness the marks of an igneous origin, can be descried far out at sea. The interior of the island is a mass of precipitous rock, from which one peak, Mount Pelée, rises to a height of four thousand five hundred feet. Here and there may be seen the craters of extinct vol-

---

[1] Bulletin de la soc. de l'hist. du prot. franç., XII., pp. 74–79.

canoes. From the almost inaccessible center of the island, long ridges of lava extend to the shores, where they form deep indentations along the coast. Between these ridges lie broad, irregular valleys of great fertility, watered by numerous streams from the surrounding heights. Amid these valleys, the rich vegetation of which contrasted singularly with the grandeur of the mountains, clothed with primeval forests, or rugged and sterile, the Huguenots noticed with special interest the *mornes*, or rounded hillocks, rising upon the lowland. Many of them were crowned with the dwellings of planters, who chose these elevated sites partly for health and partly also for safety, in view of the frequent inundations caused by the swelling of the mountain torrents.

Religious persecution had already commenced in the islands, before the arrival of the banished Huguenots. A few months after the Revocation of the Edict of Nantes, orders came to Count de Blénac, the governor-general, directing him to take measures without delay for the extirpation of heresy in the islands. The king hoped that his colonial subjects would readily follow the example of so many of their brethren in France, and renounce their errors. Should any prove stubborn, however, they were to be dealt with accordingly. The obstinate might be punished by imprisonment, or by the quartering of soldiers in their houses. An exception was made for the present in the case of the inhabitants of St. Christopher: inasmuch as the work of uprooting heresy would be attended with greater difficulty there than in the other islands, because of the facilities that the religionists enjoyed to attend heretical worship in the English part of the island, or to escape to the English altogether. Lenient measures might there be tried, before a harsher course should be adopted. The king, however, would give all to understand, that he was resolved in no wise to permit the Protestants on the islands to remove from them, for the purpose of establishing themselves elsewhere.[1]

These orders were followed by others, having reference to the companies of Huguenots sentenced to be transported to the colonies. Immediately upon their arrival, they were to be distributed among the different islands, and placed at service with the planters. No discrimination was made in favor of the "nouveaux convertis," who had hoped to procure a mitigation of their sentence by abjuring their faith. These were to be carefully watched, and compelled to perform their duties as Catholics: but they were sent off with the rest.[2]

The islands of Guadeloupe, St. Martin, St. Eustatius, and St. Domingo, received numbers of these captives. In their new homes, many died soon of grief and of exhaustion. Of those that survived, the greater number appear to have fallen into the hands of hu-

---

[1] Histoire Générale des Antilles, par M. Adrien Dessalles. Paris. 1847. Tome II., p. 63.
[2] Histoire Générale des Antilles, par M. A. Dessalles. Tome III., p. 215.

mane masters. Guiraud, one of the shipwrecked passengers of the *Espérance*, relates that he spent five months in Saint-Pierre, on the island of Martinique, and received much kindness from several persons. In fact, not a few of the merchants and planters held the same faith with the exiles. They regarded them as illustrious witnesses for the truth, and thought it an honor to acknowledge them as brethren, and to relieve their necessities.

The prisoners landed on the island of St. Domingo, were especially fortunate in finding friends. One of them, Samuel de Pechels, relates that upon reaching Port-au-Prince, he and his comrades were kindly received by the captain of the king's ship lying in the harbor. The governor treated them with great humanity. De Pechels was permitted to visit his fellow-religionists, but he soon awakened the jealousy of the priests and monks, who denounced him as hindering the others from becoming Roman Catholics; and he was sent off to another island, from which he soon succeeded in making his escape.

The first thought of the captives, upon reaching their place of banishment, was naturally that of flight. In this scheme they were joined by many of the Protestant inhabitants of the islands, whom the new policy of religious persecution now determined to leave their homes and seek refuge in the Dutch or English islands, or on the American continent. In the island of Martinique, secret arrangements were made with the masters of certain ships, for the transportation of all the Huguenot families to some foreign territory. The governor, De Blénac, hearing of the project, felt himself obliged to confer with the Jesuit fathers, and other ecclesiastics of the island. It was resolved to begin with a course of intimidation. The leading Protestants were called together in one of the churches, and gravely warned, that if they should persist in their obstinacy, they would be dealt with in all severity, according to the king's command. The result may readily be imagined. Every opportunity of escape was speedily improved. Many of the Roman Catholics favored the flight of the exiles, and helped them to effect it. Before the end of the year 1687, the king was informed that his Protestant subjects, by whole families, were leaving the islands daily.[1]

The methods of escape were various. Sometimes the Huguenot, watching upon the shore, would succeed in attracting the notice of some passing bark, and in persuading the captain to carry him with his household and his goods to a friendly port. At another time, the owner of a small sloop, or schooner, would stealthily convey his family on board, and set sail for the continent. Such an adventurer, Etienne Hamel, master of the brigantine Amorante, reached the harbor of New York in June, 1686: "a poore french Protestant," as he represents himself, "who leaving his Estate behind him

---

[1] Histoire Générale des Antilles, par M. A. Dessalles. T. II., pp. 64–66.

has been forced to fly from the Rigorous Persecution in Gardalupa [Guadeloupe] into these parts with Intent here to settle."[1] The greater number made their way to the English or Dutch islands, and thence obtained passage either to some Protestant country of Europe, or to America. A company of thirty, who had come over together in one of the vessels from Marseilles, escaped from Martinique to the English quarter of St. Christopher, and there took ship for Germany.[2]

It was at this period that a number of the French inhabitants of the Antilles came to New York. In the month of November, 1686, the governor of Canada received word from that city that within a short time fifty or sixty Huguenots had arrived from the islands of St. Christopher and Martinique, and were settling themselves there and in the neighborhood. "Fresh material, this, for banditti," wrote the governor, in reporting the fact to his royal master.[3] We have the names of fifty-four of these fugitives. The heads of families were, Alexandre Allaire, Elie de Bonrepos, Jean Boutilier, Isaac Caillaud, Ami Canche, Daniel Duchemin, Pierre Fleuriau, Daniel Gombauld, Etienne Hamel, Jean Hastier, Pierre Jouneau, Jacques Lasty, Guillaume le

---

[1] English Manuscripts in the office of the Secretary of State, Albany, N. Y., Vol. XXXVIII., p. 31.

[2] Bulletin de la soc. de l'hist. du prot. français, XII., 79.

[3] Documents relative to the Colonial History of the State of New York. Vol. IX., p. 309. M. de Denonville to M. de Seignelay, Quebec, November 16, 1686.

Chap. III.
1686.
Conte, Pierre le Conte, Josias le Vilain, Benjamin l'Hommedieu, Elie Pelletreau, Jean Neufville, Elie Papin, Antoine Pintard, André Thauvet, Jacob Theroulde, René Tongrelou, Louis Bongrand, Etienne Bouyer, Gilles Gaudineau, Jean Machet, Isaac Mercier, Paul Merlin, Jean Pelletreau, and Etienne Valleau.[1]

Most of these immigrants, it would appear, had been residing in the French islands for some years. There is reason to believe that they belonged to the number of French Protestants who had voluntarily sought a home in the Antilles, and had remained there so long as

---

[1] An Act for the naturalizing of Daniell Duchemin and others, Sept. 27, 1687. From (unpublished MSS.) "Statutes at Large of New York: 1664–1691. From Original Records and Authentic Manuscripts." Kindly communicated to me by Geo. H. Moore, LL.D.

The Sieur Boisbelleau, of Guadeloupe, came to New York the year before. The petition of Francis Basset, master, and Francis Vincent, mate, of a vessel sailing from the port of New York, August 13, 1685, shows that they were taken prisoners by the Spaniards, who carried them to the town of St. Domingo, where they were very ill used for the space of four months, and from whence, by a particular providence of God, they made their escape in a canoe to the little Goyaves. Arriving there with much difficulty, and destitute of all things necessary (the Spaniards having stripped them of their very clothes) the Sieur Boybelleau was moved with compassion towards them, for the extreme misery of such poor desolate captives that had lost all they had, and were like also in a short time to lose their lives, and brought them back in his vessel to New York. Upon this representation the ship was exempted from duties and charges.—(N. Y. Colonial MSS., Vol. XXXII. folio 86.) Denization was granted to John Boisbelleau, Sept. 2, 1685.—(Calendar of English MSS., N. Y., p. 140.) The same year, he settled at Gravesend, Long Island, N. Y., and was living there in 1687. —(Documentary History of New York, Vol. I., p. 661.)

they could enjoy some measure of religious freedom. The last eight names, however, are not found in the lists of the earlier inhabitants of the islands. It is not unlikely that Bongrand, Bouyer, Gaudineau, Machet, Mercier, Merlin, Pelletreau, and Valleau, may have belonged to the body of Huguenots transported to the islands after the Revocation of the Edict of Nantes. Many others, doubtless, of whom we have no definite knowledge, found their way to this country, and settled in South Carolina, in Virginia, in Maryland, as well as in New York and New England.

The Huguenot refugee from England who reached Boston in October, 1687, learned on the voyage, by a ship from Martinique, that nearly all the French Protestants had escaped from the islands. "We have several of them here in Boston," he adds, "with their entire families."

Too late to arrest this movement, so ruinous to its colonial interests, the French government relaxed the severity of a policy that was depopulating the islands. Orders came from the king, enjoining great gentleness toward those who persisted in their heresy, as well as toward the " new converts." These were not to be compelled to approach the sacraments, but were only to be required to attend upon religious instruction. Both the religionists and the converts, for their encouragement to remain in the islands, were relieved of the poll-tax imposed upon the inhabitants, for the first year of their residence.[1]

A modern writer states that considerable numbers of French Protestants remained in the Antilles after the period of active persecution; "submissively awaiting the happy hour when it might please the sovereign to revoke the ordinances that oppressed them, and enable them to enjoy without molestation the blessings of his reign."[2] From time to time, some of the colonists who had taken refuge in America returned to the West Indies;[3] and among the French merchants of New York, the custom long prevailed—a custom introduced by the refugees—of sending their sons upon the com-

---

[1] Ordre du Roi touchant les Religionnaires et les nouveaux Convertis envoyés aux Iles Du 1ᵉʳ Sept. 1688. Sa M⁶ a approuvé la distribution que les Administrateurs ont fait dans toutes les Isles, des Religionnaires et nouveaux Convertis qu' Elle leur a envoyés, et leur recommande de tenir la main à ce que ceux qui font encore profession de la R. P. R. abjurent, et que les autres fassent leurs devoirs de Catholiques, non pas en les obligeant par force à approcher les Sacremens; mais en les traitant avec douceur, et les obligeant seulement à assister aux instructions. Elle desire aussi qu'ils tiennent la main à ce que les Ecclesiastiques des Isles aient une application particulière à les instruire, et qu'ils fassent de leur coté tout ce qui dépendra d 'eux pour les obliger à rester dans les Isles, et de s'y faire Habitans.—Loix et Constitutions des Colonies Françoises de l'Amérique sous le Vent. Tome I., p. 469.

[2] Histoire Générale des Antilles, par M. Adrien Dessalles. Tome III., p. 215.

[3] Others remained longer in the islands, and came to America at a later day. Moses Gombeaux, commander of the sloop St. Bertram, of Martinico, petitioned the governor and council, June 8, 1726, for permission to stop in the port of New York for supplies and repairs. Moyse Gombauld

pletion of their business education, to spend some time in the islands, whither many family and social ties continued to draw them.[1]

Several Huguenot families that settled in the French West Indies, eventually removed to Bermuda, where their descendants are found at the present day. The Godet, Corbusier[2] and Le Thuillier families, went thither from the island of St. Eustatius.[3] A tradition preserved in the

---

and Anne Françoise Pintard, his wife, were members of the French Church in New York, 1736–1742. A tradition exists in the Pintard family, to the effect that "Moses Gombauld, who was son-in-law to Anthony Pintard, was imprisoned in the West Indies, and escaped by means of a rope," which had been stealthily conveyed to him by some friends, and "with which he scaled the prison walls, and so escaped."

[1] The History of the late Province of New York, by the Hon. William Smith. New York: 1829. Vol. II., p. 95, *note*.

[2] "About a century ago there was a Colonel Corbusier among the first gentry of the island." (Gen. Sir John H. Lefroy.)

[3] The following "French names from registers of births, marriages, etc., at St. Eustatius, from 1773 to 1778," were very obligingly procured for me in the year 1877, by General Sir John H. Lefroy, at that time Governor of Bermuda. There can be no doubt that these are names of French *Protestants*, inasmuch as the entries were made by the chaplain to the Dutch forces in St. Eustatius:

Romage. M. Cuvilje (child buried April 29, 1773). Sellioke. Corbusier. La Grasse (buried April 4, 1775). Raveaue. M. Collomb (buried April 16, 1776). Preveaux (buried June 2, 1776). Dubrois Godette (buried May 29, 1776). M. J. Cadette (buried June 12, 1776). Miss Lé Spere (buried Aug. 20, 1776). Zanés. Mrs. Bardin (buried Jan. 28, 1773). Danziés. M. Guizon (buried Dec. 5, 1773). Erthé. Miss Chabert (buried June 5, 1775). Panyea. M. Gilliard (buried May 20, 1776). Charitres. M. Lefevre (buried May 30, 1776). Pesant. M. Gillott (buried Sept. 19, 1777). Pancho. L'Comb. Caianna. Savallani.

Chap. III. Godet family, of Bermuda, represents that two brothers of that name fled from France at the time of the Revocation, effecting their escape by hiding themselves in empty casks, on board a ship sailing for England. From England they emigrated to the West Indies, where they found homes, the one in Guadeloupe, and the other in Antigua and St. Eustatius. The Pérot

Foissin. Lagourgue. Crochet.—Theodorus Godet, born about the year 1670, married Sarah La Roux in Antigua in 1700. He was a prosperous merchant, who resided for several years in the island of St. Eustatius, and died September 20, 1740, in Maho Bay, Guadeloupe, whither he had gone to visit his brother. He had eight children: Anne, Sarah, Theodorus, Jacob, Martin Du Brois, Mary Ann, Gideon and Adrian. Martin Du Brois, born in Willoughby Bay, Antigua, March 6, 1709, married Adriana, daughter of Lucus and Anne Benners, July 17, 1731. He died Nov. 25, 1796. His son Theodorus, born in St. Eustatius, Sept. 27, 1734, was educated in Boston, U. S. He married in Bermuda, Aug. 3, 1753, Melicent, daughter of Col. Thomas Gilbert, and had six children. He died in Bermuda in 1808. Thomas Martin Du Brois, son of Theodorus and Melicent Godet, was born in Bermuda, May 1, 1769. He married, March 25, 1795, Mary Ann, widow of William Gilbert, Esq., and daughter of the Rev. John Moore, Rector and Incumbent of Somerset Tribe. He died at St. Eustatius, Sept. 23, 1826, leaving five children. Thomas Martin Du Brois, son of the preceding, was born in Paget's Parish, Oct. 3, 1802. He married his cousin, Melicent Godet, Dec. 27, 1832. He died, May 29, 1861, leaving six children, among whom is Frederick Lennock Godet, Esq., Clerk of Her Majesty's Council, Bermuda.

Theodore Godet was naturalized in England, Sept. 9, 1698.—(Lists of naturalized Denizens; in Protestant Exiles from France in the Reign of Louis XIV. By the Rev. David C. A. Agnew. London, 1874. Vol. III., p. 61.) The name Dubrois, used in this family as a baptismal name, is that of a Huguenot family that fled in 1683 from La Rochelle to England.—(Archives Nationales, TT. No. 259.—Protestant Exiles, etc., III., p. 55.)

family, of Bermuda, is descended from Jacques Pérot, one of the Huguenot refugees in the city of New York.[1]

---

[1] Jacques, son of Jacques Pérot and Marie Cousson his wife, was born May 20, 1712, and was baptized in the French Church in New York, May 26, "apres l'action de l'apres diner."—(Records of the French Church, New York.) He was sent in early manhood by his father to Bermuda, where he settled, and married Frances Mallory. He died, February 29, 1780, leaving eight children, Martha, Mary, Elliston, John, James, William, Frances, and Angelina. Elliston, son of Jacques and Marie Pérot, born in Bermuda, March 16, 1747, was sent to New York to be educated, by his uncle, Robert Elliston, then Comptroller of the Customs, who placed him in the school kept by pasteur Stouppe, in New Rochelle, where he was a schoolmate of the celebrated John Jay. Upon his uncle's death, he returned to Bermuda. After engaging in business in the islands of Dominica, St. Christopher and St. Eustatius, he removed to the United States in 1784, and commenced business with his brother John as a merchant in Philadelphia. In 1786, he was admitted a member of the Society of Friends. He married, in 1787, Sarah, daughter of Samuel and Hannah Sansom, who died August 22, 1808. Elliston Pérot was prominently associated with many of the public enterprises of his time, and left a name that is held in high honor to this day. He died in Philadelphia, November 28, 1834, aged eighty-eight years. His brother William left a son, William B. Pérot, of Parlaville, Hamilton, Bermuda, who died in 1871, leaving a son, William Henry Perot, of Baltimore, Maryland. The family is also represented in this country by Elliston's descendants, Francis Perot, Esq., now [1884] in his eighty-sixth year, and Elliston Perot Morris, Esq., of Philadelphia, Penn.

CHAPTER IV

Approach of the Revocation.

Chap. IV.
1628.

Fall of La Rochelle.

The political importance of the Huguenots in France may be said to have ceased with the fall of their principal city, La Rochelle, in the year 1628. That importance had first appeared in the reign of Francis II. It lasted for seventy years—through the stormy times of the League, and the Civil Wars, the pacific reign of Henry IV., and the years following his reign, during which the provisions of the Edict of Nantes were carried out with some degree of faithfulness. It waned rapidly under Louis XIII., when the government showed itself increasingly disposed to set aside the provisions of that Edict. One after another of the cautionary towns and the fortified places held by the Huguenots succumbed to the royal forces. At length, after a siege of fourteen months, La Rochelle was captured, and with its fall, the part that Protestantism had played in the affairs of the state came to an end.

The higher nobility now very generally deserted the Protestant cause. Many of them had joined it during the civil wars; and so long as the Edict remained in full force, they found it for their advantage to cling to the Huguenot party. Its political consequence was not the only feature that held out inducements to those who were ambitious of preferment and distinction. The ecclesiastical system of the Reformed Church, with its presbyterian synods and assemblies, in which laymen sat with the ministers, gave opportunity to the Protestant nobles to take the lead in spiritual affairs, and like the political assemblies, provincial and national, which formed, indeed, no part of the ecclesiastical system, but which, ever since the time of the massacre of St. Bartholomew's day, had contributed not a little to the strength of the Huguenots, served to increase the prominence of the Protestant nobility.

No longer influential with the great, nor formidable in the eyes of the government, the Huguenots accepted the situation, and, after the fall of La Rochelle and Montauban, gave themselves up zealously to the pursuit of the arts of peace. A time of comparative tranquillity and prosperity ensued upon the loss of their political prestige. Throughout the provinces where they were most numerous, they engaged with fresh diligence in agriculture, manufactures, and trade. The Protestants of southern and western France surpassed all others as cultivators of the soil. In many of the seaboard towns, Huguenot merchants had long been foremost in commercial enterprise. The foreign trade of the kingdom came to be, very largely, controlled by them.[1]

---

[1] A striking testimony to this fact is given in a document already cited. (See above, page 126, *note*.) Announcing to the

Chap. IV.
1629–
1660.

Their devotion to trade and manufactures.

Inventive and industrious, they applied themselves with great success to the mechanical arts. The manufactures of woolen cloth, and linen goods, of serge, and silks, and sail-cloth, the iron-works and paper mills, and tanneries, that enriched France at this period, were founded or promoted chiefly by Protestants. In every department of labor, they were fitted to excel by their morality, their intelligence, and their thrift. The truthfulness and honesty of the Huguenot became proverbial. "They are bad Catholics," said one of their enemies, "but excellent men of business." "All our seaports," complained another, "are full of heretic captains, pilots and traders, who, inasmuch as their souls are altogether busied in traffic, make themselves more perfect therein than Catholics can well be." Religiously observing one day in seven as a day of rest, their devotion to trade was not interrupted by the many saints' days of the Roman Catholic calendar. Surrounded by watchful enemies, and schooled to self-restraint, they were prudent and circumspect in their dealings with others, and ready to combine and co-operate among themselves in their business procedures.

Meanwhile, their loyalty to the government could not be impeached. More than once the king and his ministers testified to the fact that

---

governor of Canada the Revocation of the Edict of Nantes, Louis XIV. speaks of the great number of conversions that have taken place, "*whole cities, in which almost all the merchants made profession of the Pretended Reformed Religion*, having abjured it."

the Protestants no longer caused the state any anxiety. When a discontented prince, as the Duke of Montmorency, or the Prince of Condé, sought to draw them into rebellion, for the furtherance of his ambitious schemes, he found the Huguenots firm in their attachment to the throne. A very striking declaration to this effect was made by Cardinal Mazarin, prime minister of Louis XIII., a short time before his death. The king, said he to a deputation of Protestants who came to remonstrate with him in relation to certain encroachments upon their rights, would be wanting in justice and in goodness, if he did not look with the same favor upon the Reformed as upon the Catholics, since they have been not less prompt to shed their blood and to yield up their property for his service, than they.[1] Even Louis XIV. acknowledged at a later day that his Protestant subjects had given him abundant proofs of their fidelity.

It was no political necessity, then, demanding a change in its treatment of them, that impelled the government, upon the death of Mazarin, to enter upon that course of vexatious restriction and oppression which culminated, a quarter of a century later, in the Revocation of the Edict of Nantes. The Huguenots were inoffensive to the state, and positively important to the material interests of the country. The king had confessedly no better servants than they, in the various offices, civic and military, which as yet

---

[1] Benoist, Histoire de l'Edit de Nantes, Tome III., p. 268.

were open to those of the new religion, as well as to those of the old. France had no more peaceable, moral, enterprising citizens. But the Church of Rome continued to be, as it had been from the first, the vigilant and relentless enemy of the Reformed faith. And the Church had now a pliant tool in the occupant of the throne of France. Louis XIV., like his predecessor, had pledged his word, upon ascending the throne, to maintain the provisions of the Edict of Nantes irrevocably.[1] But already the doctrine had been broached and advocated, that this perpetual edict was to be held binding only so long as the occasion for its existence might last.[2] If by any means the heretics in whose behalf that edict had been prepared, should be induced to renounce their errors, then the law would become inoperative, and might properly be revoked. To bring about this result, the king,

---

[1] "Savoir faisons que nous .... avons dit et declaré, disons et declarons par ces presentes, signées de nôtre main, voulons et nous plaît, que nosdits sujets faisans profession de ladite Religion pretenduë Reformée, jouissent et ayent l'exercise libre et entier de ladite Religion, conformément aux Edits, Declarations, et Reglemens faits sur ce sujet, sans qu'à ce faire ils puissent être troublez, ni inquietez en quelque sorte et maniere que ce soit. Lesquels Edits bien que perpetuels, nous avons de nouveau, entant que besoin est, ou seroit, confirmez, et confirmons par cesdites presentes : voulons les contrevenans à iceux être punis et châtiez, comme perturbateurs du repos public."—(Declaration, portant confirmation de l'Edit de Nantes, etc., donnée par le Roi Louis XIV. en minorité, le 8. de Juillet 1643. Benoist, Histoire de l'Edit de Nantes, tome troisième, première partie. Recueil d'Edits, etc. Pp. 3, 4.)

[2] Benoist, Histoire de l'Edit de Nantes, tome troisième, première partie, pp. 281, 282.

inspired by the clergy, bent all his energies. A series of measures, designed to hamper and repress, and more and more to intimidate and discourage the Protestants throughout the kingdom, was entered upon by the government.

One of the first of these measures was directed against the family. In 1661, a decree of the Council fixed the age at which Protestant children might lawfully renounce the faith of their parents, at fourteen years in the case of boys, and at twelve in the case of girls. Subsequent decrees prohibited parents from seeking to dissuade their children from taking this step, forbade their sending them out of the country to be educated, and finally fixed the age of conversion at *seven* years. No better device for introducing disorder and misery into the homes of the Huguenots could possibly have been adopted. The zealous emissaries of the Church availed themselves abundantly of the authority given them under these laws. The whole country soon rang with the lamentations and complaints of parents whose children were secretly enticed or openly carried off from their natural protectors. The slightest pretext answered to justify the kidnapper. The child that could be persuaded, by the promise of a toy or of a holiday, to say *Ave Maria*, or to express a willingness to attend mass, was instantly claimed as a Catholic, and either placed at once in the hands of the clergy, to be brought up as such, or returned to the parents with strict orders to bring it up as a member of the true Church. Often, indeed,

_{Chap. IV.}
_{1661.}

_{March 24.}

_{June 17, 1681.}

the capture was effected with even less formality. Children were taken without form of law, and the protests and prayers of parents were utterly unheeded by the courts of justice. This mode of persecution alone, says Benoist, was so severe, that it would seem well-nigh impossible to add anything to it.[1]

Other measures of the government deprived the Huguenots of the facilities they enjoyed for the education of their children. The Edict of Nantes had secured to them equal rights, in these respects, with their Roman Catholic neighbors. Now, these rights were gradually curtailed. In 1664, the new buildings which the Protestants of Nismes had added to their college were given to the Jesuits, and the professors were placed under the authority of the Jesuit rector. Two years later, Protestant nobles were forbidden to maintain academies for the instruction of their children. Another decree prohibited the consistories and synods of the Reformed Church from censuring parents who should send their children to Roman Catholic schools. A little later, Protestant schoolmasters were forbidden to teach children any branch of learning besides reading, writing, and arithmetic. A decree soon followed, ordaining that but a single school of the "Pretended Reformed Religion" should be kept in any one of the places where the public profession of that

---

[1] Histoire de l'Edit de Nantes, tome troisième, seconde partie, p. 19.

religion was permitted under the Edict of Nantes, and that no more than a single master should be allowed for each school. While on the one hand thus reducing the opportunities for primary instruction to the narrowest possible limits, the government on the other hand proceeded to suppress the great Protestant colleges and academies, which had been, for a century or more, the glory of the Reformed Churches of France. In 1681, the Council of State suppressed the Protestant academy which Coligny had founded at Châtillon-sur-Loing; and the more famous academy of Sedan, which had been founded by Henry IV. In 1684, the academy of Die was suppressed. In January of the next year, the academy of Saumur, "a torch" that had "illuminated all Europe" for eighty years, was extinguished. The last of these Protestant seats of learning, the academy of Montauban, ceased to exist by an order of the Council dated the fifth of March, 1685.

Chap. IV. 1671.

July 9, 1681.

September 11, 1684.

January 8, 1685.

March 5, 1685.

The Protestant churches, or "temples," as they were called, shared the fate of the schools and colleges. Upon the slightest conceivable pretext, they were closed or demolished. In 1662, twenty-three out of the twenty-five churches in the small territory of Gex, on the border of Switzerland, where the Protestants composed a majority of the population, were shut up, on the ground that the provisions of the Edict of Nantes did not extend to this territory, which had been acquired by the crown since its enactment. From that time until the

January 16, 1662.

epoch of the Revocation, in 1685, not a year passed that was not signalized by the destruction of many Huguenot houses of worship. Sometimes, this destruction was the work of the mob, incited by the clergy, and rarely punished by the authorities. More generally, it was performed by the officers of the law, at the command of the government itself. Occasionally, a reason was assigned for the suppression. Thus the "temple" of St. Hippolyte, in the region of the Cevennes, was torn down by order of the Council in 1681, because one of the worshipers failed to uncover his head when the host was passing, as he came out of the church door. The "temple" of Milhaud, in Languedoc, was demolished in 1682, because some of the Huguenots, on their way by boat to the service, had sung psalms aloud. The "temple" of Usez, in Languedoc, where three-fourths of the population were Protestants, was destroyed in 1676, for the reason that it was too near the church of the Papists, and the psalm-singing disturbed the service of the mass. An edict published in 1680 prohibited the Protestant ministers from permitting Roman Catholics to frequent their preaching, and interdicted forever the observance of "the religion" in any place where a Roman Catholic had been admitted to profess it. But in most cases, no reason whatever was given. A congregation received notice of the suppression and confiscation of its sanctuary, cemetery, and consistory-house, and all protest or appeal was vain. It was even made a crime for the shelterless flock to meet for prayer and praise under the open sky, on the site of their demolished "temple," as many congregations persisted in doing, in spite of fine and imprisonment.

{Chap. IV. 1662-1685.}

No measures taken by the government caused greater satisfaction to the Church of Rome, than those by which it thus sought to hinder the exercise of the hated religion. An assembly of the clergy of the diocese of Arles gave public thanks to the king "for the demolition of so many temples which had been raised to the idol of falsehood, for the suppression of so many colleges, which were seminaries of perdition," and declared that it regarded "these happy beginnings as auguring that the king would deal the fatal blow to the monstrous hydra of heresy."

The policy of restriction which thus bore upon the family, the school and the church, followed the Huguenot also into his daily calling. Though the Edict of Nantes expressly provided for the security of the Protestants in all their lawful avocations, the government of Louis XIV., long before the Revocation, began to close against them, one by one, the employments in which hitherto they had found means of support. They were excluded successively from all civil and municipal charges, as farmers and receivers of taxes, officers of the mint, magistrates, notaries, advocates, marshals and sergeants. The professions were commanded to repel them. They were forbidden to prac-

{Exclusion from trades and professions.}

tise as physicians or surgeons, or to exercise the functions of printers, booksellers, clerks and public messengers. The various classes of craftsmen were cautioned against admitting them. No Protestant was allowed to act as guardian of orphan children, though the parents might have been Protestants. Huguenot women were no longer suffered to act as milliners, laundresses or midwives. The ingenuity of the government seems to have been taxed to the utmost, to contrive ways of harassing and hindering the obdurate heretic, and forcing him within the pale of the Church.

But the triumph of that ingenuity was reserved for the *Dragonnades*. This method of procuring forced conversions was not altogether new. A similar method had been tried, many years before, by the troops of Louis XIII., in the conquered province of Béarn, and it had proved eminently successful. The king, in his desire for the more rapid conversion of his Protestant subjects, now suggested a renewal of the experiment. The *dragonnades* consisted simply in the military occupation of a territory whose inhabitants were at peace and defenseless. Bodies of soldiers were marched into its towns and villages, and quartered upon the Huguenot families. "If, according to a fair distribution," wrote the king, "they could entertain as many as ten apiece, you may assign them twenty." The troops had orders to prolong their stay, until their hosts should abjure. Meanwhile, they were at liberty to inflict upon them any kind of outrage, short of violation or death. The wretched families saw themselves not only impoverished, and liable to be utterly beggared by their rapacious guests, but exposed also to their licensed brutality. The historian Benoist fills many pages with particulars of these inflictions, and adds: "In short, these dragoons did, in order to compel these people to turn Catholic, all that soldiers are accustomed to do in an enemy's country, for the purpose of forcing their hosts to give up their money, or to reveal the place where they have hidden their goods. They spared neither men, nor women, nor children; neither the poor, nor the sick, nor the aged."

It was in June, 1681,—directly after the outbreak of this inhuman system of warfare upon the innocent and the defenseless,—that the king issued the declaration to which reference has already been made, permitting the children of persons of the Reformed religion to renounce it, and to embrace the Roman Catholic faith, at the age of seven years. And it would be hard to say which of these two measures produced the greater consternation among the unfortunate Protestants of France, and which awakened the deeper indignation throughout Protestant Europe. If the one decree consigned the family to the violence of a brutal soldiery, the other exposed it to the insidious arts of nuns and priests. Henceforth, no Huguenot home was safe from invasion: and Louis had at last convinced his Protestant subjects that there was no length to which he was not ready to go, to "compel them to enter"[1] the fold of Rome.

The *dragonnades* began in Poitou: but under the directions of Marillac, governor of that province, the system speedily extended to the other provinces of France. Its immediate results were highly satisfactory to the clergy and the court. It mattered little to either, that the conversions reported to them were forced, and had been procured by the most iniquitous means. France was in a fair way to be rid of the plague of heresy, and the time was at hand when the hated Edict of Nantes might be abolished because no longer operative.

These rejoicings, however, were soon disturbed by tidings that came from the provinces, the frontiers of the kingdom, and the neighboring states of Europe, that the Huguenots were fleeing from France by hundreds, and thousands, and tens of thousands. The year of the *dragonnades*, in fact, marks the beginning of that exodus, which in a little while depleted the kingdom of a great part of its best population, and enriched immensely the foreign states to which the fugitives were welcomed.

Already, from time to time,—ever since the massacre of Saint Bartholomew's Eve,—the Protestants of France had fled to those countries in considerable numbers, from increasing per-

---

[1] "Compel them to come in." These words, a horrible perversion of the command in the parable of the Great Supper, (Luke xiv., 23,) were often upon the lips of the king and the persecuting clergy.

THE EXODUS. 251

secutions at home. The last of these emigrations had occurred some fifteen years before, when the government became aware that its shipping interests were suffering seriously in consequence of the flight of so many of the seafaring inhabitants of the western provinces. But nothing like the present movement had ever been witnessed. From every part of the kingdom the report came, that whole districts were depopulated, and that the industry of the country was paralyzed.

Chap. IV. 1681– 1685.

The ingenuity of a desperate people was taxed to the utmost, to devise methods of escape. "Of those who lived near the sea-board, some would conceal themselves in bales of merchandise, or under loads of charcoal, or in empty hogsheads. Others were stowed in the holds of vessels, where they lay in heaps, men, women and children, coming forth only in the dead of the night to breathe the air. Some would risk themselves in frail barks, for a voyage, the very thought of which would once have made them shudder with fear. The guards placed by the king to watch the coast, sometimes became softened, and found such opportunities of gain in favoring the flight of the Protestants, that they even went so far as to assist them. The captains of cruisers, who had orders to intercept any vessels that might carry fugitives, themselves conveyed great numbers of them out of the kingdom: and in almost every sea-port, the admiralty officers, tempted by the profits which the shipmasters shared with

Expedients of the fugitives.

them, allowed many persons to pass, whose hiding places they would not have found it very difficult to discover. There were families that paid from four to six or eight thousand *livres* for their escape. The same thing occurred on the landward side of the kingdom. Persons stationed to guard the roads and passages, would furnish guides, at a certain price, to those whom they had been instructed to arrest, and would even serve in this capacity themselves. As for such as could not avail themselves of these advantages, for want of skill or lack of means, they contrived a thousand ways to elude the vigilance of the countless sentinels appointed to prevent their flight. Often they disguised themselves as peasants, driving cattle before them, or carrying bundles, as if on their way to some market ; or as soldiers, returning to their garrison in some town of Holland or Germany ; or as servants, in the livery of their masters. Never before had there been seen so many merchants, called by pressing business into foreign parts. But where no such expedients were practicable, the fugitives betook themselves to unfrequented and difficult roads ; they traveled by night only ; they crossed the rivers by fords scarcely known, or unused because of danger ; they spent the day in forests and in caverns, or concealed in barns and in haystacks. Women resorted to the same artifices with the men, and fled under all sorts of disguises. They dressed themselves as servants, as peasants, as nurses. They trundled wheelbarrows, they carried hods, they bore burdens. They passed themselves off as the wives of their guides. They dressed in men's clothes, and followed on foot as lackeys, while their guides rode on horseback, as persons of quality. Men and women disguised themselves as mendicants, and passed through the places where they were most exposed to suspicion, in tattered garments, begging their bread from door to door."[1]

The strain was too great; and it had been kept up too long. The Huguenots had renounced their dream of political power. For years past, their anxiety had been to escape so far as possible the notice of statesmen and of parties, and in obscurity lead quiet and peaceable lives in all godliness and honesty. But their very submissiveness and loyalty had been misinterpreted. The priest-ridden king conceived that nothing more was needed, for the subjection of these obdurate heretics to the religion of the state, than the increase of penalties and hardships. The clergy were confident that the tame and ignorant peasantry would yield, as so many of the high-born and cultured had done, under the pressure of the royal command. Many did yield outwardly; though it may well be doubted if, of all the conversions brought about by the infliction of legal disabilities, and the brutalities of the *dragonnades*, a single one was sincere. But many, of more heroic mold, resisted every

---

[1] Benoist, Histoire de l'Edit de Nantes, tome troisième, seconde partie. Pp. 948-954.

effort to detach them from their faith. And multitudes who had yielded outwardly, or who succeeded in evading punishment, were not less eager than their more courageous brethren to fly from the country, and seek refuge in Protestant lands.

Doors of escape opened speedily to the sufferers. England, where so many of their persecuted countrymen had for generations found an asylum, was foremost in its offers of hospitality. The British envoy resident in Paris kept his government informed of the measures taken by Louis XIV. against his Reformed subjects, and warmly urged the king to plead their cause. The "terrible edict" of June, 1681, at length decided Charles II. to this step. The very next month, a royal proclamation was issued, promising letters of denization under the Great Seal of England to all "distressed Protestants," "who by reason of the rigors and severities which are used towards them upon the account of their religion, shall be forced to quit their native country, and shall desire to shelter themselves under his Majesty's royal protection, for the preservation and free exercise of their religion." The refugees were assured that they should enjoy all such further privileges and immunities as might be consistent with the laws, for the free exercise of their trades and handicrafts; and that an Act would be introduced at the next meeting of Parliament, for the naturalization of all such Protestants as should come over. No heavier duties should be imposed upon them than upon his Majesty's natural-born subjects; and equal advantages with those enjoyed by native subjects should be given them for the entrance of their children into the scnools and colleges of the realm.

To render these liberal provisions effective, it was ordered, that such Protestants should be suffered to pass the customs free of all duties, with their goods and household stuff, tools and instruments of trade; and that all his Majesty's officers, both civil and military, should give them kind reception upon their arrival within any of the ports of the realm, furnish them with free passports, and grant them all assistance and furtherance in their journeys to the places whither they might desire to go. Finally, the royal proclamation ordered that collections be made throughout the kingdom, to provide relief for such of the refugees as might stand in need thereof: and the Archbishop of Canterbury and the Bishop of London were appointed to receive any requests or petitions which the refugees might wish upon their arrival to present to the king.

Holland did not linger far behind its Protestant neighbor in overtures of hospitality to the oppressed Huguenots. In September of the same year, the magistrates of Amsterdam offered them the rights of citizenship and the privileges of trade, and the States-General announced that all who should settle in their territory would be exempted for the space of twelve years from the payment of taxes. The Lutheran king of Denmark was equally prompt and liberal in promises of protection and exemption; and the Protestant cantons of Switzerland were not slow to testify their sympathy with their persecuted brethren, and invite them to take refuge within their borders.

A few years later, upon the Revocation of the Edict of Nantes, the Protestant States of Germany joined in this movement. No sooner had that crowning act of intolerance and perfidy been proclaimed to the world, than the Elector of Brandenburg, and other Protestant princes, testified their indignation, by offering the proscribed Huguenots a home, and by making the amplest provisions for them within their dominions.

And still, in France, the work of persecution went steadily forward. Louis XIV. was carrying out to the letter the counsels of his spiritual advisers, and striving to make amends for his kingly vices by crushing heresy. To prevent his Protestant subjects from quitting the country, and from availing themselves of the invitations of foreign powers, Louis lays upon them his royal behest to remain at home—and be converted. Decree follows decree, forbidding all seamen and craftsmen to remove with their families and settle themselves in other countries, upon pain of condemnation to the galleys for life. His Majesty announces to his people that "an infinite number" of conversions are taking place in all parts of the kingdom.

THE PERSECUTION CONTINUES. 257

But forasmuch as there still remain some persons who not only stubbornly continue in their blindness, but hinder others from opening their eyes, and prompt them to leave the country, thus adopting a course opposed to their salvation, to their own interests, and to the fidelity which they owe their sovereign, all persons who may be found guilty of having induced others thus to remove, shall be punished by fine and bodily inflictions.

The infatuation of Louis XIV. reached its height, when in October, 1685, he issued the famous decree, proclaiming the success of the measures taken for the extirpation of heresy, and announcing the revocation and suppression of the Edict of Nantes, the Edict of Nismes, and all other edicts and decrees made in favor of the Protestants in his kingdom.

"With that just gratitude which we owe to God," said the royal fanatic, "we now see that our efforts have attained the end we have had in view: since the best and greatest part of our subjects of that Religion have embraced the Catholic Religion. And inasmuch as by this means the execution of the Edict of Nantes, and of all other ordinances in favor of the said Religion, remains useless, we have judged that we could do nothing better, wholly to efface the memory of the troubles, the confusion and the evils which the progress of that false Religion had caused in our realm, and which had given occasion to that Edict, and to so many other Edicts and Declarations that preceded it, or that have resulted from it, than to revoke altogether the said Edict of Nantes."

The Revocation was but the finishing stroke of a policy that had been pursued with marvelous steadiness for a quarter of a century. It ordered the immediate demolition of all remaining "temples" or places of worship of the Pretended Reformed Religion. It prohibited the religionists from assembling in any house or locality whatsoever, for the exercises of that religion. Ministers of the said Religion were commanded, if unwilling to embrace the Catholic faith, to leave the kingdom within fifteen days after the publication of the present Edict, and meanwhile to perform no function of their office, under penalty of the galleys. Private schools for the instruction of children of the said Religion were prohibited, "as well as all things in general that might denote any concession whatsoever in favor of the said Religion." Parents were commanded, under heavy penalties, to send their infant children to the parish churches for baptism. All persons professing the said Religion were "most expressly" forbidden to leave the kingdom, under penalty of the galleys for the men, and of imprisonment and the confiscation of goods for the women. Such as had already left, were invited to return within four months, with the promise of liberty to resume the peaceable possession and enjoyment of their property: but should any fail thus to return, all their goods would be confiscated. Finally, it would be lawful for all his Majesty's subjects to remain within his kingdom, and to continue in their callings, and in the enjoyment of their goods, unmolested and unhindered, until such time as it might please God to enlighten them as He had enlightened the others: on condition that they perform no exercise of their pretended Religion, nor assemble themselves under pretext of the prayers or worship of that Religion.

Such was the purport of the document which amazed Europe two centuries ago, and which continues to amaze mankind. The impartial judgment of the age, and of posterity, upon this stupendous act of despotism and bigotry, has perhaps never been better expressed than in the words of a Roman Catholic cotemporary, a courtier of Louis XIV., the Duke of Saint Simon:

"The Revocation of the Edict of Nantes, without the slightest pretext, or the least necessity, as well as the various proclamations, or rather proscriptions, that followed, were the fruits of that horrible conspiracy which depopulated a fourth part of the kingdom, ruined its trade, weakened it throughout, surrendered it for so long a time to open and avowed pillage by the dragoons, and authorized the torments and sufferings by means of which they procured the death of so many persons of both sexes and by thousands together. A plot that brought ruin upon so great a body of people, that tore asunder countless families, arraying relatives against relatives, for the purpose of getting possession of their goods, whereupon they left them to starve. A plot that caused our manufactures to pass over into the hands of foreigners, made their states to flourish and grow populous at the expense of our own, and enabled them to build new cities. A plot that presented to the nations the spectacle of so vast a multitude of people, who had committed no crime, proscribed, denuded, fleeing, wandering, seeking an asylum afar from their country. A plot that consigned the noble, the wealthy, the aged, those highly esteemed, in many cases, for their piety, their learning, their virtue, those accustomed to a life of ease, frail, delicate, to hard labor in the galleys, under the driver's lash, and for no reason save that of their religion. A plot that, to crown all other horrors, filled every province of the kingdom with perjury and sacrilege; inasmuch as while the land rang with the cries of these unhappy victims of error, so many others sacrificed their consciences for their worldly goods and their comfort, purchasing both by means of feigned recantations; recantations from the very act of which they were dragged, without a moment's interval, to adore what they did not believe in, and to receive what was really the divine Body of the Most Holy One, while they still remained convinced that they were eating nothing but bread, and bread which they were in duty bound to abhor. Such was the general abomination begotten of flattery and cruelty. Between the rack and recantation, between recantation and the Holy Communion, it did not often happen that four and twenty hours intervened: and the torturers served as conductors and as witnesses. Those who seemed afterwards to make the change with greater deliberation, were not slow to belie their pretended conversion, by the tenor of their lives, or by flight."

CHAPTER V.

THE REVOCATION.

FLIGHT FROM LA ROCHELLE AND AUNIS.

<small>Chap. V.
1681–
1685.</small>
That part of western France that lies between the Loire and Gironde rivers—comprising anciently the seaboard provinces of Poitou, Saintonge, and Aunis—was inhabited, at the period of the Revocation, by a population largely Protestant. These provinces had been early visited by zealous disciples of Calvin. Poitiers, the principal town of Poitou, gave shelter to the great reformer himself, for some months in the beginning of his career; and a few young men whom <small>Calvin's disciples.</small> he gathered around him then, and who caught his fervent spirit while studying the Scriptures with him, went forth to carry the new doctrines into every nook and corner of the country. Nowhere else in France did the Reformation take a readier and a firmer hold. By the time of the outbreak of the first civil war, there were many parishes where the mass of the people had embraced the Reformed faith,[1] and the churches

---

[1] " Un grand nombre de paroisses [surtout sur les bords de la Sèvre-Niortaise et de ses affluents, et, dans le Bas-Poitou, sur ceux du Lay,] étaient presque entièrement protestantes à l'ouverture des guerres civiles."—Histoire des Protestants et des églises reformées du Poitou, par Auguste Lièvre, pasteur. Paris et Poitiers, 1856. Tome I., page 100.

were either closed, or transformed into Protestant "temples."[1]

Persecution, during the reign of Louis XIV., greatly weakened the strength of the Reformed religion in these provinces. Yet it was still sufficient to justify the king in choosing them for the scene of that species of warfare upon his Protestant subjects, which, as we have seen, he found most effectual in accomplishing forced conversions. It was in Poitou that the dragonnades were initiated by Marillac, the governor of the province: and thence they soon spread into Saintonge and Aunis.

A special interest belongs to this part of France, as the home of very many of the refugees who fled at the period of the Revocation, and who ultimately made their way to America. It will be seen in the following pages that a large proportion of the Huguenot families that came by way of England and Holland to Boston, New York, Jamestown, and Charleston, in the last years of the seventeenth century, can be traced back to the towns and villages of the country between the Loire and the Gironde. The present chapter will give the results of investigations made in this direction.

Aunis, the smallest of the thirty-three provinces into which the Kingdom of France was at

---

[1] "In Poitou they have almost all," wrote a traveler, presumed to be Sir Edwin Sandys, about the year 1599.—Europæ Speculum, 1599. P. 176. He adds that on the whole the proportion of Protestants to the Roman Catholics in France is, however, "not one to twentie."

that time divided, may be called emphatically the birthplace of American Huguenots. Aunis, indeed, could scarcely be dignified with the name and rank of a province. It was a part of Saintonge, which had been cut off from that province, and appended to the city of La Rochelle, in the fourteenth century, as a reward for the fidelity of the citizens to King Charles the Wise, during his wars with the English. This little district, commonly styled "terre d'Aunis," or "pays d'Aunis," contained only some seven hundred square miles, and was scarcely more than a suburb of its great seaport La Rochelle, which had been the stronghold of the Protestants in France for nearly seventy years, and which, though now dismantled, and spoiled of its ancient honors, was still the home of many of their wealthiest and most influential families.

La Rochelle boasted a glorious history. For almost five centuries, the city enjoyed commercial and municipal privileges of an extraordinary character. Royal charters, confirmed by successive kings, secured to the citizens the right of electing their mayor and other magistrates every year, and exempted them from all taxes and imposts. These distinguishing advantages had been granted not without reason. The Rochellese were always noted for their loyalty to the crown of France, and for the valuable services they rendered to the state under several reigns. One of the most remarkable recognitions of this fidelity was made by the king already mentioned, who conferred nobility

Vue de la Rochelle du coté des Minimes

2. Tour de la Lanterne.
3. Tour de la Chaine.
4. Tour de S. Nicolas.
5. Grosse Horloge.
6. Clocher de S. Barthelemi.
7. Clocher de S. Sauveur.
8. Bastion du Gabut.
12. Route que tiennent les vaisseaux pour entrer dans le port.

upon the mayor and magistrates of the city then in office, and upon their successors forever.

But the proudest recollections of the Rochellese dated from the period of the Reformation. Their city had early welcomed the "new doctrines" preached by Calvin's disciples. Among the first to embrace the evangelical faith were some of the monks and priests. Not a few of the nuns left their cloisters, to enter a state of life which, as they now learned, Holy Scripture declared to be honorable in all. The booksellers and the schoolmasters of the town helped to spread the teachings of the reformers. Persecution only increased the strength of the movement; and at length, so general had the change of religion become, that the Reformed, tired of holding their crowded assemblies in private houses or in halls, claimed the right to meet in the churches. For a while this right was accorded to them, and Protestants and Romanists worshiped in the same sanctuaries, the one congregation gathering together as the other dispersed. So perfect was the harmony with which this arrangement was carried out, that on a certain occasion, the priests of the church of St. Sauveur, being requested to commence their services at an earlier hour, for the accommodation of the Protestants, consented to do so, and agreed to begin matins a little before daybreak, upon condition that they should be compensated for the use of extra lights. This happy state of things, however, lasted but a few months. The religionists were compelled to return to their former places of meeting, and soon after, the "Edict of January" required them to hold their assemblies outside of the city walls.

<small>Chap. V.
1562.
January 17.</small>

In the course of the civil wars that followed, La Rochelle became the rallying point and the citadel of the Huguenot party. The vigilance of its citizens saved them from sharing in the massacre that commenced in Paris on St. Bartholomew's day; and their heroic bravery and constancy enabled them to resist the assaults of the royal army, for nine months, during the memorable siege of 1573. In the next fifty years, the city reached the height of its prosperity and renown. Famous for the strength of its fortifications, the extent of its commerce, the wealth of its merchants, the intelligence and morality of its people, La Rochelle was the pride of French Protestantism. Its "Grand Temple," the corner-stone of which had been laid by Henry, Prince of Condé, was crowded with vast congregations, that hung upon the earnest and fearless eloquence of the most learned and able pastors of the Reformed Church. During the greater part of this period, no other worship than that prescribed by the evangelical faith was performed within the city walls; and at the time of the publication of the Edict of Nantes, the Roman mass had not been said in La Rochelle for nearly forty years.

<small>November 1572 to July 10, 1573.</small>

<small>1577.</small>

Astir with political interests, holding its importance and its independence only by means of

THE SECOND SIEGE. 267

perpetual watchfulness, La Rochelle was at the same time a center of intelligence for the Protestants of France. Its college, founded in 1565, and endowed by Jeanne d'Albret and the princes, drew to itself some of the most eminent scholars of the age. Its printing presses were noted for their incessant activity, and for the rare excellence of many of their productions. La Rochelle was chosen for the holding of several of the national assemblies of the Huguenot party, and of the ecclesiastical assemblies of the Reformed churches. A free and vigorous intellectual life pervaded the place, quickened by the very anxieties and apprehensions that equally prevailed.[1]

With its second and still more terrible siege, the period of the city's independence and chief importance came to an end. In punishment for the stubborn resistance offered to his armies, and in testimony of his displeasure with a populace "whose rebellions had been the main stay and spring of the great wars that had so long

---

[1] A notable illustration may be quoted from the historian Arcère: "In the midst of the troubles of the war, [1574,] public entertainments were given in La Rochelle. A tragedy, entitled Holofernes, was represented. The author of this dramatic poem was Catharine de Parthenai, afterwards so well known under the name of the Duchess of Rohan. In this lady, the graces of a fine literary taste were blended with learning, and intellectual talent was enhanced by a heroic courage. It was she who was seen alone to stand firm upon the ruins of her defeated party, after the reduction of La Rochelle in 1628, and proudly to endure so conspicuous a reverse of fortune."—Histoire de la ville de la Rochelle et du pays d'Aulnis, par M. Arcère. A la Rochelle, MDCCLVI. Tome I., page 568.

afflicted the state," Louis XIII. ordered the complete destruction of those fortifications which had baffled the utmost skill of his soldiers and engineers. "It is our will"—so ran the royal decree—" that they be razed to the ground, in such wise that the plow may pass through the soil even as through tilled land." The special privileges and dignities which the town had enjoyed for so many centuries were abrogated; and the "Grand Temple" of the Protestants was converted into a cathedral church.

From this downfall, La Rochelle never recovered, as a place of political and military consequence. Yet it continued to be, for many years, a fountain-head of moral and religious influences for the Huguenots of France;—their "western Geneva";—and long remained exempt from many of the inflictions to which the Protestants were exposed elsewhere in the kingdom, under that repressive course which the government had already entered upon in its treatment of them. But in 1661, an old provision of the royal decree for the reduction of the city after the siege, hitherto unexecuted, was brought to notice, and carried into effect. This article prohibited all persons professing the Pretended Reformed Religion from being admitted as inhabitants of La Rochelle, unless they had resided there previously, and before the landing of the English forces under Buckingham, sent to relieve the city in July, 1627. The article was now confirmed by a civil ordinance, and in the month of November it was proclaimed with sound of trumpet through the streets of La Rochelle. Fifteen days were allowed to those whom it might concern, for their removal from within the city limits; and warning was given, that in case of disobedience they would incur a heavy fine, to be enforced if necessary by means of distraint and public sale of their effects. These tidings were heard with consternation. Many persons had come to reside in La Rochelle within the last thirty-three years. Many remembered no other home. They were bound to the place by countless ties of interest, of habit and of affection. Notwithstanding, more than three hundred families obeyed the order. Exemption, it was well understood, could be purchased by a change of religion: for the decree applied only to the Protestant inhabitants. But the tempting bait was refused. Yet the inconveniences of removal were very great. The season was most unfavorable. Rain fell in torrents for three consecutive weeks. Some, however, took their departure immediately: while others lingered, hoping for better weather, and a possible extension of time. No extension was granted. The fortnight ended, the order was sternly executed. Deputy-sheriffs entered private houses, and levied upon the furniture, putting out into the street whatever they did not seize. The dispossessed inmates were turned adrift. Children in their cradles, women in child-birth, the aged, the sick and bed-ridden, were pitilessly ejected.

Many died in the officers' hands: while others lived barely long enough to be carried out into the country by their friends.[1]

The archives of the commonwealth of Massachusetts contain an interesting memorial of this expulsion, in the petition of John Touton, doctor chirurgeon, of Rochelle in France, in behalf of himself and others. The petitioners represent that they "are, for their religion sake, outed and expelled from their habitations and dwellings in Rochelle aforesaid," and they ask "that they might have so much favor from the government here, as in some measure to be certain of their residence here before they undertake the voyage." If encouraged, they will "seek to dispose of their estates of Rochelle, where they may not have any longer continuance."[2] A list of the persons making this

---

[1] Histoire de l'Edit de Nantes. [Par Elie Benoist.] Tome troisième, première partie, pp. 431-434.

[2] "To the honoured Governor, deputy Governor and Maiistrates of the Massachusetts Colonie—The petition of John Touton of Rochell in France, Doctor Chirurgion, in behalfe of himselfe and others. Humbly shewing, that whereas your petitioner with many other protestants, who are inhabitants in the said Rotchell, (a list of whose names was given to the said honoured Govnr) who are, for their religion sake, outted and expelled from their habitations and dwellings in Rotchell aforesaid, he, your said petitioner humbly craveth, for himselfe and others as aforesd, that they may have liberty to come heather, here to inhabit and abide amongst the English in this Jurisdiction, and to follow such honest indeavours & ymploymts, as providence hath or shall direct them unto, whereby they may get a livelihood and that they might have so much favour from the Govmt here, as in some measure to be certayne of their residence here before they undertake the voyage, and what priviledges

request was sent to Governor Endicott along with the petition. Unhappily, that list has disappeared; so that we have no means of learning either the number or the names of the petitioners. That some of them carried out their purpose, is certain. Jean Touton himself is known to have come to this country shortly after:[1] and we find that about the same time, a shipmaster of La Rochelle[2] was arrested under the charge of having received emigrants bound for the English colonies in America on board his vessel. Some of these, it is more than

---

they may expect here to have, that so accordingly as they find incoridgmt for further progress herein, they may dispose of their estates of Rotchell, where they may not have any longer continuance. Thus humbly craveing you would be pleased to consider of the premisses, and your petitioner shall forever pray for your happinesse."

15 (8) 1662 The Deputyes thinke meete to graunt this pet. our honble magistes consenting thereto. William Torrey.

Consented to by ye magists. Edw: Rawson Secret. cleric. (Massachusetts Archives, Vol. X., p. 208.)

[1] John Toton [Touton] petitioned the General Court of Massachusetts, June 29, 1687, showing that he had "ever since the year 1662 been an Inhabitant in the Territory of his Majesty." He was a free denizen of Virginia "by my Lord of Effingham's favour," and was now bound to the island of Terceira on business for one William Fisher in Virginia. Learning "that all severity is used against French Protestants in that Island," he asks for letters representing him as an Englishman.—(Massachusetts Archives, Vol. CXXVI., p. 374.)

Touton was living in Rehoboth, Mass., in 1675.—(A Genealogical Dictionary of the First Settlers of New England, by James Savage.)

[2] One Brunet, a shipmaster of La Rochelle, who had embarked thirty-six young men for America. Presuming that they had been sent to the English islands [or colonies] in order to prevent their conversion to the Roman Catholic faith, the judges of La Rochelle condemned Brunet to a

probable, made their way to the city of New Amsterdam, where many of their Protestant brethren had already found a home. The directors of the West India Company at Amsterdam informed Governor Stuyvesant, in the spring of the year 1663, that they had "been approached in the name of the Protestant people of Rochelle," who were "considerably oppressed and deprived of their privileges." Subsequent letters instructed him to prepare for the coming of many families of the Reformed religion, not only from La Rochelle, St. Martin, and the surrounding district, but from many other places in France also, where the churches, it was thought, would soon be demolished. The governor was commanded "in all things to lend the helping hand" to these worthy refugees. From Stuyvesant's reply, it appears that several of the emigrants from France had reached New Amsterdam. Among them was a certain Jean Collyn, who was about to return to France on one of the Company's vessels, that he might make report of the country to others. The colonists already arrived were particularly pleased with Staten

---

fine of one thousand pounds, and "exemplary punishment," unless he should produce these persons within a year, or give satisfactory proof of their decease, or of their voluntary residence in some one of the French colonies. The Chamber of the Edict reversed this decision : but the Council re-affirmed it, on the ground that there was reason to fear that the young men might be confirmed in the profession of the Pretended Reformed Religion, should they remain in the English colonies."—(Histoire chronologique de l'Eglise Protestante de France, par Charles Drion. Tome II., p. 72.)

Island, where they proposed to settle: and they had hopes that the minister of St. Martin might be induced to come over, and undertake the pastoral office among them.[1]

Chap. V.
1664.

For the next twenty years, La Rochelle, though sharing in many of the oppressions which Protestantism throughout France was experiencing, continued to enjoy some distinctive privileges. Its "temple" remained standing, when nearly every other Protestant house of worship in the province was laid low. Its Protestant population was still large and influential; and many of the most affluent families of "the Religion" were still to be found in this ancient home of Calvinism: a home all the dearer, doubtless, because of the memories, sad as well as glorious, that enriched it.

1661–1681.

The descendant of the Huguenots who may visit La Rochelle at the present day, will find a city possessing not a few of the characteristic features that were familiar to the generation that fled from it two centuries ago. The streets, for the most part narrow and tortuous, derive a quaint and somber aspect from the long porches or arcades that border them on either side. Opening upon this covered side-walk, the entrance to a Huguenot dwelling of the olden time was often distinguishable by some pious inscription, frequently a text of Scripture, or a verse from Marot's psalms, to be read over the

Streets of La Rochelle.

---

[1] New York Colonial Manuscripts. Vol. XV., fol. 12, 106, 107, 138.

door-way. Some of these inscriptions are still legible. Small, and severely plain, this door-way led often to a dwelling that abounded with evidences of wealth and taste ; the upper stories of which were ornamented, both within and without, by rich carvings in wood and stone.

Approached from the sea, La Rochelle presents much the same appearance as of old: with its outer and inner port, separated by a narrow passage, on either side of which rise the massive forts of Saint Nicolas and La Chaîne.[1] A remnant of the ancient wall of the city connects the latter structure with the yet loftier tower of La Lanterne, originally built to serve as a beacon for ships seeking the harbor, but used in times of persecution as a prison of state. Looming up above the flat, marshy coast, the long line of which extends in unrelieved monotony as far as the eye can see, these monuments of the past remain, scarcely more gray and timeworn, perhaps, than they appeared in the days of Louis XIV. and his fleeing Protestant subjects.

It was among these scenes and associations, that the generation soon to escape from La Rochelle—the young Bernons, Faneuils, Baudouins, Allaires, Manigaults—grew up. The streets and squares, and the quays where the great commercial houses still maintained themselves, though in diminished state, had witnessed many events

---

[1] "Nous perdîmes de veüe les grosses tours et la ville de la Rochelle, puis les îles de Rez et d'Oléron, disant Adieu à la France."—Lescarbot.

of stirring interest. The house was yet standing, where Henry of Navarre, a boy of fifteen, resided, when he came with his noble mother, Jeanne d'Albret, at the beginning of the third civil war, to take refuge in the city that had just espoused the Protestant cause. The house of Guiton, the heroic mayor during the siege of 1628, was still pointed out. Nearly every dwelling, indeed, must have had its legends of heroism and of suffering, connected with that memorable siege, when twenty-five thousand, out of a population of thirty thousand, perished of hunger; and when, under those gloomy porches, the dead lay in heaps, and the living, emaciated beyond recognition, moved in mournful silence. The city walls, so bravely defended, had long since disappeared, but their outline could be traced then as now. Here was the site of the famous bastion de l'Evangile, which bore the brunt of so many assaults, in the earlier siege, that at length the royal troops refused to approach it: and there was the spot where, from the wall which had since been leveled to the ground, the women and children poured boiling pitch from a huge caldron upon the assailants. Many of the localities possessing such historic interest were associated also with the personal and domestic history of our Huguenots. One of the houses owned by Pierre Jay, at the time of his escape from France, was situated hard by the Lanterne tower. The home of Ester Le Roy, Gabriel Bernon's wife, faced upon the royal palace, once the town-hall of the Rochellese, in the days of their freedom and prosperity; and the property which she brought to her husband in dower, lay near the *pré de Maubec*, where, in the early times of Protestantism, the Calvinists, when excluded from the city, used to meet for worship.

The field, or common, known as the *pré de Maubec*, now lay within the city limits, and was included in the quarter of the *Ville neuve*, or new town. Here stood the Huguenot *prêche*, or meeting house, until destroyed after the Revocation. It was a structure much less imposing than the "Grand Temple," but it was spacious, and it had been for fifty years "the gate of heaven," to the pious religionists of La Rochelle. The chief, if not the only external ornament of this house of worship, was a finely sculptured stone, over the main entrance, displaying the arms of the kings of France and of Navarre. Within, distinguished from the plain benches that accommodated the rest of the worshipers, were high seats, provided for the magistrates of the city, the ministers, and the members of the Consistory: and on the wall near the pulpit was a tablet, the admiration doubtless of our American refugees in their childhood, inscribed with the Ten Commandments of the Law of God, in letters of gold upon a blue ground. A large bell convoked the assemblies on Sunday and on other days of observance:—a privilege enjoyed by very few of the Reformed congregations in France.

Conspicuous among the faithful who, in the

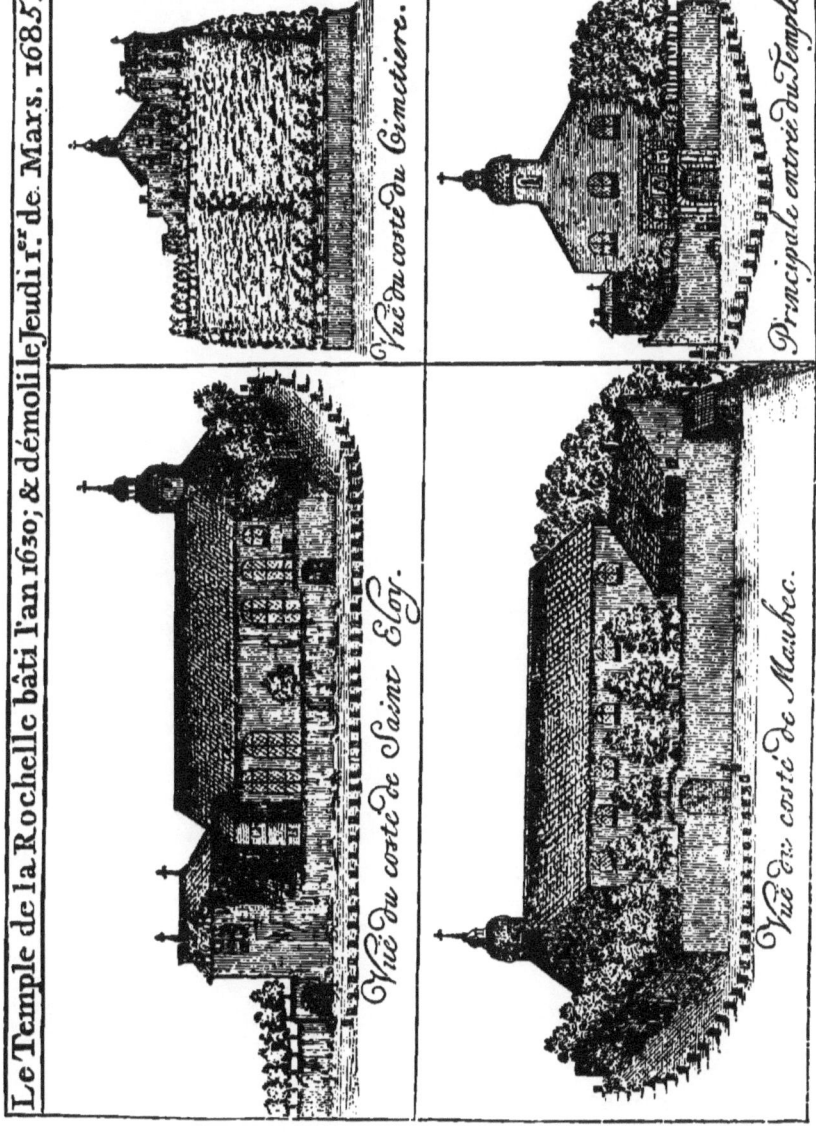

days before the Revocation, frequented the Huguenot meetings in the *pré de Maubec*, were André Bernon and Pierre Jay. The former belonged to a family of great antiquity, that originated in Burgundy, and traced back its lineage to the earliest centuries of the French monarchy. The Bernons claimed to be a younger branch of the house of the counts of Burgundy; resting the claim upon the similarity of their armorial bearings,[1] and the fact that their name was borne by several of the princes of that house. But the Bernons of La Rochelle possessed an independent claim to nobility; for they had furnished several mayors to the city; and according to ancient usage, this office conferred such rank upon the occupant and upon his heirs forever. "I might have remained in France," wrote Gabriel Bernon, the refugee, in his old age, "and kept my property, my quality, and my titles, if I had been willing to submit to slavery." For many generations, the family had been prosperous and influential. In the sixteenth century, they are mentioned as contributing for the ransom of the sons of Francis I., held as hostages by Spain after the battle of Pavia; and as sending a sum of money to Henry IV., by the hands of Duplessis-Mornay, to assist him in gaining his crown. The Bernons of La Rochelle were among the first in

---

[1] The Bernon arms are—"d'azur à un chevron d'argent surmonté d'un croissant de même, accompagné en chef de deux étoiles d'or, et en pointe d'un ours passant de même." (Filleau.)

that city to embrace the Reformed religion.[1] The branch of the family to which André belonged, was distinguished as that of Bernon de Bernonville, a designation which was now worn by his elder brother Léonard. Another branch, known as the Bernons de la Bernonière, seigneurs de l'Isleau, was also attached to the Protestant faith.[2]

---

[1] Their fidelity to that faith continued through the times of persecution that introduced and followed the Revocation. During the eighteenth century, "this family formed the nucleus of Protestantism in La Rochelle. It was in the Bernon dwelling that the Reformed were accustomed to meet for the celebration of their religious services. These meetings were not avowed, but they were known to exist, and generally they were tolerated. Whenever new orders from the government brought about a revival of persecution, the meetings wrapped themselves in the deepest secrecy; but they never ceased entirely, during the period in which that worship was denied a liberty recognized by the laws."—(The late M. L. Delayant, librarian of the Bibliothèque de la Rochelle, in a letter to the author, October 18, 1878.)
"Bernon: famille habitant la Rochelle, après avoir embrassé l'hérésie de Calvin, n' a jamais voulu se faire réhabiliter; elle a toujours été riche et considérée."—(Filleau, Dict. hist. et gén. des fam. de l'anc. Poitou, s. v.)

[2] "The name De Bernon is found in the year 1191, in the list of families who had representatives in the crusades to the Holy Land." "Transplanted into various provinces of western France, the family originated in Burgundy. It considers itself to be a younger branch of the house of the counts of Burgundy, resting this belief upon the name, which was borne by several of those princes, from the year 895, and upon the conformity of its armorial bearings with those that were borne at an early day by the counts of Mâcon. From the fourteenth century, and beginning with Raoul de Bernon, the house of Bernon possesses all the documents necessary to establish its filiation."

"The house of Bernon has formed alliances with some of the most illustrious families of the kingdom; it has rendered military services that have not been without distinction;

The ancestors of Pierre Jay had come to La Rochelle from the province of Poitou. Not improbably, they belonged to the family of that name, the seigneurs de Montonneau, whose seat was at Château-Garnier, near Civray, in Upper Poitou. As early, however, as the year 1565, Jehan Jay, who had embraced the Protestant faith, was residing in La Rochelle.

Gabriel Manigault, the father of Pierre and Gabriel, who settled in South Carolina, was the

---

and it counts among its members superior officers of the greatest merit, both military and naval. It has had several *chevaliers* of the order of Saint Louis."—Livre d'Or de la Noblesse de France.

According to the pedigree traced by M. Henri Filleau, Dictionnaire historique et généalogique des familles de l'ancien Poitou, Raoul Bernon,"who served with distinction in the wars of his time," married Charlotte de Talmont, and had a son Nicolas, chosen mayor of La Rochelle in 1357. Jean, son of Nicolas, was chosen mayor in 1398. Jean-Thomas, son of Jean, founded the two *gentilhommières*, or manors, of "Bernonière" and "Bernonville." The former derived its name from a small *château* near Pouzauges, in the province of Poitou, (now in the department of Vendée,) and the latter from a *château* on the island of Ré. Jean-Thomas left a son André, who had two sons, Pierre, sieur de la Bernonière et l'Isleau, and Jean. The latter, Jean, second son of André, had a son André. M. Filleau has not followed out the line of descent through Jean and André, the younger branch of the family; but from this point the line of descent is traced by M. Crassous as follows: André Bernon married Catharine Du Bouché in 1545. Their son Léonard married Françoise Carré, in 1578, and had two sons, Jean, *sieur de Bernonville*, and André. The younger, André, married (1) Jeanne Lescour, and (2) Marie Papin in 1605, and had two sons, Léonard, *sieur de Bernonville*, and André, to whom reference is made in the text, and who was the father of Gabriel Bernon, the refugee.—(Généalogie de la famille Bernon, à la Rochelle, dressée par M. Joseph Crassous, 1782.)

descendant of one of the earliest converts to Protestantism in Aunis. Among the first baptisms performed by a Protestant pastor in La Rochelle, was that of Sara, daughter of Jean Manigault and Louise de Foix, his wife. Jean was already one of the "anciens" or elders of the infant church: and his house was one of the places where its meetings for worship were held in secret at this early period. A century later, Isaac Manigault acted as sponsor at the baptism of Augustus Jay.

The Baudouin family of La Rochelle — whose name, in Massachusetts, has suffered the change to Bowdoin—was "one of the most ancient and important" of that city.[1] Its different branches were known by designations taken from the numerous *seigneuries* which they possessed. They were descended from Pierre Baudouin, écuyer, sieur de la Laigne, who married the daughter of Jean Bureau, mayor of La Rochelle in 1448. The Baudouins were among the first disciples of the Reformed faith in that city. Several members of this family distinguished themselves by their services to the Protestant cause during the civil wars. At the period of the Revocation, one of its branches took refuge in Prussia, another fled to the Netherlands, and a third escaped to England. It is not known to which of these branches Pierre, of Boston, belonged.

Another ancient family, which had long

---

[1] La France Protestante, deuxième edition, *s. v.*

been identified with the Huguenot cause, and which indeed has maintained its fidelity to that cause to the present day, was that of Allaire.[1] This house was represented in the Huguenot congregation, as it existed at the time of the Revocation, by several prominent members. Antoine, sieur du Bugnon : Jean, royal secretary, and Henri, counselor and lieutenant general in admiralty, were brothers. Descended from a younger branch of the same family was Pierre Allaire, whose son Alexandre came to America.

Benjamin Faneuil, a Huguenot merchant of La Rochelle, had married André Bernon's daughter Marie. His brother Pierre was the father of Benjamin, Jean and André Faneuil, who emigrated to America after the Revocation. A branch of this family, that had settled at Saintes in the province of Saintonge, took refuge after the Revocation in England.[2]

---

[1] La France Protestante, deuxième edition, s. v.

[2] For the following pedigree of the Faneuil family of La Rochelle, I am indebted to the learned genealogist M. Louis Marie Meschinet de Richemond, archiviste de la Charente-Inférieure.

Benjamin Faneuil, born in 1593, married Suzanne de l'Espine in 1616, and died in 1677. His son Pierre, born in 1618, married Marie Cousseau in 1640, and had two sons, Benjamin, who married Marie Bernon, and Pierre, who married Marie Depont. Pierre and Marie Faneuil had three sons, Benjamin, Jean and André, and two daughters, Suzanne, who married Abraham de la Croix, and Jeanne, who married Pierre Cossart.

Benjamin Faneuil married Anne Bureau, July 28, 1699, and died in New York, March 31, 1719, aged fifty years and eight months. Jean Faneuil died in La Rochelle, June 24, 1737. André [Andrew] Faneuil died in Boston, February 13, 1737.

Chap. V.
1681.

The Sigourney family bore the name of a locality in the province of Poitou, where not improbably they may have originated.¹ They were represented at this period by André Sigourney, then in middle life, who according to the family record " was comfortably settled at or near Rochelle when the Edict of Nantes was revoked."

The Sigourneys.

André Laurent, the ancestor of a noted family of South Carolina, was at this time living in the parish of Saint Sauveur, with his mother, Elisabeth Menigaut, the widow of Jean Laurent, formerly a merchant of the city. Marie Lucas, the young Huguenot girl who was to join her fortunes with his, before seeking a home in the New World, was likewise a native of La Rochelle. She was the daughter of Daniel Lucas, a merchant. The friendly relations of the two families seem to have been of long standing; and young Laurent was doubtless a frequent visitor at Périgny, a short distance out of town, where Daniel Lucas had a small farm.²

---

¹ Sigournais, now a hamlet of some eight hundred inhabitants, in the department of Vendée, four miles from Chatonnay. Near by is the château de Sigournais.

² "Elizabeth Laurens, veuve," of the paroisse St. Sauveur, is reported as having fled in 1682 to England. (Liste des familles de la religion prétendüe réformée qui sont sortis du pays d'Aulnix, Isles, et costes de Xaintonge pour aller dans lesdits pays estrangers depuis l'année 1681, jusques à la fin de May, 1685. Archives Nationales, [Paris] TT. n°· 259.) The same document mentions that " Le Sr. Daniel Lucas, marchand, sa femme et 4 enfants," took refuge, the same year, in England. " Il a une borderie à Perigny, dont son

Jean and Josué David, represented "one of the best families of La Rochelle: a family," according to La France Protestante, "not less distinguished by reason of the positions which its members have filled, than eminent for the services it had rendered." In 1572, Jean David, "pair du corps de ville," was appointed with two others to visit England, for the purpose of soliciting the help of Queen Elizabeth, and of hastening Montgomery's departure with the promised fleet for the relief of the besieged city. In 1628, Jacques David, who had twice been mayor, was sent with Philippe Vincent upon a similar embassy to Charles II., and succeeded in influencing the king to sign a treaty with the Protestants. Jean and Josué David came to New York after the Revocation.

Among the members of the "noblesse" of Aunis that continued faithful to the Huguenot cause, in these days of augmenting persecution, were several who afterwards formed part of the emigration to South Carolina. Paul Bruneau de Rivedoux,[1] écuyer, son of Arnaud Bruneau,

---

père jouit." Daniel Lucas, Mary, Augustus, James, and Peter, children, were naturalized in England, March 8, 1682. (Lists of naturalized Denizens: in Protestant Exiles from France in the Reign of Louis XIV. By the Rev. David C. A. Agnew. London: 1874. Vol. III., p. 33.) André Laurent, natif de la Rochelle, fils de feu Jean Laurent et Elizabeth Menigaut; et Marie Lucas, aussi native de La Rochelle, fille de Daniel Lucas et feu Jeanne Marchand, were married in London, Feb. 22, 1688. (Records of the French Church in Threadneedle Street, London.)

[1] Rivedoux, a little seaport on the island of Ré, at the point nearest to the mainland.

"Le fils ainé du Sr Rivedou, écuyer, son frère et 2 sœurs,"

sieur de la Chabossière;[1] Henri Bruneau, écuyer, son of Henri Bruneau de la Chabossière; Henri Auguste Chastaignier, écuyer, seigneur de Cramahé,[2] and Alexandre Thesée Chastaignier, écuyer, seigneur de l'Isle, were all born in La Rochelle. Paul Bruneau was the grandson of Jean Bruneau, counselor, an eminent citizen, whose family obtained patents of nobility in the middle of the seventeenth century.[3] He was accompanied in his flight to America by his nephew Henri, son of his deceased brother Arnaud. Henri and Alexandre Chastaignier were the sons of Roch Chastaignier, écuyer. The name belonged to a distinguished house, that traced its lineage back uninterruptedly to the eleventh century.[4] It was early and honorably identified with the Protestant cause in western France.[5] Philippe Chastaignier, the abbess of a nunnery in Poitou, entered into correspondence with Calvin, in 1549, with the purpose of abandoning the cloister, and professing the evangelical faith; a purpose which she carried out, together with eight of her nuns, leaving only one in

---

are mentioned in the Liste des familles de la religion prétendüe réformée, etc. "Année de leur départ, 1682. Lieu de leur retraite, Angleterre ou Danemark."

[1] The *château* of La Chaboissière is near La Villedieu, ten miles south of Poitiers, in Poitou.

[2] The *château* of Cramahé is about five miles southeast of La Rochelle.

[3] Filleau, Dict. hist. et gén. des fam. de l'anc. Poitou, I., p. 509.—La France Protestante, *s. v.*

[4] Filleau, Dict. hist. et gén., I., p. 612.

[5] La France Protestante, III., p. 297.

the convent.[1] The Chastaigniers who went to South Carolina, were descended from a branch of this family, established in La Rochelle, three members of which filled the office of mayor of the city.[2]

---

[1] Lièvre, Hist. des protestants et des églises réf. du Poitou, I., p. 49.

[2] Filleau, Dict. hist. et gén., I., p. 623.
The list of French and Swiss refugees in Carolina wishing to be naturalized as English, (Liste des François et Suisses Refugiez en Caroline qui souhaittent d'être naturalizés Anglois,) about the year 1695, contains these names: Paul Bruneau de Revidoux, Écuyer, fils de défunt Arnaud Bruneau de la Chabossiere, Ecuyer, et de [blank] de la Chabossiere, natif de la Rochelle, province d'Onis. Henry Bruneau, fils de défunt Henry de Bruneau de la Chabossiere, Écuyer, et de Marie de la Chabossiere, né à la Rochelle, province d'Onis. Henry Auguste Chatagner, Écuyer, Alexandre Thésée Chatagner, fils de défunt Roch Chatagner, Écuyer, et de Jeanne de Chatagner, néz à la Rochelle: province d'Onis. Élizabeth Chatagner, femme du susdit Alexandre Thésée Chatagner, fille de Pierre Buretel et d'Élizabeth Buretel. Alexandre Chatagner, Élizabeth Madeleine Chatagner, enfans des susdits, néz en Caroline.—(Habitants de Santee.)
Paul and Henry Bruneau, and Henry Augustus Chastaigner de Cramahé, had already, while in England, obtained letters of naturalization, March 20, 1686, and April 15, 1687.—(List of naturalized Denizens, in Agnew's Protestant Exiles from France, Vol. III., Pp. 41, 42.)
Arneau Bruneau, the father of Paul and Henry, probably came to South Carolina with his sons, and died there soon after. In the Secretary of State's office, Charleston, S. C., there is record of a deed of contract executed in London, February 25th, 1686, between Arnold Bruneau, seigneur of Chaboissière, and Paul Bruneau, lord of Ruedoux, [Rivedoux,] of the one part, and Josias Marylan, lord of La Forcet, of the other part, for the erection of a mill in South Carolina; the said mill to be erected on the land of either party without prejudice to the interests of the other.—(History of the Presbyterian Church in South Carolina. By George Howe, D.D. Vol. I., p. 101.)

<small>Chap. V.</small>
<small>1681.</small>

David and Elie Papin belonged to an ancient Huguenot family of La Rochelle. One of the name had served as deacon in 1561: another as minister of the church in 1612:[1] and more recently, "le sieur Papin"—whether David or Elie was intended or not, does not appear—had officiated as public "reader," or clerk, in the services of the "temple" of the Ville neuve.[2] Both became prominent members of the French refugee church in New York.

<small>Daniel Robert.</small>

Daniel Robert removed from La Rochelle to the island of Martinique at the time of the Revocation, with his wife Susanne La Tour. About the end of the seventeenth century, he came to New York, where his posterity have resided. He had left a considerable estate in France; and for years, it is said, after his arrival in America, he received legal notice from time to time, summoning him to appear at the door of a certain church, and show cause, if any he had, why certain lands or tenements in that city or in its vicinity should not be confiscated to the king, or conveyed to other members of

---

[1] La Rochelle Protestante. Recherches politiques et religieuses : 1126–1792. Par P.-S. Callot. La Rochelle, 1863. Pp. 95, 134.

[2] "Le S^r. Papin, ci-dev^t. lecteur au prèche," residing in the paroisse S^t. Sauveur, in La Rochelle, fled in 1681, with his wife and four little children, leaving a house in town, and took refuge in the island of Guernsey. (Liste des familles de la R. P. R., etc.: Archives Nationales, T^t. n°. 259.) David Papin, "marchand," is mentioned among "fugitifs de la Rochelle, 4 Octobre, 1685."—(L'Eglise Réformée de La Rochelle. Etude historique. Par L. Delmas, pasteur. Toulouse : 1870. P. 394.)

the Robert family remaining in La Rochelle.[1] The late Christopher R. Robert of New York, distinguished for his munificent charities, and particularly for the founding of Robert College, Constantinople, was a descendant of this refugee in the fourth generation.

There were other worshipers in the Protestant "prêche" of La Rochelle, before the Revocation, who bore names that have become as household words on this side of the Atlantic. It will be proper to make mention of them here, in passing, while reserving fuller accounts for the volumes of this work that will relate to the places where the Rochellese emigrants to America eventually settled.

Among the fugitives from La Rochelle who came to Massachusetts, were Louis Allaire,[2] Pierre Baudouin, Gabriel Bernon, François Bureau, Gabriel and Jacques Depont,[3] André and Benjamin Faneuil, Henri Guionneau, Jacob Peloquin, and André Sigourney. A larger number established themselves in the province of New York. The following persons became residents of the city of New York: Jean Auboyneau,[4]

---

[1] "On these occasions, although he was not easily roused to anger, he would become very angry, and for a while be much agitated, tearing the papers indignantly to pieces, and throwing them into the fire."—(Family record.)

[2] Son of Jean Allaire and Jeanne Bernon, of La Rochelle. —(Allaire Genealogy.)

[3] Nephews of Gabriel Bernon, whose sister Suzanne married Paul de Pont, of La Rochelle.—(Bernon Papers and Genealogy.)

[4] Le nom d'une famille de La Rochelle qui y fut des premières à embrasser les principes de la Réforme.—(La France

Chap. V.
1681.

Daniel Bernardeau,[1] Marie Billard, widow of Etienne Jamain,[2] Jeanne Boisselet, wife of Jean Carouge,[3] Pierre and Samuel Bourdet,[4] Pierre Chaigneau,[5] Jean and Josué David, Benjamin D'Harriette,[6] Etienne Doucinet,[7] Auguste

---

Protestante.) Louis, married in 1573, had a son Louis, pastor of several churches, among them the church of La Rochelle (1607–1610). He died in 1668, leaving several sons, one of whom, Pierre, had a son Pierre, born in 1672, and a son Jean, born in 1674. (Ibid.) Jean Auboyneau was in New York in 1697.

[1] A Rochellese family. Daniel Bernardeau and Marie Monier, his wife, were in New York in 1701.

[2] Marie Billard, veufue d'Estienne Jamain de la Rochelle, died in New York May 5, 1689.

[3] Invoice of goods found in the house of John Carrouge, deceased April 5, 1689.—(Wills, Surrogate's Office, New York. No. 14. Pp. 167, 168.) Enterrement, 6 Avril, 1689, Jeanne Boisselet, femme du sieur Carrouge, native de laro^{lle} [La Rochelle] en le Royaume de France.—(Records of the French Reformed Church of New York.)

[4] Pierre and Samuel Bourdet were members of the French Church in New York, as early as the year 1689, when Samuel was the husband of Judith Piaud, of La Rochelle.—(See below.) Comp. Estienne Bourdet, one of the fugitives from La Rochelle in 1685.

[5] Pierre Chaigneau (liste des religionnaires fugitifs de La Rochelle dont les biens ont été saisis, 1685–1688 ; quoted by Delmas, l'Eglise Réformée de la Rochelle, p. 395). Peter Chaigneau, naturalized in England, March 21, 1688.—(Agnew, III., 49.) He was made freeman of the city of New York, May 29, 1691. Pieter Chaigneaig, van Rochel, married Aeltje Smit, in the Dutch Church, New York, May 13, 1693.

[6] "Famille de fervents protestants rochelois."—(La France Protestante, I. p. 724.) Benjamin d'Harriette was the son of Susanne Papin, by her first husband, Benjamin d'Harriette, of La Rochelle. She married in London, November 9, 1686, Elie Boudinot, veuf, (Livre des Mariages de l'Eglise françoise de la Savoye,) with whom she came to New York, accompanied by her son, who was made freeman of the city in 1700.

[7] "Le nommé Doucinet," and wife, of the paroisse St.

and Marie Grasset,[1] Marie Anne Guichard,[2] René Het,[3] Guillaume Huertin,[4] François Hullin,[5] Auguste Lucas, Auguste Jay, Gabriel Le

Sauveur, La Rochelle, fled to England in 1682.—(Liste des familles de la R. P. R., etc., Archives Nationales, TT. n°. 259.) Stephen Doussiner, Susan, *wife*, Mary and Marianne *children*, were naturalized in England, March 8, 1682. —(Agnew, III., 31.) They were in New York November 4, 1688.

[1] Augustus and Mary Grasset, naturalized in England, March 8, 1682, came as early as 1689 to New York, where Grasset became a leading merchant and government official, and one of the "chefs de famille" of the French Church. He was murdered in the negro insurrection, April 7, 1712. Marianne Grasset, "van Rochel," was married in the Dutch Church, New York, April 30, 1692, to Henri de Money, "met attestatie van de Fransche Kercke."

[2] Marie Guichard and sister, of the paroisse St. Barthelemy, La Rochelle, fled in 1684 to England.—(Arch. Nat., TT.) Marie Anne Guichard, French Church, New York, March 6, 1706.

[3] Son of Josué and Sarah Het, of La Rochelle. He was a merchant of New York, and agent in that city, with André Fresneau, of the Royal West Indies Company of France.—(Dr. E. B. O'Callaghan; in Historical Magazine, new series, vol. IV., p. 266.)

[4] Guilleaume Huertin, maistre de navire, demeurant à presant en cette ville, et cy-devant à la Rochelle, was married in Bristol, England, by M. Descairac, January 2, 1698, to Elizabeth Bertrand, veuve de Jean Bertrand, marinier. He was the son of le sieur Guilleaume Huertin, of La Rochelle, maistre de navire du Roy, décédé en ung voiage des Indes; and of Suzanne Croiset his wife.—(Régistres de l'Eglise Françoise Protest°. Episcop°. de Bristol, Non-Parochial Registers, etc. Foreign Churches. Somerset House, London.) Guilleaume Huertin came with his son Guillaume, born in Bristol, November 12, 1699, to New York, and died there in 1718.

[5] François Huslin and his wife, of the paroisse St. Barthelemy, La Rochelle, fled to England in 1683.—(Arch. Nat., TT.) He was naturalized there, July 2, 1684, and was made a freeman of the city of New York, May 29, 1691.

Chap. V.
1681.

Boiteux,[1] Etienne Jamain,[2] François Louraux,[3] Jacques Merie,[4] Paul Merlin,[5] Pierre Morin,[6] (ancestor of John Morin Scott,) Elie Nezereau,[7]

His wife Elizabeth died Dec. 23, 1694. He died in September, 1702.

[1] Gabriel Le Boiteux, naturalized January 5, 1688, made freeman of the city of New York, August 3, 1688, was perhaps a brother of Paul and Pierre Le Boiteux, fugitives from La Rochelle, whose goods were seized February 4, 1685, and who established themselves as merchants in Amsterdam. Gabriel became a prominent merchant in New York, and was one of the first Elders of the French Church (in 1688).

[2] Etienne, Arnaud, Nicolas, and perhaps Elie, sons of Etienne Jamain, marchand de la Rochelle, were in New York at an early day. Etienne was high constable in 1705; Elie in 1710. Nicolas was one of the "chefs de famille" of the French Church in 1704.

[3] François Louraux, natif de la Rochelle, décédé le 22 Juin, 1689, was interred in the cemetery of the French Church in New York.

[4] Jacques Merie, or De Maree, "van Rochel," was married, November 27, 1692, in the Dutch Church of New York, to Cornelia Roos, widow of Elias Provoost.

[5] Paul Merlin, born at Rochelle, was naturalized in New York, September 27, 1687.

[6] Pierre Morin, natif de la Rochelle, France, fils de Pierre Morin, marchand au dit lieu, married Marie Jamain, June 12, 1692, in the French Church in New York. He was naturalized in England, October 10, 1688, with his first wife Frances, and was made freeman of New York, June 11, 1691. Three sons and four daughters were baptized in the French Church.

[7] Born in La Rochelle [1639]: died in New York, March 28, 1719, aged eighty years.—(Inscription upon his tombstone, in Trinity Church-yard, New York.) He was naturalized in England, March 20, 1686, and came over in the ship Robert, with pasteur Peiret, in October, 1687. He was made freeman of New York, December 5, 1687. He was engaged in trade with the West Indies, and died in Kingston, Jamaica, in March, 1709, leaving by will fifty pounds to the Elders of the French Reformed Protestant congregation in New York, for the use of the poor. A former will mentioned his nephews James, Martin and Lewis, his cousin Elias Nezereau, and his deceased niece, Jane Barbauld, of London.

David and Elie Papin, Etienne Perdriau,[1] Gédéon, son of Alexandre Petit,[2] Jeanne Piaud, wife of Simeon Soumain, Judith Piaud, wife of Samuel Bourdet,[3] Daniel Robert and Jean Sevenhoven.[4] The settlers of New Rochelle, in Westchester county, New York, were, as it might be presumed, for the most part Rochellese. The leading member of the settlement was Alexandre Allaire, of whom mention has already been made. With him were associated Louis Bonneau,[5] Jean Bouteiller,[6] Jacques

---

[1] Daniel Perdriau, of La Rochelle, was a refugee in Cork, Ireland, in 1695.—(Régistre du Temple de Soho, Somerset House, London.) Etienne, Elizabeth, and Marie Perdriau, were members of the French Church in New York, 1689–1699. Stephen, mariner, was made freeman in 1702.

[2] Will proved in New York, March 20, 1688.

[3] La veuve Piaud, ses 3 filles et un neveu, de la paroisse de St. Sauveur, La Rochelle, fled to England in 1681.—(Arch. Nat., TT.) Jeanne, probably one of the daughters, was married to Simeon Soumain before coming to America; their son Simon was baptized in the French Church in Threadneedle street, London, June 10, 1685. Judith, probably another daughter, was married to Samuel Bourdet.

[4] Jean Sevenhoven, van Rochel, was married to Mary Lescuye [L.'Escuier], in the Dutch Church of New York, September 22, 1693.

[5] Famille Rocheloise (La France Protestante). There is no evidence that Louis was related to Antoine, of La Rochelle, who went to South Carolina. (See below.) But the baptismal name Louis was frequently given in the family that remained in France.—(Callot, La Rochelle Protestante, p. 105.)

[6] Born at Rochell.—(Act of Naturalization, New York, September 27, 1687.) Boutellier was one of the founders of the settlement of New Rochelle: but he left for the island of St. Christopher, September, 1690, and died there in the following year, leaving his lands in the settlement to his godchild Jeanne, daughter of Alexandre Allaire.—(Town Records of New Rochelle.)

Chap. V.
1681.

Flandreau,[1] Daniel Gombaud,[2] Jean Hastier,[3] Bartholomew and Isaac Mercier,[4] Daniel Rayneau,[5] Ambroise Sicard,[6] André and Peter

---

[1] Jacque Flandreaux, de la Rochelle, married in London, December 15, 1695, Madeleine Mesnard, de la ville de Saintes.—(Régistre des Baptemes et Mariages dans l'Eglise de Glass House street et de Leicesterfields. Somerset House.) He was in New Rochelle in 1698.

[2] Daniel Gombaud, born at Rochell.—(Act of Naturalization, New York, September 27, 1687.) He settled in New Rochelle before 1693. Like his namesake, perhaps kinsman, Moses Gombeau, (see above, p. 234) he had resided in Guadeloupe before coming to America. He was accompanied to New York by Agnes Constance Le Brun, "born at Guadeloupe," who afterwards became the second wife of Gabriel Le Boiteux.

[3] John Hastier, born at Rochell.—(Act of Naturalization, etc.) He, or another Jean Hastier, had resided in the island of St. Christopher. He was one of the early settlers of New Rochelle, but removed to New York in 1694 or 1695, and was made freeman of that city, August 26, 1695. He died about the year 1698.

[4] Isaac Mercier, born at Rochell, was naturalized in New York, Sept. 27. 1687. He had obtained denization the year before, Sept. 3, 1686.—(Act of Naturalization, etc.) He became a leading member of the settlement of New Rochelle. Bartholomew, perhaps his brother, arrived in the province two years earlier, coming from Boston "to settle in the city" of New York.

[5] Daniel Rayneau, the ancestor of the Renaud family in America, is believed to have emigrated from La Rochelle.—(History of Westchester County, N. Y., by the Rev. Robert Bolton. Revised Edition. Vol. II., page 757.) He first went to Bristol, England. A Bible in the possession of one his descendants contains this statement: "Mémoire du jour que nous avons parti de Bristol ce fut le sixieme d'Avril 1693."

[6] Ambroise Sicard was a refugee from La Rochelle—(History of Westchester County, etc., II., 758), who came to America with his three sons, Ambroise, Daniel and Jacques. The Records of the French Church in New York begin with the entry of the baptism of Madelaine, daughter of Ambroise Sicard [junior] and Jeanne Perron, his wife, November 24, 1688. The Sicards settled in New Rochelle as early as the year 1692.

Thauvet,[1] Jacob Theroulde.[2] Of the settlers of Ulster County, New York, Jean and Etienne Gascherie,[3] and Jean Thévenin, were from La Rochelle. Several members of the Huguenot family of L'Hommedieu fled from La Rochelle after the Revocation. Pierre and Osée, or Hosea, were the sons of Pierre L'Hommedieu and Marthe Peron his wife. The husband died before the year 1685. Marthe accompanied her children to England, and came to America with Pierre, who settled in Kingston, Ulster County, New York.[4] Benjamin and John L'Hommedieu,

---

[1] Andrew Thauvet, born at Rochelle, was naturalized in New York, September 27, 1687.—(Act of Naturalization, etc.) He was one of the first purchasers of land in New Rochelle, November 12, 1688, and with Peter Thauvet bought one thousand acres, May 31, 1690. He was appointed a justice of the peace, December 14, 1689. Peter Thauvet, merchant, was made freeman of the city of New York, June 24, 1701. He married Susanne Vergereau, May 29, 1700, and died in 1704.

[2] "Jacob Theroulde, born at Rochell, Sarah, his wife, Marianne and Dorothy, their daughters, born at the island of St. Christopher's," were naturalized in New York, September 27, 1687.—(Act, etc.) Theroulde had obtained denization in New York, with liberty to trade or traffic, the year before, June 14, 1686. He purchased lands in New Rochelle as early as 1690, but in 1701 sold them, and went back to St. Christopher. His wife Sarah was a daughter of Gerard and Allette Douw, of that island.

[3] Several of this name are mentioned among the fugitives from La Rochelle. John and Stephen, sons of Judith Gascherie, were naturalized in England, April 15, 1687, and came to Kingston, N. Y., as early as 1696.

[4] Marthe Péron, veuve de Pierre L'Hommedieu ; 29 Septembre, 1685. Osée L'Hommedieu ; 4 février, 1685.—(Liste des religionnaires fugitifs de la Rochelle dont les biens ont été saisis ; 1685–1688.) Osée, goldsmith, son of Pierre and Marthe L'Hommedieu, was in London in 1702. The will of Pieter L'Hommedieu, late of Kingstown, Ulster County,

"born at Rochell," were naturalized in New York, September 27, 1787. Benjamin had obtained letters of denization some months before. He settled on the east end of Long Island, in the village of Southold, and married the daughter of Nathanael Silvester, of Shelter Island.[1]

Of the settlers of Staten Island, several were natives of this city.[2] So, too, were Pierre and Moïse Chaillé,[3] of Maryland, Antoine Duché,[4]

New York, signed February 10, 1691-2, and proved March 30, 1692, mentions his mother Martha. (Wills, Surrogate's Office, New York; No. IV., p. 181.) He leaves property in trust "till Mr. August Jea [Jay] doth returne." Auguste Jay, his partner in business, was then in France.

[1] Hosea L'Hommedieu fled from La Rochelle several months previous to the flight of his brother Pierre and their mother Marthe. Perhaps he was accompanied by Benjamin and Jean, who may have been his brothers. The interesting tradition among the descendants of Benjamin L'Hommedieu agrees perfectly with these facts. "Benjamin and a brother left France together. Their widowed mother went with them to the shore at La Rochelle, and as a parting gift confided to one a Bible, and to the other a silver watch. They fled to Holland, and thence came to America. The watch is now in the possession of Professor Eben Norton Horsford, of Harvard University." (Communicated by the Reverend A. S. Gardiner, a descendant of Benjamin L'Hommedieu.)

A monument in memory of Nathanael Sylvester has been recently erected on Shelter Island, by the daughters of Professor Horsford, descendants of Benjamin L'Hommedieu and of Patience Sylvester, his wife.

[2] Among them Etienne Mahault, who had been for some time an inhabitant of St. Christopher. He died on Staten Island in 1703.

[3] The name occurs among the "persécutés en Aunis," in 1681, under the intendant Demuin.—(Benoist, V. 1021.) La France Protestante mentions the famille de Challais, of La Rochelle, 1679. The tradition of the Chaillé family in America is, that Pierre Chaillé escaped from La Rochelle on

of Pennsylvania, Antoine Pintard,[1] of New Jer-
board of an English vessel, and took refuge in England, [where he was naturalized Sept. 9, 1698,] that he was the spokesman chosen by his fellow-refugees to refuse a message addressed to them by Louis XIV., inviting them to return to France; that he entered the English navy; that while in England he married a lady of Huguenot birth, named Margaret Brown; and that he removed to America, establishing himself at first in Boston. His son, Moses Chaillé, as early as 1710, was a resident of Maryland, where his descendants are to be found at present. (Communicated by Professor Stanford E. Chaillé, M.D., of the University of Louisiana.)

[1] Jacques Duché, paroisse St. Sauveur, La Rochelle, fled to England in 1682, with his wife and eight children, and his son-in-law. He had a house in town.—(Arch. Nat.) He was naturalized in England, March 8, 1682, with his wife Mary, and his sons Arnold and Anthony.

[1] According to the family tradition, Antoine Pintard came from La Rochelle. His petition for denization, addressed in 1691 to the governor and council of New York, "sheweth, that he being a Native of the Kingdome of France, was by the severity used by that prince towards those of the Reformed Churches oblidged to depart that Relme." Since that time, being the space of four years, he has been an inhabitant of this his Majesty's government of New York.—(Historical Manuscripts in the Office of the Secretary of State, Albany, N. Y., Vol. XXXVII., page 80.) Pintard first settled in Shrewsbury, New Jersey, then within the jurisdiction of the province of New York. There his house took fire, and he lost all his property. He removed to the city of New York, and began life anew as a merchant. He was an Elder of the French Church in New York, and in 1729 resigned the office of treasurer of the poor-fund (receveur des deniers des pauvres) which he had held until then: "à cause de son grand âge." He died about the year 1732.—(Will of Anthony Pintard, Senior, late of Shrewsbury, but now of the city of New York: dated February 4, 1729; proved May 11, 1732.—Secretary of State's Office, Trenton, New Jersey.)

Anthony Pintard left three sons—Anthony, John, and Samuel—and six daughters: Magdala, Catharine, Margaret, Isabella, Flòrinda, and Anna Frances. Magdala married James Hutchins. (June 30, 1728, jour de l'ascension, Jacques, son of Jacques and Magd. Hutchins, born in Shrewsbury,

Chap. V.
1681.

sey, Jean L'Orange,[1] and George de Rochelle,[2] whose descendants settled in Virginia : while of the South Carolina Huguenots, Jeanne Berchaud,[3] wife of Jean Boyd, Antoine Bonneau,[4]

New Jersey, in 1727, was baptized in the French Church, New York.) Catharine married first John Searle, and secondly the Rev. Robert Jenney. Margaret married Joseph Leonard. Isabella married Isaac Van Dam. Florinda married George Spencer. Anna Frances married Moses Gombaud. (See above, p. 235.)

The marriage license of Anthony Pintard (junior?) and Katharine Staleboth, of Neversink in East Jersey, is dated May 4, 1692.—(Wills, Surrogate's Office, New York ; No. IV., p. 184.)

[1] La veuve du Sr Lorange, paroisse St. Sauveur, La Rochelle, fled to England in 1682, leaving " quelque bien en Poitou."—(Arch. Nat.) La veuve Lorange and Jean Vilas L'Orange, were inhabitants of Manakintown, Virginia, 1701, 1714.

[2] George de Rochelle, from La Rochelle or its neighborhood, fled in the reign of Louis XIV. to the United Provinces, and thence came to America. (Tradition.) George Rupell was in South Carolina in the early part of the eighteenth century. A son or grandson removed to Albemarle, Virginia. Descendants of the emigrant are to be found in several of the Southern States.

[3] Jeanne, femme de Jean Boyd, fille de Elie Berchaud de la Rochelle, inhabitant of Santee, 1696.—(Liste des François et Suisses Refugiez en Caroline qui souhaittent d'être naturalizés Anglais.)

[4] Antoine Bonnaud, tonnelier ; sa femme : paroisse St. Barthelemy, La Rochelle, fled in 1685. Antoine Bonneau, né à la Rochelle, fils de Jean Bonneau et de Catherine Roi, and Catherine du Bliss, his wife, applied to be naturalized, 1696, with Antoine and Jean-Henri, leurs enfans nez en France. Jacob, leur fils né en Caroline.—(Liste des François, Réfugiez en Caroline, etc.) Anthony Bonneau, senior, cooper, was " made free of this part of the province," by the Lords Proprietors of South Carolina, March 10, 1697. (An Act for making Aliens free of this part of the Province, and for granting liberty of conscience to all Protestants. Trott's Laws of South Carolina, page 61.)

Henri and Paul Bruneau, Pierre Buretel,[1] Alexandre and Henri Chasteignier, César Mauzé,[2] Henri Peronneau,[3] and Pierre Videaul,[4] came also from La Rochelle.

At no great distance from the city, and within the same territory of Aunis, there were several smaller places inhabited by families that subsequently fled to America. Eleven miles to the north-east, was the town of Marans, famous in the wars of the League. Completely sur-

---

[1] Charles Burtel, fugitif du département de La Rochelle.—(Arch. Nat.) His property was seized, May 4, 1688. Le Sr. Pierre Burtel, sa femme et sa fille, fled to Holland in 1684.—(Arch. Nat.) He was naturalized in England, April 15, 1687. Pierre Buretel, né à la Rochelle, fils de Charles Buretel et de Sara Bonhier: Elizabeth Chintrier sa femme.—(Liste des François et Suisses Refugiez en Caroline, etc.) Peter Buretel, chirurgeon, was made free of the city of New York, June 11, 1708. Marie Chintrier, wife of Saviott Broussard, alias Deschamps, who obtained letters of denization, March 12, 1696; and Françoise Chentrier, widow of André Stuckey, 1707, were perhaps of the same family with Buretel's wife.—(Patents, Albany, N. Y., Vol. VII., p. 9.—Records of the French Church in New York.)

[2] Elie Mauzé, 1682, and la veuve Mauzé, 1684, both fled from La Rochelle to England, (Arch. Nat.,) where Elias was naturalized in 1682, and Cæsar Mozé was naturalized April 15, 1687.—Cæsar Mozé was in South Carolina in the same year.

[3] Henri Peronneau, né à la Rochelle, filsde Samuel Peronneau et de Jeanne Collin. (Liste des François et Suisses Refugiez en Caroline, etc.)

[4] Pierre Videaul, né à la Rochelle, fils de Pierre Videaul et de Madelaine Burgaud, was among the inhabitants of Santee who applied, about the year 1696, to be naturalized; with his wife Jeanne Elizabeth and their daughter Jeanne Elizabeth, born in London, and with their children Pierre Nicholas, Marianne, Marthe Ester, Judith, Jeanne and Madelaine, born in Carolina.—(Liste des François et Suisses Refugiez en Caroline, etc.)

rounded by water, or by salt marshes, it formed a picturesque island, approached only from the south-east by a causeway. Taken by the forces of the duke of Guise, in 1588, Marans was retaken by Henry of Navarre after the battle of Coutras. When the Huguenot army was about to advance to the assault of this place, the troops kneeled down, according to their custom, in prayer. The Roman Catholic soldiers, witnessing this procedure, exclaimed: "They are praying to God: now they will beat us, just as they did at Coutras!"

Marans was the home of Elie Boudinot,[1] a prosperous merchant, and an earnest adherent of the Protestant faith. The family to which he belonged had been identified for several generations with the Huguenot cause. "Compelled to abandon his country in order to avoid the continual persecution to which he was subjected because of his profession of the Gospel," Boudinot came to America, where his descendants have been conspicuous for their fidelity to the same principles, and their zeal in spreading them.[2]

---

[1] Seigneur de Cressy: so designated on the fly-leaf of a book of his, in the possession of his descendants.

[2] The will of Elias Boudinot is recorded in the city of New York, and contains some interesting particulars.

Au nom de Dieu amen. Je soubsigné Elie Boudinot marchant demeurant cydevant à Marant au gouvernement de La Rochelle en France ayant esté constraint d'abandonner ma patrie pour eviter la continuelle persecution quon me fezait pour la profession de l'Evangille mestent retirè en ce lieu avecq Suzanne Papin ma femme et nos enfans.... Je recomande mon ame a la sainte et Glorieuse Trinité au

Benon and Mauzé, villages lying east of La

Pere qui l'a crée au Fils qui la rachettée et au Saint Esprit quy la illuminée et santifiée Desclarant que je veux vivre et mourir en la créance et profession de la religion reformée en laquelle jay esté par la grace de Dieu eslevé et mon corps estre jnhumé duement Et comme par le contract de mariage entre la ditte Suzanne Papin ma femme et moy passé par André Mucot nottaire royal a Londre le onziesme novambre mil six cent quatre vingt-six ma ditte femme apportionna Benjamin et Suzanne D'hariette ses Enfans Chacun cent soixante huit livres sterlin payable par moy ou mes herittiers lorsquils seront en age ou pourveus par mariage Jay satisfait a la dite cloize ayant payé a deffunt Pierre Bellin marit [mari] de la ditte Suzanne D'hariette, 168£ sterlin suivant leurs quittance deux signée Jay aussy payé au dit Benjamin D'hariette pareille somme de cent soixante huit livre sterlin suivant sa quittance les dittes deux sommes payée en argent de ce lieu avecq le change suivant le cours. Comme il a pleu a Dieu me donner de mon present mariage quatre enfans qui sont Jean Benjamin Madelaine et Suzanne Boudinot Je desclare Suzanne ma femme leurs mere Tutrice et Curatrisse laquelle je laisse dame et maîtresse de tous generallement les biens meubles marchandize argant debtes et tous effects quy se trouveront mapartenir a la charge de donner a chacun de mes dits enfans Jean, Benjamin, Madelaine et Susanne Boudinot la somme de deux cents cinquante livres argent de ce lieu et cella lors quils seront en age ou pourveus par mariage a quoy je les apotionne chascun et herittiers les ungs des autres et comme Elie Boudinot mon fils est de mon premier mariage quy depuis quelque temps cest marié et en consideration de son dit mariage je luy ay donne trois cent livres argent courant de ce lieu partye an faveur comme herritier de deffunte Janice Barand ma femme sa mere pour sa potion quy luy venoit de reste des effects quil avoit plut a Dieu me faire la grace de retirer de France et comme aprez ma mort mon dit fils Elie demanderoit a venir a partager tant avecq la ditte Suzanne ma femme quavecq ses autres freres et soeurs de mon dit present mariage dans tous les effets qui je peus laisser pour eviter tous troubles embaras ou contestation qui pouroit survenir dans le dit partage je veux et ordonne que la ditte Suzanne ma femme paye trois mois apres mon deceds a mon dit fils Elie Boudinot la somme de cent cinquante livres argent de ce lieu

Chap. V.
1681.

Rochelle,[1] are noticeable as the places where three Huguenot families transplanted to New York, originated. Mauzé was the home of Louis

---

ayant cours et ce pour touttes succession et pretention de tous les meubles marchandize argent debtes et autres effects generallement quy se trouveront a moy apartenir et apres la ditte somme de cent cinquante livres payée mon dit fils ne poura faire aucune demande a la ditte Suzanne ma femme ny a ses freres et soeurs soubs quelque pretexte de succession que ce soitt.—Et comme j'ay laissé du bien en France et autres effets suivant les contracts obligation promesse et billets et par mes livres de conte le tout laissé entre les mains de deffunt mon nepveur Jean Boudinot marchant a Marenes avecq ma procuration generalle pour agir pour moy et pour retirer de mes effets ce quil pouroit en cas de quelque Remize le tout sera partagé par mes dits enfans du premier et segond lit par egalle portions et sil plaisoit a Dieu Comme je len prie de tout mon coeur de restablir en France la liberté de nostre sainte religion et que mes dits enfans y retournasse ils partageront entreux tous les biens meubles et Immeubles quy se trouveront a moy apartenir et ce par egalle portion se sont là mes derniere vollontés et Intention voullant et entandant quelle sortes leurs plain et entier effet et pour plus forte execution dicelle jay nommé pour executeur et administrateur et pour faire valloir mon dit present testament monsieur Paul Drouilhet mon bon amy marchant en ce lieu lequel je prie daccepter cette commission comme len jugant tres digne et capable et de le faire executeur en tous ses points contre tous et envers tous revoquant par ce mien dit present Testament tous ceus quy se pouront trouver cy devant faits par moy en foy de quoy jay escrit ce present signé de ma main cellé de mon cachet en presence des tesmoings sousignés a New York le quatorziesme novembre milceptcent....Eslie Boudinot. Tesmoins Gabriel Broussard Henry Pichot.

Proved October 26, 1702.
Record of Wills, VII., pp. 35-36.

[1] Benon, sixteen miles from La Rochelle, is now a village of a thousand inhabitants. Mauzé, with eighteen hundred inhabitants, lies seven miles further east.

Guion,[1] and of Pierre Elisée Gallaudet;[2] and

1681.

[1] Louis Guion, of Mozé [Mauzé] en Aunis, and Marie Morin, his wife, presented their son Louis, born August 21, 1694, for baptism in the French church in Glasshouse street, London.—(Registre, etc., in the custody of the Registrar-General, Somerset House.) Louis Guion, who bought land in New Rochelle, N. Y., in 1690, was doubtless related to him. The family tradition represents that he came from La Rochelle, and that his son Louis, twelve years of age in 1698, (census of New Rochelle,) was born at sea.

[2] A memorandum, partly undecipherable, in the possession of the Gallaudet family in America, states that " Peter Elisha Gallaudet" was "born in Mozé [Mauzé], pays d'Aunis, seven leagues from old Rochelle and four from Niort en Poitou. His estate between his sister * * * the name of the place called 3 Punall [?] à Saint Gelais between Niort and Surin. His father's name Joshua Gallaudet, born and bred at Mosé. His mother's name Margaret Prioleau, daughter to Elisha [Elisée] Prioleau, minister of Exoudun * * *"—Communicated by E. M. Gallaudet, LL.D.

Elisée Prioleau was the son of Elisée, minister of Niort, 1639-1650. He was minister of Exoudun, Poitou, 1649-1663.—(Lièvre, Hist. des prot. et des églises réf. du Poitou, III., 288, 306.) Samuel, a younger son of the pastor of Niort, was minister of Pons in Saintonge, from 1650 to 1683. He was succeeded in that charge by his son Elie Prioleau, who came after the Revocation with some members of his flock to Charleston, S. C.

Dr. Pierre Elisée Gallaudet was a resident of New Rochelle, N. Y., as early as the year 1711. Several of his descendants have illustrated the name by their distinguished philanthropic services, particularly in promoting the improvement of the condition of deaf-mutes. The Rev. Thomas Hopkins Gallaudet, LL.D., founder of the first institution in America for the instruction of the deaf and dumb, (born in Philadelphia, Dec. 10, 1787, died in Hartford, Conn., September 9, 1851,) was the great-grandson of the Huguenot emigrant. Two of his sons, the Rev. Thomas Gallaudet, D.D., Rector of St. Ann's Church for Deaf-Mutes, in the city of New York, and Edward Miner Gallaudet, Ph.D., LL.D., President and Professor of Moral and Political Science, National Deaf-Mute College, Washington, D. C., continue the good work with which their father's memory is honorably associated.

Benon, that of Pierre Vergereau and his brother Jean.¹

Off the coast of Aunis, and nearly opposite the city of La Rochelle, lies the island of Ré, a spot that may be said to rival that city in its claim upon the attention of Americans of Huguenot descent: for it was the native place, or the place of refuge, of many families that ultimately found their way to the New World. The Isle of Ré is but sixteen miles long, with an average breadth of less than three miles. Its principal towns are St. Martin, La Flotte, and Ars. Like the main shore, from which it is separated only by the narrow strait of Perthuis,² the land is low and sandy, and abounds in briny lagoons and marshes, that yield rich supplies of sea-salt, and furnish employment to many of the inhabitants. At the time of the Revocation, the population of the Isle of Ré was almost wholly Protestant.³ The fishermen and

---

¹ Jean Vergereau, natif de Benon en Aunis, married Marie Mahault, in the French church in New York, June 16, 1697. Pierre, apparently his brother, was a witness to the marriage. His son Pierre, goldsmith, became prominent in the affairs of the French church, and was an elder in 1740 and long after. He married Susanne Boudinot.

² At the narrowest part, this channel is little more than two miles in width.

³ The inhabitants of the island of Ré, at the present day, are in large proportion descended, it may be presumed, from the "nouveaux convertis," or the nominally converted Protestants, who remained in the country after the Revocation of the Edict of Nantes. They are said to exhibit marked traits of character, which we may perhaps regard as indicative, in some measure, of their Huguenot origin. "Très-sobre, travailleur acharné, appréciant et désirant

seamen and salters of this region had been among the earliest converts to the evangelical faith, a century and a half before: and their seclusion and obscurity had shielded them in a measure from molestation on account of their belief. Of late, also, many Huguenots of means, leaving their abodes in the interior of the country, had sought this island as a retreat where they might hope to escape observation, and whence, if need there should be, they might wing their flight to a friendlier shore beyond seas. This fact serves to explain the presence of some persons, concerning whom there is reason to believe that they had come from the neighboring provinces of Poitou, Saintonge, and Angoumois, to sojourn here.

Among the French Protestants who came to Boston, in Massachusetts, was Adam De Chezeau,[1] a native of the Isle of Ré. Ezéchiel Carré,

---

l'instruction, le paysan rétais," writes an intelligent observer, "est estimable entre tous. Plus que tout autre habitant natif d'une petite île, il a la volonté et l'aptitude de tout faire par lui-même: il est à la fois marin, pêcheur, cultivateur, saulnier, vigneron, maçon, charpentier. A première vue, on peut sourire de quelques-unes de ses habitudes: après réflexion on y reconnaît l'empreinte de véritables et rares qualités. Vraiment bon, il ménage les animaux qui l'aident à son travail au point de les gâter et de les rendre volontaires et ombrageux comme des enfants trop aimés."—(D. Lancelot: La Rochelle et son arrondissement. La Rochelle: 1877. Pp. 43, 44.)

[1] De Chezeaux, famille originaire de l' île de Ré.—(Bulletin historique et littéraire: Société de l'histoire du protestantisme français. Vol. XXIV., pp. 477, 526.) Adam de Chezeau, mariner, with others, "forced to leave their native country of France on account of the Protestant religion, for which" they "have been greatly persecuted and distressed,"

Chap. V.
1681.

the pastor of the Narragansett colony,[1] and Pierre and Daniel Ayrault,[2] who accompanied him, were from the same place. Nicolas Filoux,[3] and Paul Collin,[4] ancestors of families that settled in Connecticut, were inhabitants of the island. In New York, Pierre and Abraham Jouneau,[5] Ezéchiel Barbauld,[6] Elie and Guil-

petitioned the General Court of Massachusetts for denization in February, 1731.—(Mass. Archives, Vol. XI., p. 488.)

[1] Ezechiel Carreus, Retensis, was admitted in 1670 to the study of philosophy and theology in the Académie of Geneva.—(Livre du Recteur: Catalogue des Etudiants de l'Académie de Genève, de 1559 à 1859. Genève, 1860. P. 158.)

[2] Pierre Ayrault, fugitif de l'île de Ré. (Archives Nat., TT. n°. 259.) But see below.

[3] Nicolas Pierre Filoux fled from the Isle of Ré in 1685. (Arch. Nat.) Nicolas Fillou, natif de l'île de Ré en France, died in New York, March 1, 1690.—(Records of the French Church in New York.) Pierre, perhaps a son of Nicolas, was in New York in 1697: possibly the ancestor of the Fillou or Philo family of Norwalk, Connecticut, reputed to be of Huguenot descent.

[4] Paul Collin and his wife fled from the Isle of Ré in 1683 to Dublin, Ireland.—(Arch. Nat) Paul Collin, one of the settlers of Narragansett in 1686, was probably, like Pierre, who settled in South Carolina, a son of Jean Collin and Judith Vasleau of the Isle of Ré. (He was sponsor at the baptism of a child of Pierre Valleau, in New York, July 19, 1721.) Paul appears to have removed to Milford, Connecticut, after the breaking up of the Narragansett colony, and was probably the father of John Collin, born in 1706, ancestor of the Hon. John F. Collin, of Hillsdale, N. Y.

[5] Peter Jouneau, born at the Isle of Ré, was naturalized in New York, September 27, 1687. Abraham Jouneau was one of the fugitifs de l'Ile de Ré.—(Arch. Nat.) He was made a freeman of the city of New York in 1701, and was an Elder of the French Church in 1724. Philip Jouneau was made a freeman in 1702. Was he a son of Philippe Jouneau, pasteur à Barbezieux, Angoumois, en 1682 ?

[6] Ezekiel Barbauld was naturalized in New York, September 21, 1728, and made free of the city in the same year.

laume Cothoneau,[1] Etienne Valleau,[2] Marie Du Tay, wife of Jean Coulon, and Jeanne Du Tay, wife of Jacques Targé,[3] René Rezeau,[4] Jacques

---

Possibly a son of Ezéchiel Barbauld, natif de St. Martin dans l'île de Ré, pastor of several of the French churches in London.

[1] Elie Cottoneau, Guillaume Cottoneau, fugitifs de l'Ile de Ré, (Arch. Nat.) were among the principal settlers of New Rochelle, N. Y., 1694.

[2] Estienne Vasleau, marchand, fled from the Isle of Ré in 1682 to England.—(Arch. Nat.) Estienne Vallos, Mary, his wife, Estienne, junior, Arnaud, their sons: Sarah and Mary, daughters, born at the Isle of Ré, were naturalized in New York, September 27, 1687.—(Act.) Etienne Valleau, probably the son, settled in Kingston, Ulster County, N. Y.

Esaie Valleau, who settled in New Rochelle, N. Y., was probably related to Etienne. He was also from the Isle of Ré.—(Arch. Nat.) The name is still extant in the city of New York. Isaiah Valleau died in that city, December 26, 1875, at the house of his son, Henry Valleau, aged seventy-four years.

[3] Marie du Tay, de l'île de Ré, was married, April 27, 1692, in the French Church in New York, to Jean Coulon. Jeanne du Tay, wife of Jacques Targé. "Dutaies," fugitif de l'île de Ré. (Arch. Nat.)

[4] René Rezeau, maçon, of the Isle of Ré, with his wife [Anne Coursier], fled in 1685, "à la Caroline."—(Arch Nat.) They presented their daughter Ester for baptism in the French Church in New York, January 1, 1689. Jacques Rezeau, de St. Martin en Ré, was married in that Church, March 10, 1705, to Marie Contesse. René settled on Staten Island. Several of the earlier settlers of Staten Island were were also natives of the Isle of Ré. Among these were Jean Belleville, of St. Martin en Ré, and perhaps François Martineau—an Isle of Ré name—who became members of the Dutch Church in New York, July 28, 1670; (Harlem, Its Origin and Annals, by James Riker, p. 301;) Jacques Guion, of St. Martin's en Ré, who received a grant of land on Staten Island in 1664, (Ibid. p. 20,) and Paul Regrenie, who obtained a grant in 1674.—(Marie Regreny, of St. Martin en l'île de Ré : register of marriages in Leicester Fields Chapel, London.)

Chap. V.
1681.

Erouard,[1] Elie Mestayer,[2] Daniel Jouet and Marie Coursier, his wife,[3] Jacques Bertonneau,[4] Jean, François, Ester, and Madeleine Vincent,[5]

[1] Jacques Erouard, de l'île de Ré, and Elizabeth Brigaud his wife ; and Marie Eroüard, de l'île de Ré, wife of Jean Brigaud, were in London, 1695, 1697.—(Registers, etc., Somerset House.) Jacques Eroüard and Jeanne Jabouin his wife presented their children for baptism in the French Church, New York, 1755–1763. Charles Eroüard and Ester Coutant his wife, were members of the French Church, New Rochelle, 1759–1761. The name has been transformed into Heroy.

[2] François and Philippe Metayer, fugitifs de l'Ile de Ré.—(Arch. Nat.) François Mestayer, de l'Ile de Ré, aged seventy-eight years, received aid from the Royal Bounty fund, in London, 1705. Elie Mestayer, sponsor at the baptism of Abraham Jouneau's child, French Church in New York, March 20, 1720.

[3] Daniel Jouet, fils de Daniel Jouet et d'Elizabeth Jouet, natif de l'isle de Ré · et Marie Coursier sa femme, fille de Jehan Coursier et de Anne Perrotau.—(Liste des François et Suisses Refugiez en Caroline, etc.) Their children Daniel and Pierre were born in that island. A daughter Marie was born in Plymouth, England. Two sons, Ezéchiel and Jean, and two daughters, Elizabeth and Anne, were baptized in the French Church, New York. Jouet was one of the Narragansett colonists. He removed to New York, and thence to South Carolina.

[4] " Mr Bertonneau," a member of the French Church in New York, received assistance in 1694. Sara Bertonneau, née en l'isle de Ré, widow of Elie Jodon and wife of Pierre Michaud, was in South Carolina in 1696.

[5] Madeleine Vincent, wife of Jean Pelletreau, was "born at St. Martins."—(Act of Naturalization, New York, 1687.) Her brothers Jean and François, sailmakers, came to New York at the same time. François Vincent, voilier, who fled to England in 1681, was of Soubise.—(Arch. Nat.) He had probably pursued his trade in that place, twenty miles south of La Rochelle, previous to his flight. François was naturalized in England, March 21, 1682, and a week later he sailed from London with his wife Anne Guerry and his children Anne and Françoise for America.

EMIGRANTS FROM THE ISLE OF RÉ.

Olivier Besly,[1] Grégoire Goujon,[2] Marie Gallais,[3] Pierre and Daniel Bontecou,[4] were natives

---

[1] Besly, famille protestante de la Rochelle et de l'Ile de Ré.—(La France Protestante.) Jean and Etienne Besly, fugitifs de l'isle de Ré.—(Arch. Nat.) Oliver Besly was one of the leading inhabitants of New Rochelle, N. Y., in 1694.

[2] Grégoire Gougeon was among the "persécutez en Saintonge, Aunix, Ile de Ré et environs," mentioned by Benoist, Histoire de l'Edit de Nantes, Vol. IV., p. 1021. Grégoire Goujon, fugitif de l'Ile de Ré.—(Arch. Nat.) A merchant of New York, and a member of the French Church in that city in 1701. His wife was Renée Marie Graton. He bought land in New Rochelle, May 30, 1701. His daughter, Renée Marie, became the second wife of pasteur Louis Rou, of New York, November 3, 1713.

[3] Jean Galais, fugitif de l'Ile de Ré.—(Arch. Nat.) John Gallais, and Mary his wife were naturalized in England in 1686. La veuve Galay was one of the colonists of Narragansett. Marie Gallais, French Church in New York, 1691.

[4] Pierre Bondecou, sa femme, cinq enfans, fugitifs de l'Ile de Ré, had gone, it was supposed, to "la Caroline," in 1684. (Arch. Nat.) They were in New York as early as July 24, 1689, when Pierre Bontecou and his wife Marguerite presented their daughter Rachel for baptism in the French Church. Daniel Bontecou, undoubtedly the son of Pierre, was born about the year 1681, and died in the city of New York in November, 1773, aged ninety-two. "This gentleman," writes M. du Simitière, "I knew very well for many years. In the summer of the year 1770, being in company with him, he told me that he was born at La Rochelle from the descendant of the famous Dutch navigator Bontecoe [Bontekoe], that his parents fled from France for the sake of religion when he was an infant, that they went to England, and soon after came to New York, that he had then resided there eighty-two years. Mr. Bontecoe was for many years an Elder of the French Church in New York, and at the abovementioned time enjoyed good health, sound judgment, and tolerable memory."—(Du Simitière MSS., Philadelphia Library Company.) The descendants of Pierre Bontecou are numerous, and are to be found chiefly in the State of New York. The family is at present represented by Charles Hubbard Bontecou, Esq., of Lansingburgh, N. Y., and others.

Chap. V.
1681.

of the Isle of Ré. The families of Rappe[1] and Ribouleau,[2] in Pennsylvania, originated in the same locality. Of the settlers of Manakintown, Virginia, Paul Bernard,[3] Janvier[4] and Abraham Sallé,[5] were natives of Ré. And of the Huguenots who went to South Carolina,

---

[1] Gabriel Rappe fils, fugitif de l'Ile de Ré, had fled, it was thought—between 1681 and 1685—to "la Caroline."—(Arch. Nat.) He was in Pennsylvania in 1683, when Capt. Gabriel Rappe, with others, promised allegiance to the king and fidelity and lawful obedience to William Penn, proprietor and governor.—(Penn. Archives, Vol. I., p. 26.) Gabriel Rappe was naturalized, July 2, 1684.

[2] Nicolas Ribouleau, who appeared before the provincial council at the same time with Rappe, was doubtless from the same place. Several refugees of this name are mentioned, as fugitives from the isle of Ré.

[3] Paul Bernard le jeune, sa femme, deux enfans, fugitifs de l'île de Ré, 1685, were believed to have gone to "la Caroline." Joseph Bernard and wife were among the settlers of Manakintown, Virginia, 1701.

[4] Philippe Janvier, sa femme, trois enfans, fled to England from the Ile de Ré in 1683.—(Arch. Nat.) Pierre Janvier and Marie Boynaux were married in the Swallow Street French Church, London, December, 1711.—(Régistre, etc.) "Thomas Janvier, the ancestor of the families of this name in this country, was a Huguenot."—(An Address, embracing the Early History of Delaware, and the Settlement of its Boundaries, and of the Drawyers Congregation. By Rev. George Foot. Philadelphia, 1842, p. 56.) He was living in the town of New Castle, Delaware, as early as 1707.—(Historical Sketch of the Presbyterian Church of New Castle, Delaware. By the Rev. J. B. Spotswood, D.D. Pp. 15, 21.)

[5] "Abraham Salle, son of John Salle, by Mary his wife: born at Saint Martins in France," petitioned the governor and council for denization, New York, 1700. The children of Abraham Sallé and Olive Perault his wife, baptized in the French Church, New York, were Abraham, born October 31, 1700, and Jacob, born July 28, 1701. Sallé removed to Manakintown, Virginia.

Jacques and Jean Barbot,[1] Moïse Le Brun,[2] Daniel Garnier, and Elizabeth Fanton his wife,[3]

---

[1] "Jacques Barbot, Marchand ; sa femme ; 1685 ; à la Caroline. Jean Barbot."—(Archives Nationales, Tᴛ., nº. 259.) I have not met these names among those of the refugees in America ; nor that of "le sieur Laboureur : sa femme et ses enfans," who is also represented as having fled from the Isle de Ré in 1685, and as having gone to "la Caroline."

[2] Moyse Le Brun, né à l'isle de Ré, fils de Moyse Le Brun et de Marie Tauvron.—(Liste des François et Suisses Réfugiez en Caroline.) La veuve Le Brun was aided by the French Church in New York, and she and her son were sent to Carolina, their passage being paid, Sept. 12, 1694.—(Records of the French Church in New York.)

Agnes Constance Le Brun, "born at Guadaloupe," was naturalized in New York in 1687, together with Daniel Gombaud and his wife.—(Act of Naturalization, N. Y.) She lived for some time in New Rochelle, probably with Gombaud, who may have been her guardian : and was received a member of the Dutch Church of New York, September 14, 1691, by certificate from the French Church in New Rochelle.—(Records of the Reformed Protestant Dutch Church, City of New York. Liber A.)

[3] Daniel Garnier, Marchand : sa femme, six enfans, et Rachel Fanton sa sœur, sortis de l'Isle de Ré en 1685 ; lieu de leur retraite, la Caroline.—(Archives Nationales.) Daniel Garnier, né en l'Isle de Ré, fils de Daniel Garnier et de Marie Chevallier ; Elizabeth Fanton, sa femme ; Etienne, Rachel, Margueritte, Anne, leurs enfans néz en l'Isle de Ré : inhabitants of Santee in 1696.—(Liste des François et Suisses Réfugiez en Caroline.) An older daughter had married Daniel Horry, since deceased. Elizabeth Garnier, veuve Daniel Horry, fille de Daniel Garnier et de Elizabeth Fanton, native de l'Isle de Ré. Elizabeth Marye, Lidie Marye, filles de Daniel Horry et de la ditte Elizabeth Garnier, néez en Caroline.—(Id.)

Isaac Garnier, cordwainer, perhaps also of the Isle of Ré, if not related to the above, was a member of the French Church in New York as early as the year 1692. He had several children baptized in that church, and was one of the "chefs de famille" in 1704 and after. He was made a freeman of the city in 1695.

Chap. V.
———
1681.

Chap. V.
1685.
Arnaud France,[1] Daniel Huger,[2] Daniel Jodon and Sara Bertonneau his mother,[3] Isaac Mazicq,[4]

---

[1] Arnaud France ; sa femme; deux enfans: sortis de l'Isle de Ré en 1685 ; lieu de leur retraite, à la Caroline. —(Archives Nationales.) The name does not occur in any lists of refugees in America.

[2] Daniel Huger, Marchand: sa femme: deux enfans ; sortis de l'Isle de Ré en 1682 ; lieu de leur retraite, à Londres.—(Archives Nationales.) Daniel Huger and Jeanne his wife were naturalized in England, March 8, 1682. The wife's name may have been Jeanne Marguerite. Daniel Huger, né à Loudun, [en Poitou,] fils de Jean Huger, et Anne Rassin ; Margueritte Perdriau, sa femme; Margueritte leur fille, née à la Rochelle ; Daniel et Madeleine, leurs enfans, néz en Caroline : refugees in South Carolina, 1696. —(Liste des François et Suisses Réfugiez, etc.)

[3] Daniel Jodon, fils d'Elie Jodon et de Sara Jodon, né en l'Isle de Ré. Sara, femme de Pierre Michaud, fille de Jacques et Elizabeth Bertonneau, [see above,] née en l'isle de Ré, ci-devant femme de Elie Jodon : refugees in South Carolina, 1696.—(Liste des François et Suisses Réfugiez, etc.)

[4] Isaac Mazic, fugitif de l'Isle de Ré. (Archives Nationales, TT. n°· 259.) The same document mentions Estienne and Paul Mazic. Isaac Mazicq, natif de l'Isle de Ré, fils de Paul Mazicq, et de Hélesabeth Vanewick, Marianne Le Serrurier, sa femme, Marie Anne Mazicq, leur fille, née en Caroline.—(Liste des François et Suisses Refugiez, etc.) "Isaac Mazyck, the ancestor of the numerous and respectable families in South Carolina bearing the name, arrived at Charleston, with many other Huguenot refugees, from England, in December, 1686. His father, Paul Mazyck, or Paul de Mazyck, was a native of the Bishopric of Liege, and a Walloon. Paul married Elizabeth Van Vick, or Van Wyck, of Flanders. He removed to Maestricht, in the Netherlands, and afterwards to St. Martin, in the Isle de Ré, opposite La Rochelle. Stephen Mazyck emigrated to England, thence to Ireland, and resided many years in Dublin, where he died. Isaac fled from France to Amsterdam. He was a wealthy merchant, and succeeded in transferring to that commercial city the sum of fifteen hundred pounds sterling. From Amsterdam he went to England with his funds, and sailed from London with an interest in a cargo of one thousand

EMIGRANTS FROM OLÉRON.

Pierre Mounier,[1] and Etienne Tauvron,[2] came from Ré; while Isaac Biscon[3] and Jean Héraud were from the neighboring island of Oléron.

The flight of these families, as of so many others, from France, occurred chiefly between the years 1681 and 1686. It was in 1681, as we have seen in a preceding chapter, that the severities inflicted by the government upon the subjects of the Reformed religion, with a view to coerce them to embrace "the king's religion,"

---

pounds. This investment enabled him, in Charleston, to lay the foundation of the wealth which he afterwards acquired, and which he liberally dispensed in aid of the religious and charitable institutions of the city. He is believed to have been one of the founders of the Huguenot Church in Charleston, to which he left in his will one hundred pounds, the interest of which he directed to be paid annually forever for the support of a Calvinistic Minister of that Church. In his family Bible, under date of 1685, is this record: 'God gave me the blessing of coming out of France, and of escaping the cruel persecution carried on there against the Protestants: and to express my thanksgiving for so great a blessing, I promise, please God, to observe the anniversary of that by a fast.'"—(History of the Presbyterian Church in South Carolina. By George Howe, D.D. Vol. I., p. 102.)

[1] Pierre Mounier: fugitif de l'Isle de Ré.—(Archives Nationales.) Peter Mousnier was naturalized in England April 15, 1687. Pierre Mounier, natif de l'isle de Rée, fils de Louis Mounier et Elizabeth Martineaux, et Louise Robinet sa femme, fille de Louis Robinet; refugees in South Carolina, 1696.—(Liste des François et Suisses Réfugiez, etc.)

[2] Estienne Tauvron, né à l'isle de Ré, fils de Jacques Tauvron et de Marie Brigaud. Madeleine, sa fille, née a l'isle de Ré. Ester, née à Plymouth.

[3] Jean Biscon, fugitif de l'Isle d'Oléron.—(Archives Nationales.) Isaac Biscon and wife, admitted into the colony of Massachusetts, February 1, 1691; and Samuel Biscon, South Carolina, 1717, were probably of the same extraction.

reached a point that must have seemed to them the height of barbarity and oppression, in the enactment of a law permitting children of the age of seven years and upward to forsake the faith of their parents. Before this period, the Huguenots of La Rochelle, though exposed to some of the penalties and disabilities endured by their brethren throughout France, had long enjoyed an exceptional tranquillity. During this time, many a Protestant family had made its way from another province to find, in some one of the villages of Aunis, or in the city itself, a comparative freedom from religious persecution. But with the appointment of Demuyn, "a mortal enemy of Protestantism," as governor of Aunis, in 1674, the tribulations of the long favored Rochellese may be said to have begun in earnest. The laws which we have elsewhere rehearsed, shutting out all Protestants from civil employments, from the learned professions, from trades of various kinds, were now enforced, so far as practicable. No class was exempt from annoyance and indignity. The families that prided themselves upon their noble rank, in virtue of descent from persons who had filled the highest municipal offices, were informed that they could retain their honors only on condition of renouncing heresy. Ministers of the Gospel were threatened, silenced, imprisoned. The citizens of La Rochelle, as early as the summer of 1681, saw the towns and villages around them visited by bands of soldiers, quartered on defenseless Protestant families; and they knew that, sooner or later, they too must experience the horrors of the *dragonnades*. Already, numbers from Poitou were flying before the storm of persecution. More than one hundred of these, discovered in La Rochelle, whither they had come to embark for England or Holland, were thrown into the tower of *La Lanterne*. At length the decree went forth for the suppression of the Huguenot worship, in that city that had so long been the stronghold or the refuge of the Calvinists of France. It was ordered that the "temple" be demolished within one month, and that the Protestants themselves perform the work of destruction. Not one, however, was found willing to take part in it; the government employed workmen for the purpose, charging the expense of the demolition to the homeless congregation: and in five days it was completed. A few weeks later, the Protestant heads of families were summoned to an interview with the governor, Arnou, who had succeeded Demuyn in this position. They were commanded, in the king's name, to renounce the heresy of Calvin: and they were informed that, "should they withstand their sovereign's order, and stubbornly close their hearts against the Holy Ghost, His Majesty would consider himself discharged from responsibility for the pains and calamities that would befall them, beginning in this world, in punishment for their hardness of heart."

October came—the fatal month of the Revocation—and with it, the *dragonnades*. It was on the first day of this memorable month, that a letter was addressed by a Protestant of La Rochelle to some unknown person in Boston, Massachusetts, picturing in quaint but touching language the wretched condition of his fellow-religionists, and expressing their desire to seek refuge in America. "God grant that I and my family were with you; we should not been exposed to the furie of our enemies, who rob us of the goods which God hath given us to the subsistence of our soule and body. I shall not assume to write all the miseries that we suffer, which cannot be comprehended in a letter, but in many books. I shall tell you briefly, that our temple is condemned, and rased, our ministers banished forever, all their goods confiscated, and moreover they are condemned to the fine of [one] thousand crowns. All t'other temples are also rased, excepted the temple of Ré, and two or three others. By act of Parliament we are hindered to be masters in any trade or skill. We expect every days the lord governour of Guiene, who shall put soldiers in our houses, and take away our childeren to be offered to the Idol, as they have done in t'other countrys.

"The country where you live (that is to say New England) is in great estime; I and a great many others, Protestants, intend to go there. Tell us, if you please, what advantage we can have there, and particularly the boors who are accoustumed to plough the ground. If some body of your country would hazard to come here with a ship to fetch in our French Protestants, he would make great gain. All of us hope for

God's help, to whose Providence we submit ourselves, etc."[1]

The fears of this writer were soon realized. A few days later, "seven to eight thousand fusileers, just come, as it was said, from converting the Protestants in Béarn," entered La Rochelle. They were quartered in the houses of Protestants only. To one family, five soldiers were assigned, to another ten, to a third, an entire company. The scenes of disorder and outrage already witnessed in the villages of Poitou and Saintonge, were repeated in the homes of the Rochellese. "At first, these men appeared in the character of merchants in search of gain: but suddenly they were seen to be transformed, as it were, into so many lions and tigers; so that all who could escape abandoned their houses, which the soldiers at once pillaged, selling the furniture. Upon those who could not or would not leave their homes, they vented all their fury, until many who would no longer bear it, yielded to violence."[2] Three hundred families, tormented beyond all endurance, gave way,

---

[1] The above extract from the letter in question was discovered by the late Rev. Abiel Holmes, D.D., corresponding secretary of the Massachusetts Historical Society, in the MSS. collected by the Rev. Thomas Prince, and deposited in the library of that society. The document was entitled a "letter written from Rochel, the 1st of October 1684." The date is evidently a mistake for 1685. From certain peculiarities of phraseology, spelling, etc., I am convinced that the writer was Gabriel Bernon.

[2] Histoire des Réformez de la Rochelle depuis l'année 1660 jusqu' à l'année 1685 en laquelle l'Edit de Nantes a été revoqué. [Par A. Tessereau.] Amsterdam: chez la veuve de Pierre Savouret, dans le Kalver-Straat, 1689.

and suffered themselves to be enrolled among the "new converts" of Rome. Eight hundred families, however, stood firm: though the governor, having again sent for them, threatened to destroy them [*les abîmer*], if they persisted in their obstinacy. And now, four companies of the dreaded dragoons entered La Rochelle; and the heart-broken Huguenots saw them come by fifties and hundreds into their dwellings, sword in hand, with oaths and curses, as if storming a foreign city. Nothing remained for the unfortunate citizens but recantation, imprisonment or flight. Many succumbed to the temptation to purchase security and comfort, by outwardly conforming to the Church of Rome, though scarcely disguising their repugnance for her doctrines and worship. Others did not go so far, taking refuge in a verbal recantation, against which their consciences protested, and which they hastened to disavow, so soon as they were able to make their escape from France. Some utterly refused, as they expressed it, to "bow the knee to Baal," and suffered every loss and indignity that a brutal soldiery and a merciless priesthood could inflict upon them, rather than forsake the faith of their fathers. Multitudes fled to other lands, leaving their houses and their goods to be confiscated, severing all the ties that bound them to their country and their race, and carrying with them the virtues that were to contribute immensely to the worth and prosperity of the peoples that received them. By the time the Edict of Fontainebleau appeared, revoking the "irrevocable and perpetual" Edict of Nantes, Protestant La Rochelle, to all appearance, had ceased to exist.

The "large house" of Pierre Jay, "below the Bourserie," had been one of the dwellings especially marked for intrusion, when the fusileers from Béarn entered La Rochelle. Finding that the annoyances which they inflicted upon the Huguenot merchant did not avail to convert him, the governor withdrew these soldiers, and substituted for them a number of the dreaded dragoons. The situation of the family soon became intolerable. A visit to the parish priest, a word spoken, or a signature, would have sufficed at any moment to rid them of their tormentors: and many of their friends and neighbors were hastening to purchase exemption in this way from barbarities which they could no longer endure. Jay did not recant. He determined, if possible, to remove his wife and children from the house, unobserved by the dragoons, and to put them on board a vessel about to sail for Plymouth. The difficulties in the way of carrying out this plan, especially the latter part of it, were very great. The king's ships were cruising in the channel, with strict orders to search every vessel that might leave the coast; and companies of cavalry had been recently stationed by the governor of Aunis in the neighborhood of every place of embarkation along the shore. Jay, however, succeeded, and having insured the safety of his family, he remained at home, doubtless with the design of rescuing at least some portion of his property from the general wreck. It was not long, of course, before the fugitives were missed. Jay was arrested, and imprisoned in the tower of La Lanterne, under charge of having violated the severe law forbidding all connivance at the escape of Huguenots from the kingdom. Through the intervention of some influential Roman Catholic friends, he recovered his liberty. Any effort to secure his property, by sale, or collection of debts, now seemed hopeless. But it so happened that about this time several merchant ships, in the cargoes of which he was interested, were expected to arrive in the harbor of La Rochelle. Of one of these—both vessel and cargo—he was sole owner. It was a ship engaged in trade with Spain. Jay resolved to escape, in the first of these vessels that might make its appearance. To this end he instructed a pilot, upon whose fidelity he could depend, to watch for its arrival, and cause the ship to be anchored at a place agreed upon off the Isle de Ré. The vessel expected from Spain was the first to arrive. The friendly pilot lost no time in acquainting his employer with the fact: and favored by the darkness, Jay succeeded in reaching the pilot-boat, where he lay concealed for several hours, so near to one of the king's ships that he could hear the voices of the crew. At length, the wind sprang up, the cruiser sailed on, and Jay was enabled to board his own vessel, and soon joined his wife and children at Plymouth. The property they had

Vue du Port de la Rochelle du côté du bo petite Rive.

1. TOUR DE S. NICOLAS.
2. " DE LA CHAINE.
3. " DE LA LANTERNE.
4. GROSSE HORLOGE.
5. PLACE BARENTIN.

been able to carry with them, together with the proceeds of the sale of the ship and its cargo, sufficed to maintain the refugees in comfort during their remaining years.

But the anxieties of this Huguenot family were not over. The elder of Pierre Jay's two sons, Auguste, now a young man just come of age, was absent from La Rochelle at the time of his parents' flight, having been sent by his father upon a voyage to some part of Africa. On his return to La Rochelle, he found his home deserted, his father's property confiscated, and his religious faith interdicted. By the kindness of an aunt, Madame Mouchard, young Jay was able to secrete himself, until an opportunity was found for his escape from France. He reached the West Indies in safety, and made his way to South Carolina, where he intended to settle, but finally established himself in the city of New York.[1]

The fortunes of Gabriel Bernon, the emigrant to Massachusetts, were not less varied. His father, André Bernon, the merchant of La Rochelle to whom reference has been made on a preceding page, died some years before the Revocation,[2] leaving five sons and five daughters,

---

[1] The life of John Jay: with Selections from his Correspondence and Miscellaneous Papers. By his son, William Jay. New York: 1833. Vol. I., pp. 3–6.

La Rochelle d'Outre-Mer: Jean Jay. Par L. M. de Richemond. Revue Chrétienne, 1879, p. 547

[2] He was living at the time of Gabriel's marriage, when he signed the marriage contract, 23 August, 1673. His wife, Suzanne Guillemard, was then already deceased.—Bernon Papers, MS.

all of whom had reached maturity.[1] André, the eldest, was a prosperous banker, and an "ancien" of the Huguenot church. When Arnou, the cruel governor, called before him the heads of families that remained steadfast in their faith, after the first domiciliary visits of the soldiery, and threatened them with utter ruin should they persist in their obstinate course, André Bernon exclaimed with tears, "Sir, you would have me lose my soul! since it is impossible for me to believe what the religion you bid me embrace teaches." "Much do I care," was the brutal reply, "whether you lose your soul or not, provided you obey."[2] André Bernon did not long survive the destruction of his beloved church and the dispersion of his brethren. He died soon after

---

[1] André Bernon's sons were: André, Samuel, Jean, (born in 1659,) Gabriel, (born April 6, 1644,) and Jacques. His daughters were: Esther, Jeanneton, (married Jean Allaire,) Eve, (married Pierre Sanceau,) Suzanne, (married Paul de Pont,) and Marie (married Benjamin Faneuil).

[2] "Il y en avoit encore plus de huit cents [familles] qui tenoient bon. Le sieur Arnou (Intendant) fit venir de ces derniers chés lui le Samedi 6 Octobre, et après leur avoir reproché qu' ils etoient des opiniatres enragés et des rebelles aux volontés de leur souverain, il les menaça de les abymer, à moins qu'ils ne lui donnassent parole de se faire instruire. Tous, à la reserve d'un ou de deux, temoignèrent de la fermeté. Ce fut alors que le S'r André Bernon, qui avoit été un des anciens du Consistoire, et qui étoit un des bons marchans de la ville, lui dit en pleurant, et d'une manière qui en fit pleurer d' autres. *Vous m' allez damner, Monseigneur, puisqu' il m' est impossible de croire ce qu' enseigne la Religion qu' on veut que j'embrasse ;* à quoi le sieur Arnou répliqua avec insulte, *Je me soucie bien que vous vous damniez ou non, pourvû que vous obéissiez.*"

the Revocation, and was buried by night in his own garden at Périgny.[1]

Samuel and Jean, the second and third sons of André Bernon, senior, forsook the faith of their parents, and became zealous Romanists. Samuel's conversion had occurred long before the Revocation, in 1660,[2] shortly after his marriage with the daughter of a Huguenot minister, who was himself on the point of conforming to the Church of Rome.[3] Some of his letters to Gabriel, in reply to his brother's unsparing strictures upon that Church, are extant, and reveal at once the sincerity of the writer, and his credulous acquiescence in the errors and fabrications of Rome. Jean was a more recent proselyte. Educated for the Protestant ministry, he became pastor of the Reformed church of Saint Just,[4] near Marennes, in the province of Saintonge: but at the time of the Revocation, he followed the example of his brother Samuel, and like him

---

[1] Histoire des Réformez de la Rochelle, etc., pp. 297-281, 302.

[2] Filleau, Dictionnaire historique et généalogique des familles de l'ancien Poitou. Vol. I., p. 313.

[3] Marie Cottiby, daughter of Samuel Cottiby, pastor at Poitiers, 1653 to 1660. Complaint of his conduct while pastor having been made to the Synod of Loudun, Cottiby hastened to abjure Protestantism. He was rewarded with the office of king's attorney for the district of La Rochelle. —(Lièvre, Histoire des protestants et des églises réformées du Poitou, III., 78, 79.) La France Protestante, deuxième édition, vol. II., p. 390, erroneously states that Samuel Bernon's *father*, as well as his father-in-law, abjured Protestantism on this occasion.

[4] Pasteur de S. Just, 1661-77, mais qui abjura à la Révocation.—La France Protestante.

Chap. V.
1685.

escaped the miseries that befell others of his kindred. Samuel, "sieur de Salins"—his Huguenot name,[1] the only trace he retained of a Huguenot extraction—lived in comfort, if not in luxury, in the city of Poitiers, in Poitou, "having acquired a large fortune while engaged in commercial transactions, both in America and Europe."[2] Jean, "sieur de Luneau,"[3] resided in Marennes, or in the neighboring parish of Saint Just, where he had exercised his Protestant ministry, and where he seems to have acquired an estate, perhaps the reward of his abjuration.[4] He sometimes joined with Samuel in endeavors to persuade his fugitive brother Gabriel, in America, and his sister Esther, then in England, to come back to France, renounce their heresy, and live under that king whose subjects they were by birth. " Our brother de St. Jeux [St. Just]," writes Samuel to Gabriel, " can better than I explain to you the difficulties upon matters of religion that may prevent you from returning to your dear country. He has very correct ideas on these matters; I do not think

Fervent Proselytes.

---

[1] Samuel : "nom inusité alors chez les catholiques, et en honneur chez les protestants."—Histoire de la colonie française du Canada. I. Note XXI.
[2] Filleau, Dictionnaire des familles de l'ancien Poitou. I., p. 313.
[3] Sgr du fief de Feusse et du fief Luneau.—Filleau.
[4] Jean Bernon is repeatedly mentioned by Samuel in his letters to Gabriel, as "notre frère de St. Jeux"—*i. e.*, St. Just. Gabriel names him but once. In an inventory of his property on leaving La Rochelle, "mons^r. Jean Bernon mon frère" is mentioned as owing him a sum of £140, under the head " Dettes douteuses."

that he makes as much use of them as he should."[1]

Gabriel Bernon, fourth son of André, had reached the age of forty-one at the time of the Revocation.[2] Associated with his father, and succeeding him in business, he was now one of the leading merchants of La Rochelle. His accounts show very extensive commercial relations with the chief towns of the neighboring provinces—Poitiers, Limoges, Angoulême, Niort, Châtellerault, Loudun, and other places; and a foreign trade with Martinique, St. Christopher, Cayenne, and St. Domingo. More important than any of these transactions, however, had been the trade with Canada. In Quebec, as we have seen already, he was recognized as the principal French merchant, and as having rendered great services to the colony. But he was also an inflexible Huguenot: and the clergy, to whom just now the destruction of heresy was the only consideration, were bent upon his ruin. "It is a pity," wrote the governor of Canada, "that he cannot be converted. As he is a Huguenot, the bishop wants me to order him home this autumn, which I have done, though he carries on a large business, and *a great deal of*

---

[1] Jean Bernon died in or before the year 1714.

[2] "Le Mardy douziesme Apruil mil six cents quarante quattre a esté Baptizé par Monsr. Vincent; Gabriel fils de André Bernon et de Suzanne Guillemard—parrain Gabriel Prieur marrayne Marie Guillemard; Il est né le sixiesme dudit mois Signé G. Prieur P. Vincent. Cy dessus est Extraict du papier des Baptesmes du Consistoire de la Rochelle. A. Bernon."—Bernon Papers, MSS.

money remains due to him here." Recantation or ruin—the Huguenot merchant was to make his choice. Gabriel Bernon reached La Rochelle in the height of the persecution that had commenced in the spring preceding. He was thrown into prison, where he languished for some months.[1] An interesting memorial of this period of suffering is preserved by one of his descendants in Rhode Island: a French psalter, of microscopic size, given him, it is said, by a fellow-prisoner in the tower of La Lanterne. After some months, he was released, perhaps through the influence of his Roman Catholic brothers: and soon after, having made such disposition of his remaining property as he could make, he found means to escape from France to Holland. His wife, Esther Le Roy, endeavored to accompany him, but was arrested in the attempt. She feigned conversion, was released, and soon rejoined her husband.[2]

André Sigourney, and Charlotte Pairan his wife, were living in comfortable circumstances in La Rochelle, when the quartering of troops commenced. Determined not to renounce their faith, they laid their plans for escape, and suc-

---

[1] His goods were seized on the thirteenth of October, 1685. His imprisonment probably extended from this date to the beginning of May, 1686, when, upon his release, he prepared a balance-sheet, showing the condition of his affairs. This document is headed "A la Rochelle, le 10 May 1686. Extrait de ce quy mest Dh'eu en Divers endroits, dont Jay mis les partes en mains de mons^r. Sanceau, le 10e May 1686."

[2] *La France Protestante*: deuxième edition, vol. II., p. 391.

ceeded in quietly transferring a portion of their effects to a vessel in the harbor. The day fixed upon for the attempt to leave, was a holiday. The family provided a bountiful feast for the soldiers billeted upon them, and while these were in the height of their carousal, they departed unobserved. The weather was stormy, and they had a rough and perilous passage across the channel, but reached England safely.

Often, the happiness of those who effected their escape was overcast by sadness, in view of the failure of others in the same attempt.

Many of our refugee families left behind them those near and dear to them; the men—if steadfast in their faith—liable to be shut up in prisons; the women, sent to convents, worse than prisons. Pierre Sanceau, Gabriel Bernon's brother-in-law, reached England almost penniless. "As for my poor wife and daughter," he says, "they are still in La Rochelle. They have been repeatedly sent to the convents. Just now, they are out, but on warning."

The two sons of Roch Chastaignier, seigneur de Cramahé, who fled from La Rochelle, and reached South Carolina, had an elder brother, Hector François Chastaignier, who sought to make his escape at the same time, but was captured. Thrown into prison, and subjected to the most shameful maltreatment, he displayed a heroic fortitude and a constancy worthy of the early martyrs.[1]

---

[1] In the lists of persons who suffered persecution in Aunis, we recognize not a few namesakes of our American

refugees. Benoist, the historian of the Edict of Nantes, mentions the following: G. Cothonneau, E. Dechezault, C. Ayrault, I. Valleau, P. Valleau, Chaillé, Etienne Jouneau, Daniel Renault, Philippe Janvier, Grégoire Gougeon, Beaudoin, France, Du Tay, Nicolas Rappe, Alaire, Mercier, Papin. Samuel Pintard—doubtless a relative of the refugee in New York—was in 1695 a galley-slave upon the ship La Grande.

APPENDIX.

ERRATA.

VOLUME I.

Page vi., line 31, for "1879," read "1877."
Page viii., line 4, for "John William," read "William John."
Page 31, lines 14, 15, for "two furlongs," read "six furlongs."
Page 35, lines 22, 23, read "impetuous."
Page 121, line 7, for "were," read "was."
Page 175, line 3 from foot, for "the time," read "at the time."
Page 222, *note*, line 4, for "Benoist, V.," read "Benoist, IV."
Page 224, last line,   "   "   "   "
Page 263, line 25, read "The present chapter and the following one."
Page 276, line 11, for "after," read "shortly before."
Page 320, *note*, line 2, for "1659," read "1639."

VOLUME II.

Page 97, lines 3, 22, for "Orléannais," read "Orléanais."
Page 124, line 6 from foot, for "Paul," read "Jean."
Page 125, lines 11, 12, from foot, for "Marguerite," read "Louise."
Page 148, margin, for "1684–1686," read "1681–1686."
Page 218, line 2 from foot, for "Edict," read "Edit."
Page 241, line 20 from foot, omit "au."

APPENDIX.

LETTER OF THE MINISTERS RICHER AND CHARTIER TO CALVIN.

[See above, pages 41, 42.]

RICHERIUS ET CHARTERIUS CALVINO.

* * * Quum enim ad eum locum pervenissemus in quo is erat qui partim sua autoritate, partim consilio, partim sumptibus (quantum ei licet) huius ecclesiæ primordia curat, qui et huius nostri instituti dux et caput est, in Gallia multa nobis resolvenda fuerunt in quibus sapientia divina clarissime apparuit. Alia præterea illic gesta sunt, verum talia quæ nos consolare potius quam tristitia afficere deberent: præsertim quum videremus multos verbi Dei cupidos, et ea quæ nobis necessaria essent polliceretur qui præstare poterat, tum ad libros emendos, tum ad vestimenta comparanda, tum ad itineris sumptus faciendos. Quum autem pervenissemus Lutetiam, ecclesiam Christi illic congregatam optime verbo Dei comperimus, unde maxime sumus consolati, videntes adimpleri Davidis vaticinium quo prævidebat Christi regnum in medio inimicorum suorum stabile fore, quod te nostris ad te literis iam intellexisse confidentes pluribus verbis non prosequemur. Peracto Lutetiæ omni nostro negotio appulimus portuum maris vulgo appellatum Honnefleur: die autem Novembris 19 ingressi sumus naves quarum ministerio huc usque tandem pervenimus hancque insulam quam appellant de Couligni introivimus die 7 Martii, ubi cœlitus nobis paratum invenimus et patrem et fratrem Nicolaum *Villagaignonem*. Patrem dico quia nos uti filios amplectitur, alit et fovet, fratrem vero quia nobiscum unicum patrem cœlestem Deum invocat, Iesum Christum solum esse Dei et hominum mediatorem credit, in eius iustitia se coram Deo iustum esse non dubitat, spiritus sancti interno motu apud se ipsum experitur se vere membrum Christi esse: cuius rei testimonia non pauca vidimus. Delectatur enim verbo Dei, cui ne doctorum quidem antiquorum dogmata, quamvis multis sacra videantur, præferre instituit. Carnis certe indicium hoc vix admittit, quandoquidem antiquitas apud eum multum potest: eo usque tamen pervenit ut animum suum sancto puroque Dei verbo regi sinat. Honeste et prudenter familiæ suæ præest, quæ illius ecclesiæ speciem præferre videtur quam in domo suo habebant Priscilla aut Aquilla aut illius quæ apud Nympham erat. Quo fit ut speremus brevi futurum ut inde prodeant amplissimæ

1557.

1557. ecclesiæ quæ laudem Dei celebrent et Christi regnum augeant. Is enim optimum sinceræ veræque christianæ religionis exemplar et dux se ipsum præbuit, tum in audiendis publicis concionibus et orationibus, quibus aderant et omnes eius domestici, tum in percipienda sacra coena Christi quam avidissime et religiosissime excepit. Priusquam autem ad hoc cœleste convivium accederet, publicam fidei suæ confessionem clara voce protulit, et Solomonem imitatus locum in quo eramus congregati precibus Deo se dicare declaravit, seque et sua omnia ad eius gloriam propagandam parata esse professus est.

Sed ne historiam texere potius quam te nostrarum rerum certiorem facere videamur, reliquorum narrationem tabellario familiarissime tibi cognito relinquentes, a quo privatis colloquutionibus quæcunque nobis acciderunt poteris intelligere, scriptis nostris finem imponemus: modo te rogaverimus ut tuas præces in conspectu Dei effundas, quo perperficiat Christi ædificium quod in his terræ finibus inchoatum est, et admoneas omnes quos Deum timere et exanimo venerari cognoscis, ut idem tecum agant. Hoc autem Eleutheropoli [*Genevæ*], cui te ministrum evangelii præposuit, iam absolutum præcamur ut conserveret, foveat, in tranquillo et pacato statu retineat, simulque suas ecclesias ubique sua paterna clementia congregatas cœlesti fortitudine muniat. Collegas tuos omnes saluta, si lubet, nostro nomine, nominatim autem Nicolaum *Galazium, P. Viretum* et Theodorem *Bezam*. Insulæ Couligniensi quæ prima Francorum exculta fuit habitatio in Antarctica Gallia. Cal. Aprilis anno 1556.[1]

Tui fratres quos evangelii ministros esse iussisti.

G. CHARTERIUS,   RICHERIUS,
tuus in Christo.   tuus in Christo.

Corpus Reformatorum, Vol. XLIV. Joannis Calvini Opera quæ supersunt omnia. Ediderunt Gulielmus Baum, Eduardus Cunitz, Eduardus Reuss, Theologi Argentoratenses, Vol. XVI. Brunsvigæ, 1877. No. 2613. Richerius et Charterius Calvino. A Monsr. despeville. Pp. 440-3.

(Translation.)

* * * For, when we had come to that place in which he resided who, partly by his influence, partly by counsel, partly by expenditure of money (so far as he can) looks to the first beginnings of this church, who also is leader and head of this undertaking of ours, we had many things to settle in which the Divine wisdom most clearly appeared. Moreover, other matters were done there, but such as ought rather to cheer than to sadden us: especially since we saw many persons eager for the word of God, and he who could afford it promised those things that we needed both for the purchase of books, and the obtaining of clothing, and the expenses of the journey. When, however, we reached Paris, we ascertained that a church of Christ had there been gathered in the

---

[1] In anno manifestus error.

best manner according to God's word, whereby we were most greatly cheered, seeing the fulfillment of David's prophecy who foresaw that Christ's kingdom would be established in the midst of His enemies. Being confident that you already understand this by our letters to you, we shall say no more. All our business being transacted at Paris, we pushed on to the seaport commonly called Honfleur. On the 19th day of November we embarked on vessels, by means of which we at length came hither, and entered upon this island which they call de Couligni, on the 7th day of March, where we found there had been provided for us by Heaven, both as father and brother, *Nicholas Villegaignon*. I style him father, because he embraces, nurtures and cherishes us as sons; and brother, because with us he invokes God as his only heavenly Father. He believes Jesus Christ to be the only Mediator between God and men, he does not doubt that in His justice he is just before God, by the inner moving of the Holy Ghost within him he knows from experience that he is in truth a member of Christ: of which thing we have seen not a few proofs. For he delights in the word of God, to which he purposes to prefer not even the tenets of ancient doctors, however many may hold them sacred. This certainly scarcely leaves room for the judgment of the flesh, since antiquity has great weight with him: to this point, however, has he come that he permits his mind to be governed by the holy and pure word of God. Honestly and prudently does he preside over his family, which seems to present the appearance of that church which Priscilla and Aquila had in their house, or of that which was in the house of Nymphas. Hence we hope that there shall shortly come forth from it most illustrious churches that shall publish abroad the praise of God and increase the kingdom of Christ. For this man has shown himself a most excellent exemplar of and guide to sincere and true Christian religion, both by attending upon public meetings and sermons, at which also all those of his house were present, and in partaking of the holy Supper of Christ, which he has received with the utmost eagerness and devotion. But before approaching this heavenly feast, he made with a clear voice a public profession of his faith, and, imitating Solomon, declared that he dedicated the place wherein we were gathered by prayers to God, and announced that he and all his goods were consecrated to the spread of His glory.

But lest we should seem to be weaving a tale, rather than informing you respecting our affairs, we shall leave the narration of the rest to the bearer, who is most familiarly known to you, from whom you will be able to learn in private conversation whatever has happened to us, and shall close our letter.

Only we shall ask you to pour out your prayers in God's sight, that He may perfect the building of Christ that has been begun in these ends of the earth, and to exhort all those whom you know to fear and heartily to reverence God, to unite with you in doing the same thing. This also we now pray earnestly for Eleutheropolis [the "Free City"—sc., Geneva], over which He has placed you as a minister of the Gospel, that He may preserve, foster, maintain it in tranquillity and peace, and at the same time arm with heavenly

1557. courage His churches everywhere gathered through His fatherly mercy. Salute all your colleagues, if you please, in our name, and by name Nicholas des Gallars, Pierre Viret and Théodore de Bèze. On the Island de Coligni which is the first civilized habitation of the French in Antarctic France, April 1st, 1556.[1]
 Your brethren whom you bade to be ministers of the Gospel.

G. CHARTIER,   RICHER,
Yours in Christ,   Yours in Christ.

LETTER OF THE MINISTER RICHER TO AN UNKNOWN CORRESPONDENT.

[See above, pages 41, 42.]

RICHERIUS INCERTO.

Gratia et pax a Deo per Iesum Christum.
 Nolui oblatam occasionem præterire, frater, quin tuam humanitatem de rebus nostris certiorem facerem : inprimis notum tibi esse velim beneficium, quod a Domino hactenus accepimus, ut eiusdem bonitati digneris nobiscum gratias referre. Id utique est quemadmodum optamus. Quandoquidem omnium nostrum talem pro sua bonitate habuit curam, ut per tam varia terrarum et maris discrimina, omnes nos ad portum sanos et incolumes perduxerit. Satan quidem, ut est sui similis, diversis nos in itinere exposuit periculis : sed ut filii (etsi hoc nomine indigni) experti sumus semper tanti patris manum auxiliatricem : quam etiam benigne exporrigit in dies magis ac magis erga nos. Altero die postquam appulimus *Villagagno* voluit verbum Dei publice prædicari : deinde subsequenti hebdomada sacrosanctam Christi cœnam administrari expetivit, quam et ipse cum aliquot e suis domesticis religiose adiit, reddita primum suæ fidei ratione cum magna ecclesiæ quæ aderat ædificatione. Quid commodius nostro instituto contingere poterat ? Quid demum votis omnibus nostrum respondisset opportunius, quam ut his tesseris apud nos vera appareret ecclesia ? Talibus beneficiis dignatus est nos prosequi benignus ille summus pater. Regio hæc autem, quod sit inculta raroque habitatore, nihil fere profert quod nostrates vel gustare vellent. Milium quidem, ficus sylvestres et quasdam radices quibus farinam ad viaticum conficiunt, suis gignit incolis. Panem vero non habet, nec vinum aut quid vino proximum profert. Imo nec fructum aliquem (quem noverim) quo quandoque usi fuerimus. Nihilominus tamen nobis bene est, et recte valemus : imo ut me exempli vice proferam, vegetior sum solito : sed et id omnibus aliis commune est. Beneficium aeri adscriberet physicus, qui adeo temperatus sit ut nostro respondeat Maio. Sed ne tanta

---

[1] That is " avant Pâques," Old Style, but New Style, Thursday, April 1, 1557.

APPENDIX. 333

summo illi maximo et optimo numini irrogetur iniuria, dicam quod sentio. Hoc modo paternum suum affectum nobis aperit bonus ille cœlestis pater, qui hic in tam barbaro et agresti solo suum nobis ministrat favorem, adeo ut experiamur viaticum hominis pendere non e pane, sed e verbo Dei, cuius favor hic nobis est omnium delitiarum loco. Unum est quod nos non mediocriter urget et angit, populi scilicet barbaries, quæ tanta est ut maior esse non possit. Non affero, quod sint anthropophagi, quod tamen illis adeo vulgare est ut nil magis: sed doleo crassam mentis eorum hebetudinem, quæ mediis in tenebris tamen est palpabilis. De virtute patris quamvis ethica* nihil norunt prorsus, bonum a malo non secernunt, denique vitia quæ natura in cæteris gentibus naturaliter arguit loco virtutis habent: saltem vitiorum turpitudinem non agnoscunt, adeo ut hac in re a brutis parum differant. Cæterum quod omnium perniciosissimum est, latet eos an sit Deus, tantum abest ut legem eius observent, vel potentiam et bonitatem eius mirentur: quo fit ut prorsus sit nobis adempta spes lucrifaciendi eos Christo: quod ut omnium est gravissimum, ita inter cætera maxime ægre ferimus. Audio quidem qui mox obiiciet eos tabulam rasam esse, quæ facile suis possit depingi coloribus, quod nativo huiusmodi colorum splendori nihil habeat contrarium. Sed norit ille quantum impediat idiomatum diversitas. Adde quod desunt nobis interpretes, qui Domino sint fideles. Proposueramus quidem illorum ministerio et industria uti: scilicet reperimus illos ipsissima esse Satanæ membra, quibus nihil magis invisum quam sanctum Christi evangelium. Proinde hac in re nobis operæ pretium est sistere gradum, patienterque exspectare, donec adolescentuli, quos Dominus a *Villagagnone* barbaris huius patriæ tradidit erudiendos, norint naturalem ipsorum distinguere linguam. Ad hoc enim illi apud eos degunt et versantur. Faxit Deus ut sit hoc illis citra aliquod animarum suarum periculum. Nam ubi hoc munere nos donarit Altissimus, speramus hanc Idumeam futuram Christo possessionem. Interim expectamus frequentiorem populum, cuius conversatione et formetur hæc natio barbara, et nostra ecclesia suum accipiat incrementum. Abundaremus utique omni bonorum copia, si hic frequens adesset populus. Nam quod tenuis et modica sit annona, id efficit rarus habitator, et somnolentus agricola. Sed iis omnibus prospiciet Altissimus. Nos vero nostratum omnium ecclesiarem precibus commendari obnixe cupimus. Ex Gallia antarctica, pridie Aprilis, 1557.

                                 Tuus P. RICHERIUS.

Joannis Calvini Opera quæ supersunt omnia. Volumen XVI., p. 433. No. 2609. Richerius incerto. Primitiæ Brasilianæ.

1557.

*Ethnica!

(*Translation.*)

Grace and peace from God through Jesus Christ.

I was unwilling to neglect the opportunity that offered, brother, to inform your excellence respecting our affairs. First of all, I would wish you to know the favor we have thus far received from God, in order that you may deign with us to render thanks to His goodness. That certainly is as we wish. Since in His goodness

1557. He has had such a care of all ours, that through so various dangers of land and sea, He has brought us all safe and sound to port. Satan, indeed, as he is ever like himself, exposed us on the way to different dangers : but as sons (although unworthy of this name) we have always experienced the helping hand of so great a Father: which also He benignantly extends to us more and more from day to day. The day after our arrival, *Villegagnon* wished the word of God to be publicly preached: then on the following week [Lord's Day] he asked that the holy Supper of Christ should be administered, which he also himself religiously approached with some of those of his household, after first having made a profession of his faith, to the great edification of the church that was present. What could have happened more favorable to our design? What indeed would have more opportunely answered all our wishes, than that by these tokens a true church might appear among us? With such favors has the supreme Father deigned to follow us. This region, however, because it is uncultivated and sparsely inhabited, produces scarcely any thing that our men will even taste. It brings forth for its inhabitants, indeed, millet, wild figs, and certain roots with which they prepare flour for sustenance. But it has no bread, nor does it produce wine or any thing resembling wine; nay, not even any fruit (that I know) which we have ever used. Nevertheless, we are in good condition and very well: nay, to bring myself forward as an example, I am more vigorous than usual : but this is also the common experience of all the rest. A natural philosopher would ascribe the benefit to the air, which is so mild as to correspond with our month of May. But lest so great a wrong should be done to that greatest and highest Being, I shall say what I think. In this way does our heavenly Father show us his paternal affection, who here in so barbarous and savage a soil ministers to us His favor, so that we learn from experience that man's sustenance depends not on bread, but on the word of God, whose favor is here in lieu of all delights to us. There is one thing that burdens and grieves us not a little, namely, the barbarism of the people, which is so great that there cannot be greater. I do not refer to the fact that they are man-eaters, a thing so common with them, however, that nothing is more common: but I mourn the gross dullness of their minds, which in the midst of the darkness still can be felt. Of a father's virtue, however moral,* they know nothing whatever; they do not discern good from bad ; in fine, the vices which nature among other nations naturally condemns they hold as virtue: at least they do not recognize the baseness of vices, so that in this matter they differ little from the brutes. But what is most pernicious of all, they know not whether there be a God, so far are they from observing His law, or admiring His power and goodness: hence it arises that the hope of gaining them for Christ is quite taken away from us : which as it is of all things most grievous, so among others we are most distressed by it. I hear, indeed, some one objecting that these men are a *tabula rasa*, which can easily be painted with its colors, because it contains nothing contrary to such a native resplendence of colors. But let him know how great

* Or, albeit heathenish.

APPENDIX.   335

an obstacle is the diversity of language. Add to this that we have a lack of interpreters that are faithful to the Lord. We had intended, indeed, to employ the services and activity of those [we had]: but we have found them to be the very limbs of Satan, to whom nothing is more hateful than Christ's holy Gospel. Therefore in this matter it is best for us to pause and wait patiently, until some young men, whom the Sieur de *Villegagnon* has given over to be taught to the barbarians of this country, shall have learned to comprehend the native tongue of the latter. For, with this end in view, they are spending their time and occupying themselves among them. God grant that this may be without any peril to their souls! For when the Most High shall have vouchsafed us this gift, we hope that this Edom will be Christ's possession. Meanwhile we are expecting a more numerous population, by association with which both this barbarous nation may be fashioned, and our church may be increased. Certainly we should have an abundance of good things, if there were here a large population. For that the harvest is light and moderate is occasioned by the fewness of the inhabitants and the sluggishness of the tillers of the soil. But for all these things the Most High will provide. We earnestly desire to be commended to the prayers of all our churches. From Antarctic France, the day before the Calends of April [March 31st] 1557.   Your P. RICHER.

1557.

Complete extant Works of John Calvin. Volume XVI., p. 433. No. 2609. Richer to an uncertain correspondent. First fruits of Brazil.

LETTER OF VILLEGAGNON TO CALVIN.

[See above, pages 42, 43.]

VILLEGAGNON CALVINO.

Exprimi non posse puto quo me affecerint gaudio tuæ literæ, et qui ad me una venere fratres. Huc me redactum invenerunt, ut mihi magistratus gerendus esset et munus ecclesiasticum subeundum. Quæ mihi res maximam anxietatem obtulerat. Ozias ab hac vitæ ratione me avertebat: sed præstandum erat ne operarii nostri quos mercede traduxeram gentis adducti consuetudine eius se vitiis contaminarent, aut religionis desuetudine in ἀπόστασιν devolverentur. Quam mihi sollicitudinem ademit fratrum adventus. Adiecit hoc etiam commodi quod si qua ex causa post hac erit nobis laborandum aut periculum incurrendum, non deerunt qui sint mihi solatio et me consilio iuvent. Cuius rei facultatem abstulerat periculi nostri suspicio. Qui enim fratres mecum a Francia traiecerant, rerum nostrarum iniquitate permoti alius alia causa illata Ægyptum repetiverant. Qui fuerunt reliqui homines egentes mercede conducti quos pro tempore nancisci potueram, eorum hæc erat conditio ut ab eis mihi potius esset metuendum quam petendum solatium. Hæc autem huius rei causa est. Ubi

1557. appulimus simul omnis generis se nobis opposuere difficultates, ut vix inirem rationem quid potissimum esset agendum. Regio erat incultissima, nulla erant tecta, rei frumentariæ nulla copia. Sed aderant homines feri, ab omni cultu et humanitate alieni, moribus et disciplina penitus a nobis discrepantes, sine religione, honoris, virtutis, recti aut iniusti ulla notitia, ut me subitet dubitatio an in bestias humana specie præditas incidissemus. Contra hæc incommoda erat summo studio et celeritate nobis prospiciendum et comparandum remedium, dum naves ad reditum instruebantur, ne eo subsidio destitutos indigenæ, rerum nostrarum capti cupiditate, nos imparatos opprimerent et interficerent. Huc quoque accedebat Lusitanorum infida vicinitas, qui [*etsi*] quam incolimus regionem tueri non potuerunt huc tamen [*nos*] esse intromissos ferunt ægerrime et insano odio prosequ [*untur*]. Eam ob rem uno tempore hæc omnia se nobis agenda proponebant. Receptui nostro locus deligendus, expurgandus et complanandus, munitiones circumducendæ, propugnacula excitanda, tecta ad impedimentorum custodiam exstruenda, materia conquirenda, et adverso colle locis impeditissimis, humeris ob bestiarum penuriam comportanda. Præterea quod indigenæ in diem vivant et agriculturæ non studeant nullo certo loco cibaria congesta reperiebamus, sed erat victus noster e lonquinquo carptim petendus. Qua ex re manum nostram, quantulacunque esset, disteneri oportebat et minui. His adducti difficultatibus qui meæ amicitiæ causa sequuti fuerant rebus nostris diffisi, ut supra demonstravimus, pedem retulerunt. Ego quoque non nihil commotus sum. Sed quum mecum reputarem amicis affirmasse, me hac ratione e Francia movere ut quam curam prius rebus humanis impenderam eius studii comperta vanitate regno Christi excolendo adhiberem, iudicavi me in voces et hominum reprehensionem incursurum et nomini meo iniuriam facturum, si labor aut periculi opinio a cœpto me deterreret. Præterea quum Christi negotium gerendum esset, credidi hunc mihi non defuturum sed ad felicem exitum perducturum. Ergo me confirmavi vimque omnem ingenii intendi in rationem eius rei perficiendæ quam summa vitæ meæ devotione susceperam. Hac autem via id assequi me posse existimavi, si vitæ integritate hoc meum propositum comprobarem, et quam operariorum manum traduxeram ab infidelium consortio et familiaritate averterem. In eam sententiam animo meo inclinato non sine Dei providentia factum esse visum est ut in hæc negotia involveremur, sed id accidisse ne otio corrupti libidini et lasciviæ operam daremus. Præterea succurrit nihil esse tam arduum quin conando superari possit. Proinde ab animi fortitudine petendum esse auxilium et continenti labore familiam exercendam : huic nostro studio Dei beneficientiam non defuturam. Itaque in insulam duobus millibus passuum a continenti remotam transmissimus, ibique domicilio nostro locum delegi, ut adempta fugæ facu [*ltate manum nostram in*] officio continerem, et quod feminæ sin[*e viris suis non essent, ad*] nos commeaturæ delinquendi occasionem [*præriperem*. *Accidit tamen*] ut e mercenariis 26 voluptatis illecti cupiditate in m[*eam vitam conspiraverint*]. Sed die constituta consilio exsequendo res mi[*hi per unum ex*] consciis enunciata es ipso momento quo ad me opprimen[*dum*] armati admaturabant, hoc modo periculum effugimus. Quinque e meis domesticis ad arma convocavi et adversum ire cœpi. Tum tantus coniuratis incessit terror tantaque perturbatio, ut nullo negotio facinoris autores quatuor, qui mihi fuerant designati, corripuerimus et in vincula coniecerimus. Eo casu reliqui consternati positis armis delituerunt. Postridie unum catenis exsolvimus ut causam suam diceret liberius. Sed effuso cursu in mare se præcipitem egit et suffocavit. Reliqui ut e vinculis causam dicerent adducti sine quæstione ultro exposuerunt quæ per indicem comperta habuimus. Unus ex ipsis, paulo ante a me castigatus quod se scorto coniunxisset, iniquiore esse mente cognitus est, et ab se coniurationis initium factum esse, atque scorti patrem muneribus devinxisse, ut eum e nostra potestate eriperet, si scorti copulam prohibere contenderem. Hic suspendio sceleris pœnas luit: duobus reliquis delicti gratiam fecimus, ita tamen ut in catenis terram exercerent. In aliis quid esset peccati exquirendum esse mihi non putavi, ne compertum scelus inultum omitterem, aut si supplicio castigare vellem, quum facinus ad multitudinem pertineret, non superessent qui opus a nobis institutum perficerent. Itaque dissimulata animi mei offensione peccatum condonavimus, et omnes animo bono esse iussimus. Non ita tamen a sollicitudine nos abduximus quin quid in unoquoque esset animi ex studio curaque sua quotidiana diligentissime venaremur. Et quum labori eorum non parcerem, sed assidua mea præsentia ad opus eos urgerem, non solum pravis consiliis vitam præclusimus sed brevi tempore insulam nostram munitionibus [*et validi*]ssimis propugnaculis sæpivimus. Interim pro ingenii mei [*captu e*]os monere et a vitiis deterrere non desistebam, atque [*ment*]es eorum christiana imbuere religione, indictis a me mane [*et*] vesperi publicis et quotidianis precibus: qua cautione et diligentia reliquam anni partem quietiorem habuimus. Cæterum eam quam exposuimus curam nobis ademit navium nostrarum adventus. Hinc enim nactus sum viros a quibus non solum mihi sit minime cavendum, sed quibus salutem meam tuto possim committere. Hac oblata mihi facultate decem ex omni copia delegi, apud quos imperii nostri potestatem deposui, decernens ut nullæ res posthac nisi consilio gerantur. Adeo si quid in quemquam durius statuerem, nisi consilii autoritas et consensus accederet, infirmum esset et inane. Hoc tamen mihi reservavi ut lata sententia supplicii veniam dare mihi liceat. Sic omnibus prodesse, nemini nocere possum. Hæ demum sunt artes quibus dignitatem nostram retinere tueri et propugnare constitui.

Addam consilium quod literis tuis adhibuisti, summa animi contentione operam daturus ut ne vel tantillum ab eo deflectamus. Hoc enim certe nec sanctius nec rectius nec sanius ullum esse persuasum habeo. Quamobrem etiam tuas literas in senatu nostro legendas, deinde in acta transscribendas curavimus ut, si quando a cursu aberrare contigerit, earum lectio ab errore revocet. Dominus noster Iesus Christus ab omni malo te tuosque collegas protegat, spiritu suo vos confirmet vitamque vestram ad opus ecclesiæ suæ quam longissime producat. Fratribus meis carissimis *Cepha* et *de la Fleche* fidelibus plurimam salutem meis verbis velim impertias. Collignio e Francia antarctica prid. Cal. Aprilis 1557.

1557.

1557.   Si ad *Renatam* Franciæ heram nostram quidpiam literarum dederis, hanc quæso meo nomine diligentissime saluta. Tui amantissimus cupidissimus et ex animo

N̂ᶦ[1]

Ioannis Calvini Opera quæ supersunt omnia. Volumen XVI., p. 437, No. 2612. Villegagnon Calvino. Historiam novæ suæ coloniæ in Francia antarctica, quam vocat, enarrat.

(*Translation.*)

I deem it impossible to express with what gladness your letters, and the brethren that came to me with them, have affected me. They found me reduced to this necessity, that I must discharge the office of magistrate and take upon me the ecclesiastical functions. This thing had brought me very great anxiety. Ozias dissuaded me from this mode of life: but I had to discharge it lest our workmen whom I had brought over on hire, led by the custom of that class, should contaminate themselves with vices, or through disuse of religion should fall into apostasy. This solicitude the coming of our brethren removed from me. There was this additional advantage that, should there hereafter from any cause be labor or danger to be undergone by us, there will not be wanting those that will be a comfort and will help me by their counsel. The possibility of this had been taken away by the suspicion of our danger. For the brethren that had come over with me from France, induced by the unfavorable condition of our affairs, one alleging one reason, another another, had sought Egypt again. Those who remained, needy men hired for pay, whom I had according to circumstances been able to find, were of such a condition that I had rather to entertain fear than to seek consolation from them. This was the reason. The moment we arrived, difficulties of every kind presented themselves to us, so that I scarcely could determine what was best to be done. The region was most uncultivated, there were no houses, there was no store of grain. But there were here savages, strangers to all civilization and gentleness, altogether dissimilar to us in manners and training, without religion, with no knowledge of honor, virtue, justice or injustice, so that the doubt entered my mind whether we had not fallen upon beasts possessed of human form. For these disadvantages we had to look out and provide a remedy, while the ships were made ready for a return, lest the natives, seized upon by the desire for our property, might overwhelm us destitute of help and unprepared, and might slay us. To this was added the treacherous proximity of the Portuguese, who, although they were unable to retain the region which we inhabit, nevertheless are very greatly annoyed that we have entered it, and pursue us with insane hatred. Consequently all these things presented themselves to be done at

---

[1] Nicolaus (*Durand de Villegagnon*). Siglum ita scriptum est ut etiam V repræsentetur.

one and the same time : a spot was to be selected for our reception, 1557. and was to be cleared and leveled; fortifications were to be thrown about it, defenses were to be reared, houses were to be erected for the protection of our effects, timber was to be obtained, and to be carried up hill, through places very difficult of passage, on the shoulders of men, on account of the lack of beasts of burden. Moreover because the natives live as best they can from day to day and do not practice agriculture, we found stores of food brought together in no certain place, but our means of subsistence had to be sought, now here and now there, from afar. Hence our band, small as it was, had to be scattered and diminished. Influenced by these difficulties those who had followed me out of friendship, being distrustful of our success, as I have above shown, retired. I also was somewhat disturbed. But when I bethought myself that I had asserted to my friends, that I was moved to depart from France for this reason, that, having discovered the vanity of the pursuit of human affairs, I might devote the care I had previously given to them, to the promotion of the kingdom of Christ, I judged that I should incur the talk and censure of mankind and wrong my own name, should toil or belief of danger deter me from my undertaking. Moreover when Christ's business was to be transacted, I believed that He would not desert me but would lead me to a happy issue. Therefore I took heart and bent the whole energy of my mind to the mode of carrying to its completion the matter I had undertaken with the supreme devotion of my life. This I thought I might attain in this way : namely, if I should attest my purpose by the integrity of my life, and preclude the band of workmen, which I had brought over with me, from association and familiarity with the unbelievers. My mind being inclined to this opinion, it seemed to have been brought to pass not without the providence of God that we should be involved in these occupations, but that this had happened in order that we might not be corrupted by idleness, and give ourselves up to lust and wantonness. Moreover it occurred to me that nothing is so hard but that it can be overcome by effort. Therefore help must be sought from fortitude of mind, and the household must be trained by constant labor: to this zeal of ours the kindness of God would not be lacking. So we crossed to an island distant two miles from the continent, and there I chose a spot for our habitation, in order that, the opportunity of flight being taken away, I might keep our band in the path of duty; and, since the women would not come to us without their husbands, I might remove the occasion for committing sin. It happened, however, that twenty-six of the hired men, enticed by desire, conspired against my life. But, on the day appointed for the execution of the plan, the matter being announced to me by one of the culprits at the very moment when armed men were preparing to overwhelm me, we escaped the danger in the following manner: I called five of my domestics to arms and advanced to meet the assailants. Then such terror and confusion took possession of the conspirators, that without any trouble we arrested and put in chains the four instigators of the crime who had been pointed out to me. The rest, thrown into consternation

1557. by this incident, laid down their arms and skulked away. The next day we relieved one of them of his chains in order that he might more freely plead his cause. But starting off on a run he threw himself into the sea and was drowned. The rest having been brought out to plead in chains, without being put to torture, of their own accord confessed what we had already learned through the informer. One of them, having been punished by me, a short time before, because he had had to do with a dissolute woman, was known to be particularly ill-affected, and to have bribed the woman's father to rescue him from our power, in case I should apply myself vigorously to prevent his intercourse with her. This man paid the penalty of his crime by being hung: the other two I pardoned, but ordered that they should be set at work in the fields in chains. I thought it best not to investigate the culpability of the rest, lest I might leave a discovered crime unpunished, or, if I wished to punish with death, as the crime involved a great number of persons, there might not survive enough men to accomplish the work begun by us. Therefore, dissembling the offense committed, we forgave the sin and bade all be of good cheer. We could not so free ourselves, however, from solicitude, as not to make most diligent search to discover what was every man's disposition from his zeal and daily pursuits. And inasmuch as I did not spare the labors of the men, but urged them on to the work by my continual presence, not only did we preclude their life from bad designs, but, in a short space of time, we surrounded our island with fortifications and very strong defenses. Meantime, according to the power of my understanding, I ceased not to admonish them and deter them from vices, and to imbue their minds with the Christian religion, having appointed public daily prayers morning and evening. In consequence of this caution and religion, we had more quiet during the rest of the year. But the advent of our ships took away the care which we have set forth. For here have I found men, not only from whom I need in no wise stand on my guard, but to whom I can securely commit my safety. Since the ability has thus been offered to me, I have selected out of my entire force ten men in whose hands I have placed the power in our government, decreeing that hereafter nothing shall be done without the council. Thus if I should decide with too much harshness against any one, the sentence will be of no effect and void, unless the authorization and agreement of the council be added. I have, however, reserved for myself the right to pardon, in case a sentence to death has been rendered. Thus I can benefit all, be hurtful to no one. These are the arts by means of which I have determined to retain, protect and defend our dignity.

I shall add, respecting the advice which you have given in your letters, that I shall give the greatest attention in order that we may not turn aside from it even in the slightest particular. Of this I am persuaded, that no advice is more holy, or just, or sound than this. Wherefore also we have had your letters read in our senate, and then transcribed upon the records, in order that, if at any time it should chance that we stray from the course, the reading of them may recall us from our error. May our Lord Jesus Christ protect you and your colleagues from all evil, may He confirm you by His Spirit, and lengthen out as far as possible your life for the work of His Church. I beg you to salute in my name my very dear brethren the faithful *Cephas* and *De la Fleche.* At Coligny in Antarctic France, the day before the Calends of April [March 31st,] 1557.

1557.

Should you write to *Renée of France,* our Mistress, I beg you to salute her most diligently in my name.

Your most loving, eager and from the heart,
N_i^a [1]

Complete extant Works of John Calvin. Volume XVI., p. 437. No. 2612. Villegagnon to Calvin. He narrates the history of his colony in Antarctic France, as he calls it.

COMMISSION OF HENRY IV. TO DE MONTS.

[See above, pages 86-88.]

"Commission du Roy au Sieur de Monts, pour l'habitation ès terres de la Cadie, Canada, & autres endroits en la Nouvelle France. Ensemble les defenses à tous autres de trafiquer avec les sauvages desdittes terres.

1603.

"Henry par la grace de Dieu Roy de France & de Navarre, A nôtre cher & bien amé le sieur de Monts, Gentil homme ordinaire de nôtre Chambre, Salut. Comme nôtre plus grand soin et travail soit & ait toujours esté, depuis nôtre avenement à cette Couronne, de la maintenir et conserver en son ancienne dignité, grandeur & splendeur, d'etendre & amplifier autant que legitimement se peut faire, les bornes & limites d'icelle. Nous estans dès long temps a, informez de la situation & condition des païs & territoire de la Cadie, Meuz sur toutes choses d'un zele singulier & d'une devote & ferme resolution que nous avons prinse, avec l'aide & assistance de Dieu, autheur, distributeur & protecteur de tous Royaumes & etats, de faire convertir, amener & instruire les peuples qui habitent en cette contrée, de present gens barbares, athées, sans foy ne Religion, au Christianisme, & en la creance & profession de nôtre foy & religion ; & les retirer de l'ignorance & infidelité où ilz sont. Ayans aussi dès longtemps reconeu sur le rapport des Capitaines de navires, pilotes, marchans & autres qui de longue main ont hanté, frequenté, & traffiqué avec ce qui se trouve de peuples esdits lieux, combien peut estre fructueuse, commode & utile à nous, à nos états & sujets, la demeure, possession & habitation d'iceux pour le grand & apparent profit qui se retirera par la grande frequentation & habitude que l'on aura avec les peuples qui s'y trouvent, & le trafic & commerce qui se pourra par ce moyen

---

[1] Nicholas (*Durand de Villegagnon*). The abbreviation is thus written in order that the V may also be represented.

1603. seurement traiter et negocier. Nous pour ces causes à plein confians de vôtre grande prudence, & en la conoissance & experience que vous avez de la qualité, condition & situation dudit païs de la Cadie : pour les diverses navigations, voyages, & frequentations que vous avez faits en ces terres, & autres proches & circonvoisines : nous asseurans que cette nôtre resolution & intention, vous estant commise, vous la sçaurez attentivement, diligemment, & non moins courageusement, & valeureusement executer & conduire à la perfection que nous desirons, Vous avons expressément commis & établi, & par ces presentes signées de nôtre main, Vous commettons, ordonnons, faisons, constituons & etablissons, nôtre Lieutenant-general, pour representer notre persone, aux païs, territoires, côtes & confins de la Cadie : A commencer dés la quarantiéme degré jusques au quarante-sixiéme. Et en icelle étendue ou partie d'icelle, tant & si avant que faire se pourra, établir, étendre & faire conoitre nôtre nom, puissance & authorité. Et à icelle assujettir, submettre & faire oheir tous les peuples de la dite terre, & les circonvoisins : Et par le moyen d'icelles & toutes autres voyes licites, les appeller, faire instruire, provoquer & émouvoir à la conoissance de Dieu, & à la lumière de la Foy & religion Chrétienne, la y établir : & en l'exercice & profession d'icelle maintenir, garder, & conserver lesdits peuples, & tous autres habituez esdits lieux, & en paix, repos & tranquillité y comander tant par mer que par terre : Ordonner, decider, & faire executer tout ce que vous jugerez se devoir & pouvoir faire, pour maintenir, garder & conserver lesdits lieux souz nôtre puissance & authorité, par les formes, voyes & moyens prescrits par nos ordonnances. Et pour y avoir égard avec vous, commettre, établir & constituer tous Officiers, tant ès affaires de la guerre que de Justice & police pour la premiere fois, & de là en avant nous les nommer & presenter : pour en estre par nous disposé & donner les lettres, tiltres & provisions tels qu'ilz seront necessaires. Et selon les occurrences des affaires, vous mémes avec l'avis de gens prudens & capables, prescrire souz nôtre bon plaisir, des loix, statuts & ordonnances autant qu'il se pourra conformes aux notres, notamment és choses & matieres ausquelles n'est pourveu par icelles : traiter & contracter à méme effet paix, aliance & confederation, bonne amitié, correspondance & communication avec les dits peuples & leurs Princes, ou autres ayans pouvoir & commandement sur eux : Entretenir, garder & soigneusement observer, les traittez & alliances dont vous conviendrez avec eux : pourveu qu'ilz y satisfacent de leur part. Et à ce defaut, leur faire guerre ouverte pour les contraindre & amener à telle raison, que vous jugerez necessaire, pour l'honneur, obeissance & service de Dieu, & l'établissement, manutention & conservation de notredite authorité parmi eux : du moins pour hanter & frequenter par vous, & tous noz sujets avec eux, en toute asseurance, liberté, frequetatiô & cômunication, y negotier & trafiquer aimablement & paisiblement. Leur donner & octroyer graces & privileges, charges & honneurs. Lequel entier pouvoir susdit, Voulons aussi & ordonnons : Que vous ayez sur tous nosdits sujets & autres qui se transporteront & voudront s'habituer, trafiquer, negotier & resider esdits lieux, tenir, prendre, reserver, & vous approprier ce que vous voudrez & verrez vous estre plus commode & propre à vôtre charge, qualité & vsage desdites terres, en departir telles parts & portions, leur donner & attribuer tels tiltres, honneurs, droits, pouvoirs & facultez que vous verrez besoin estre, selon les qualitez, conditions & merites des personnes du païs ou autres. Sur tout peupler, cultiver & faire habituer lesdites terres le plus promptement, soigneusement & dextrement, que le temps, les lieux, & commoditez le pourront permettre : en faire ou faire faire à cette fin la decouverture & reconnoissance en l'etenduë des côtes maritimes & antres contrées de la terre ferme, que vous ordonnerez & prescrirez en l'espace susdits du quarantiéme degré jusques au quarante-sixiéme, ou autrement tant & si avant qu'il se pourra le long desdites côtes, & en la terre forme.* Faire soigneusement rechercher & reconoitre toutes sortes de mines d'or & d'argent, cuivre & autres metaux & mineraux, les faire fouïller, tirer, purger & affiner, pour estre convertis en vsage, disposer suivant que nous avons prescrit par les Edits & reglemens que nous avons fait en ce Royaume du profit & emolument d'icelles, par vous ou ceux que vous aurez établis à cet effet, nous reservans seulement le dixiéme denier de ce qui proviendra de celles d'or, d'argent, & cuivre, vous affectans ce que nous pourrions prendre ausdits autres métaux & mineraux, pour vous aider & soulager aux grandes dépenses que la charge susdite vous pourra apporter. Voulans cependant ; que pour vôtre seureté & commodité, & de tous ceux de noz sujets qui s'en iront, habituëront & trafiqueront esdites terres : comme generalement de tous autres qui s'y accommoderont souz nôtre puissance & authorité, Vous puissiez faire batir & construire vn on plusieurs forts, places, villes & toutes autres maisons, demeures & habitations, ports, havres, retraites, & logemens que vous conoitrez propres, vtiles & necessaires à l'execution de ladite entreprise. Etablir garnisons & gens de guerre à la garde d'iceux. Vous aider & prevaloir aux effets susdits des vagabons, personnes oyseuses & sans aveu, tant és villes qu'aux champs, & des condamnez à banissement perpetuels, ou à trois ans au moins hors nôtre Royaume, pourveu que ce soit par avis & consentement & de l'authorité de nos Officiers. Outre ce que dessus, & qui vous est d'ailleurs prescrit, mandé & ordonné par les commissions & pouvoirs que vous a donnez nostre trescher cousin le sieur d'Ampville Admiral de France, pour ce qui concerne le fait & la charge de l'Admirauté, en l'exploit, expedition & execution des choses susdites, faire generalement pour la conquéte, peuplement, habituation & conservation de ladite terre de la Cadie, & descétes, territoires, circonvoisins & de leurs appartenances, & dependances souz nôtre nom & authorité, ce que nous mémes ferions & faire pourrions si presens en personne y estions, iaçoit que la cas requit mandement plus special, que nous ne le vous prescrivons par cesdites presentes : au contenu desquelles, Mandons, ordonnons & tres-expressement enjoignons à tous nos iusticiers, officiers & sujets, de se conformer : Et à vous obeïr & entendre en toutes & chacunes les choses sudites, leurs circonstances & dependances. Vous donner aussi en l'execution d'icelles

1603.

*Ferme.

1603.

tout ayde & confort, main-forte & assistance dont vous aurez besoin & seront par vous requis, le tout à peine de rebellion & desobeïssance. Et à fin que persone ne pretende cause d'ignorance de cette nôtre intention, & se vueille immiscer en tout ou partie, de la charge, dignité & authorité que nous vous donnons par ces presentes : Nous avons de noz certaine science, pleine puissance & authorité Royale, revoqué, supprimé et declaré nuls & de nul effet ci apres & des à present tous autres pouvoirs & Commissions, Lettres & expeditions donnez & delivrez à quelque persone que ce soit, pour découvrir, conquerir, peupler & habiter en l'étenduë susdite desdites terres situées depuis le dit quarantieme degré, iusques au quarantesixiéme quelles qu'elles soient. Et outre ce mandons & ordonnons à tous nosdits Officiers de quelque qualité & condition qu'ils soient, que ces presentes, ou *Vidimus* deuëment collationné d'icelles par l'vn de nos amez & feaux Conseillers, Notaires & Secretaires, ou autre Notaire Royal, ilz facent à votre requéte, poursuite & diligence, ou de noz Procureurs, lire, publier & registrer és registres de leurs iurisdictions, pouvoirs & détrois, cessans en tant qu'à eux appartiendra, tous troubles & empichemens à ce contraires. Car tel est nôtre plaisir. Donné à Fontaine-bleau le huitiéme jour de Novembre ; l'an de grace mil six cens trois : Et de nôtre regne le quinziéme. Signé, HENRY, Et plus bas, Par le Roy, POTIER. Et scellé sur simple queuë de cire iaune.

(*Translation.*)

[See above, page 97, note.]

"The Patent of the ffrench Kinge to Mounsieur De Monts for the inhabitinge of the countries La Cadia, Canada, and other places in New ffraunce."

(British State Papers, Colonial, 1574-1621, Vol. I., No. 10.)

Henery by the grace of God Kinge of ffrance and Navarre. To our deare and welbeloved the Lord of Monts, one of the Ordinary Gentlemen of our Chamber, greetinge. As our greatest care and labour is, and hath alwaies beene, since our cominge to this Crowne, to maintaine and conserue it in the auntient dignity, greatnes and splendour thereof, to extend and amplifie, as much as lawfully may bee done, the bounds and limitts of the same. Wee beinge of a longe time informed of the scituaçon and condiçon of the lands and territories of La Cadia moved above all thinges with a singuler zeale, and devout and constant resoluçon wch wee have taken with the helpe and assistance of God Authour Distributour and Protectour of all Kingdomes and estates to cause the people wch doe inhabite the countrey, men at this pñte * time barbarous, Atheists without faith or religion, to be conuerted to Christianity, and to the beleife and profession of our faith and religion, and to drawe them from the ignorance and vnbeleife wherein they are, havinge also of a longe time knowen by the relaçon of the Sea Captaines, Pylotts, Merchants and others, who of longe time have haunted, frequented, and trafficked with the people that are found in the said places, how fruitfull, commodious, and profitable may bee

*presente.

vnto vs, to our estates and subiects, the dwellinge possession and habitaçon of those countries, for the great and apparant profit wch may bee drawen by the greater frequentaçon and habitude wch may be had with the people that are found there, and the Trafficke and commerce wch may bee, by that meanes safely treated and negotiated. Wee then for these causes fully trustinge on your great wisedome, and in the knowledge and experience that you have of the qualitie, condiçon and situaçon of the said Countrie of La Cadia: for the divers and sundry navigaçons, voyages, and frequentaçons that you have made into those parts and others neere and borderinge vpon it. Assuringe our selues that this our resoluçon and intention, beinge committed vnto you, you will attentively, diligently, and no less couragiously and valorously execute and bringe to such perfecçon as wee desire: Have expressely appointed and established you, and by these presents, signed with our owne hands, doe committ, ordaine, make, constitute and establish you, our Lievtenant generall, for to represent our person in the countries, territories, coasts, and confines of La Cadia. To begin from the 40 degree to the 46. And in the same distance, or part of it, as farre as may bee done, to establish, extend, and make to bee knowen our name, might and authoritie. And vnder the same to subiect, submit and bringe to obedience all the people of the said land and the borderers thereof: And by the meanes thereof and all lawfull waies, to call, make, instruct, provoke and incite them to the knowledge of god, and to the light of the faith and Christian religion, to establish it there: And in the exercise and profession of the same, keepe and conserue the said people, and all other inhabitants in the said places, and there to commaund in peace, rest, and tranquillity as well by sea, as by land: to ordaine, decide and cause to be executed all that wch you shall iudge fitt and necessary to bee done, for to maintaine, keepe and conserue the said places vnder our power & authority by the formes, waies and meanes prescribed by our lawes. And for to have there a care of the same with you to appoint, establish and constitute all Officers, as well in the affaires of warre, as for Justice and policie, for the first time, and from thence forward to name and present them vnto vs, for to bee disposed by vs, and to give lres,* titles, and such provisoes, as shalbee necessarie. And accordinge to the occurrences of affaires your selfe with the aduice of wise, and capable men, to prescribe vnder our good pleasure, lawes, statutes, and ordinances conformable, asmuch as may be possible, vnto ours, specially in thinges and matters that are not provided by them. To treate and contract to the same effect, peace, alliance, and confederacy, good amity correspondency, and communicaçon with the said people and their princes, or others, havinge power or commaund over them: To entertaine, keepe and carefully to obserue, the treatises, and alliances wherein you shall covenant with them; vpon condiçon that they themselves performe the same of their part. And for wont thereof to make open warre against them, to constraine and bringe them to such reason as you shall thinke needfull, for the honour, obedience, and seruice of god, and establishment, maintenance and conseruaçon of our said authoritie amongst them:

1603.

*lettres.

1603. at least to haunt and frequent by you, and all our subjects with them, in all assurance, libertie, frequentaçon, and communicaçon there to negociate and trafficke lovingly, and peaceably. To give *favours. and graunt vnto them fovours*, and priviledges, charges and honours. W^{ch} intire power abovesaid, we will likewise and ordaine, that you have over all our said subiects that will goe in that voyage with you and inhabite there, trafficke, negociate and remaine in the said places, to retaine, take, reserue, and appropriate vnto you, what you will and shall see to bee most commodious for you, and proper for your charge, qualitie, and vse of the said lands, to distribute such parts and porçons thereof, to give and attribute vnto them such titles, honors, rights, powers and faculties as you shall see necessary, accordinge to the qualities, condiçons and meritts of the persons of the same Countrie or others. Cheifely to populate, to manure, and to make the said lands to be inhabited as spedily, carefully, and skilfully, as time, places and commodities may permitt. To make thereof, or cause to bee made to that end, discouerie and view alonge the maritime Coasts and other Countries

The contents of the Patent being from 40 to 46. of the maine land, wch you shall order and prescribe in the foresaid space *of the* 40 *degree to the* 46 *degree, or otherwise*, asmuch and as farre as may bee, alonge the said Coast, and in the firme land. To make carefully to be sought and marked all sorts of mines of gold and siluer, Copper, and other Metalls and Mineralls, to make them to be digged, drawne from the earth, purified, and refined for to bee conuerted into vse, to dispose accordinge as wee have prescribed by Edicts and orders, wch wee have made in this Realme of the profitt and benefit of them, by you or them whom you shall establish to that effect, reseruinge vnto vs onely the tenth peny, of that wch shall issue from them of gold, silver and copper, leavinge vnto you that wch wee might take of the other said Metalls and Mineralls, for to aide and ease you in the great expences that the foresaid charge may bringe vnto you; Willinge in the meane while that aswell for your securitie and commoditie, as for the securitie and commoditie of all our subiects, who will goe, inhabite, and trafficke in the said lands: as generally of all others that will accommodate themselues there vnder our power and authoritie; you may' cause to bee built, and frame one or many fforts, places, Townes, and all other houses, dwellings and habitaçons, Ports, havens, retiringe places and lodgings, as you shall knowe to bee fitt, profitable and necessary for the performinge of the said enterprise. To establish garrisons and souldiers for the keepinge of them. To aide and serue you for the effects abovesaid with the vagrant, idle persons and masterlesse, as well out of Townes as of the Countrey: and with them that bee condemned to perpetuall banishment, or for three yeares at the least out of our Realme: Provided alwaies that it bee done with the aduice, consent, and authoritie of our officers. Over and besides that wch is above mençoned (and that wch is moreover prescribed commaunded and ordained vnto you by the Commissions and powers wch our most deare Cousin, the lord of Ampuille Admirall of ffraunce hath given vnto you for that wch concerneth the affaires and the charge of the Admiralitie, in the exploit, expediçon and executinge of the thinges abovesaid) to doe

generally whatsoever may make for the conquest, peoplinge, in-   1603.
habitinge and preseruaçon of the said land of La Cadia, and of the
Coasts, territories adioyninge, and of their appurtenances and dependencies, vnder our name and authoritie, whatsoever our selues
would and might doe, if wee were there present in person, although
that the case should require a more spiall* order then wee prescribe   *speciall.
vnto you by these presents. To the contents whereof wee com-
maund, ordaine, and most expressely doe inioyne all our Justices,
Officers, and subiects to conforme themselues: And to obey and
give attention vnto you, in all and everie the things abovesaid,
their circumstancies and dependencies. Also to give vnto you in
the executinge of them, all such aide and comfort, helpe and assistance, as you shall have need of, and whereof they shall be by you
required, and this vpon paine of disobedience and rebellion. And
to the end no body may pretend cause of ignorance, of this our
intention, and to busie himselfe in all, or in parte of the charge,
dignitie, and authoritie wch wee give vnto you by these presents:
Wee have of our certaine knowledge, full power, and regall authoritie, revoked, suppressed and declared voide, and of none effect
hereafter, and from this present, all other powers and Comissions,
ltres† and expediçons given and deliuered to any person soeuer, for   † lettres.
to discover, people, and inhabite in the foresaid extention of the
said lands scituated from the said 40 degree to the 46, whatsoever
they bee. And furthermore wee command and ordaine all our said
officers of what qualitie and condiçon soever they bee, that after
those pnts‡ or the duplicate of them shallbee duely examined by   ‡ presents.
one of our beloved and trustie Counsellors, Notaries, and Secreta-
ries, or other Notarie Royall, they doe vpon our request, demaund,
and sute, or vpon the sute of any our Atturneys, cause the same
to be read, published, and recorded in the records of their iurisdic-
çons, powers, and precincts, seekinge, as m[u]ch as shall apper-
teine vnto them, to quiet and appease all troubles and hinderance
wch may contradict the same. ffor such is our pleasure. Given
at ffountain-bleau the 8 day of November: in the yeare of our Lord
1603: And of our Raigne the 15. signed Henery: and vnderneath,
by the Kinge, Potier; And sealed vpon single labell with yellow
waxe.

Indorsed:—" The copie of the ffrench Kings Patent to Mounsieur de Monts of La Cadia Canada &c.
    granted 8 Noveb 1603,
      fro 40 to 46 degrees.
                    Acadia, Canada,
                          &c.
                      Novr 1603."

1621.

PETITION OF THE WALLOONS AND FRENCH.

[State Papers, Holland, 1622,[1] Jan.-Mar., Bundle No. 145.]

[See above, pages 158-163.]

Sera treshumblement supplié Monseigneur L'Ambassadeur du Serenissime Roy de Lagrande Bretagne de nous donner auis et responce sur les articles quj s'ensuiuent.

i

Premierement sil plairoit a sa majesté de permettre a cincquante ou soixante familles tant de Wallons que françois tous de la religion refformée d'aller s'habituer en Virginie terre de son obeissance ; & sil ne luy plairoit pas prandre leur protection et sauuegarde enuers et contre tous et les maintenir en leur religion.

ij

Et a cause quaus-dites familles se pourroit trouuer pres de trois cens personnes, quaussi ils souhaiteroient mener auecq eus quantité de bestail, tant pour la culture de la terre que pour leur entretien : et qua ces causes il leur seroit besoin d' auoir plus d'une nauire : sj sadicte majesté ne voudroit point les en accommoder d'une esquippée et munie de canons et aues armes, sur lequelle ils accompliroient (auecq celle quils pourroient fournir) leur voyage retourner querir des commodités aus lieus concedes par sadite majesté ensemble transporter celles du pays.

iij

Si arriues ausdict pays, elle ne leur voudroit pas permettre de choisir entre les lieus non encore cultiues par ceus quil a pleu a sadite majesté y enuoyer, vne place commode pour leur demeure.

iiij

Sj audict lieu est eu, ils ne pourroient pas ædiffier vne ville pour leur seureté, la munir de fortiffications requises, dans laquelle ils pourroient eslire gouuerneur et majistrats pour lexercice tant de la police que de la iustice ; soubs les lois fundamentales qujla pleu ou plaira a sadicte majesté establir ausdites terres.

v

Sj sadite majesté ne leur voudroit pas donner canons et munitions pour la manutefion de ladite place, leur octroyer droit en cas de necessité de batre poudre, composer boullets, et fondre canons sous les panonceaus & armes de sadite majesté.

---

[1] A clerical mistake for 1621. See above, page 163, note.

APPENDIX.

vj

Si elle ne leur voudroit pas conceder vne banlieue ou territoire de huit mille angloises la ronde cest a dire seze mille de diametre dans lequel ils pourroient cultiuer champs pres vignes et autres commodites lequel territoire soit conjointement soit diuiseur ils tiendroient de sadite majesté a foy et hommage telle que trouuerra raisonnable sadite majestñ sans quautre y peut demourer sans prandre lettre de baillette dens des terres y contenues dans lesquelles ils se reserueroient droit seignoirial subalterne et sil ne seroit pas permis a ceus d'entreus quj pourroient viure noblement de se dire tels.

vij

Sils ne pourroient pas chasser esdites terres a poil et a plume pescher en mer et riuieres couper arbres de haute futaye et autres tant pour la nauigation que autres negoces selon leur volunté en fin se seruir de tout ce quj seroit tant dessus que dessous terre sauue les droits royaus aleurs plaisir et volunté et du tout traffiquer auecq les personnes quj leurs seroient permises.

Lesquelles choses sestendroient seulement ausdites familles et aus leurs sans que ceus quj viendroient denouueau audit territoire sen peussent preualloir quentend que ils leurs concederoient selon leur puissance et non audela sj sadite majesté ne leur concedoit de nouueau.

Et pource quils ont entendu que sadite majesté a establj vne maison commune a Londres dans laquelle non ailleurs on doit descharger les marchandises quj viennent desdites terres considerant quil est plus que raisonnable que ceus quj par leur labeur et industrie ont donne au public la iouissance de ceste terre iouissent les premiers des fruits dicelle se sousmetteront aus constitutions quj pour cet effet y ont esté establies lesquelles pour meilleur entretien leur seront communiques.

Soubs lesquelles conditions et priuileges ils prometteroient foy et obeissance telle que doiuent fidelles et obeissans subjects a leur Roy et souuerain Seigneur se sousmetteront aus lois generallement establies ausdites terres de tout leur pouuoir.

> Sur ce que dessus mondict Seigneur lAmbassadeur donnera auis sil luy plaist comme aussj sj son plaisir seroit de faire expedier ledict priuilege en forme deue le plustost que faire se pourra a cause du peu de temps quj reste dicy au mars (temps commode pour lembarquemt) pour faire lacceuil de tout ce quj est requis ce faisant obligera ses seruiteurs a prier Dieu pour laccomplissemt de ses saincts deseins et pour sa santé et longue vie.
> JESSE DE FOREST.

Indorsed :—Supplicaoñ of certaine Wallons and French who are desirous to goe into Verginia.

[Inclosed in Sir Dudley Carleton's letter dated 19 July, 1621.]

1621.

ANSWER OF THE VIRGINIA COMPANY.

[State Papers, Colonial, Vol I., No. 55.]

[See above, pages 163–165.]

The humble answere of so many of His Maties Councell for Virginia as could at present bee assembled, they being in His Highnes name required by the R^t Ho^ble Sr George Calvert Principall Secretary of State, to deliver their opinion concerning certaine Articles putt vp by some Walloones and ffrenchemen desirous to goe to Virginia.

for the ffirst — If it stand wth His Maties gratious favour they do not conceive it any inconvenience at present to suffer sixtie families of Walloones and ffrenchmen not exceeding the number of 300 persons to goe and inhabite in Virginia, The sayd persons resoluing and taking oath to become His Maties and His Successours faithfull and obedient subjects: and being willing as they make profession to agree in points of faith, So likewise to bee conformable to the forme of gouvernm^t now established in the Churche of England.

for the second — They esteeme it so Royall a favour in His Matie, and so singula[r] a benefitt to the sayd Walloones and ffrenchemen to bee admitted to live in that fruitefull land vnder the proteccion and gouvernm^t of so mighty and pious a Monarch as His Matie is, that they ought not to expect of His sacred Matie any ayde of shipping or other chargeable favour. And as for the Company for Virginia their stock is so vtterly exhausted by theese three last yeares supplies, as they are not able to giue them any farther helpe in that kinde, then onely in point of advise & Councell, for the cheapest transportation of themselues and goodes, and the most frugall and profitable managing of their affayres, if His Royal Matie please so to command them.

ffor the 3. 4. 5. 6. 7. Articles — They conceiue that for the prosperity and principally the securing of the plantacion in His Maties obedience, it is not expedient that the sayd ffamilies should sett downe in one grosse and entire bodie wch the demaundes specifyed, but that they should rather bee placed by convenient numbers in the principall Citties, Borroughes and Corporacions in Virginia, as themselues shall choose, There being giuen vnto them such proporcion of land and all

APPENDIX. 351

other priviledges and benefitts whatsoever in as ample manner as to the naturall Englishe, And this course they out of their experience do conceiue likely to proue better, and more comfortable to the sayd Walloons and ffrenchemen, then that other wch they desire.   1621.

All theese their opinions they do most humbly submitt to the most excellent wisdome of His sacred Matie

signed by
JOHN FERRAR, Deputy.

Indorsed :— " xj. August 1621 Copie of the answere made by the Virginia Company to the request made by the Wallons and Frenche to plant themselues in Virginia."

THE WALLOON AND FRENCH PETITIONERS.

[See above, pages 162, 173, *seq*.]

" The Signature of such Walloons and French as offer themselves to goe into Verginia," is preserved in the British Public Record Office, London. (State Papers, Colonial, Vol. I., No. 54.*) An application kindly made in my behalf, in November, 1880, by Arthur Giraud Browning, Esq., of London, for permission to have a photograph of this document made, was most courteously granted. An engraving of the petition appears in the present work. The original measures eighteen by thirteen and a half inches. The signatures, accompanied with a statement of the calling of each person, are arranged in the form of a "round robin," encircling the " promise" made by the signers to fulfill, the conditions set forth in their communication to the English ambassador.

With the valued help of the Librarian of the Walloon Library in Leyden, I have ascertained that the greater number of these petitioners were members of the Walloon Church in that city. The investigation made has also enabled me to present the names, many of which are written very indistinctly, with greater correctness. Several of them were not to be found in the Walloon records of Leyden; and it is likely that the signers belonged to other cities. Many names reappear in those records after an interval of three or four years. The persons thus named may have emigrated to New Netherland, and returned to " Fatherland," as dominie Michaelius wrote, August 11, 1628, that " a portion of them" were about to do.

" Signatures :"

f   5 [6] enfans Jesse de Forest tincturier
f   2 enfans Nycolas de la Marlier tainturier
fme   Jan Damont laboureur

352 APPENDIX.

1621.
fme	3 enfans	Jan Gille laboureur
f	5 enfans	Jan de Trou paigneur en laine
fme	5 enfans	Phlipe Maton teinturie et deux serviteur
fme	4 enfans	Anthoyne de Violate vigneron de vingne
fme	5 enfans	Ernou Catoir paignier
fme	1 enfans	Anthoin Desendre laboureur
fme	4 enfans	Abel de Crepy ouvrier de la navette
fme	4 enfans	Adrien Barbe tainturier
fme	1 enfans	Michelle Censier ticheran de drape
fme	1 enfans	Jerome Le Roy tischeron de drape
	Jeune fils	Claude Ghiselin tailleur dabits
fme	1 enfans	Jan de Crenne facteur
fme	2 enfans	Louis Broque laboureur
Homme a marier		
Jeune fils [erased]		Mousnier de la Montagne estudient en medicine.
Homme a marier		
Jeune fils [erased]		Mousnier de la Montagne pharmacien et chir-[urgien.
fe	2 enfans	Jacque Conne laboureur de terre
fe		Henry Lambert drapier de drap
fme	4 enfans	Jorge le ca[ ] charger
fme	2 enfans	Michel du Pon chapiller
f	4 enfans	Jan Billt [Billet ?] laboureur
f	2 enfans	Polle de Pasar tiseran
fme		Antoine Gremier gardener
fme	5 enfans	Jean Gourdeman laboureur
fme	4 enfans	Jean Campion painnier
	Jeune fils	Jan de la Mot laboureur
fme	1 enfans	Antoinne Martin
	Jeune homme	Franchois Fourdrin passeur de peau
fme	5 enfans	Jan le Ca laboureur
f	2 enfans	Theodor du Four drapier
	Jeunne fs	Gillam Broque laboureur
f	4 enfans	Gouerge Woutre
fme	6 enfans	Jan Sage sairger
fme	2 enfans	Mari Flip au nom de son mari munier
	Jeune fils	P. Gantois Estudiant en Theologie
Homme a marier		Jacques de Lechielles brasseur
fe	6 enfans	Jan le Rou imprimeur
fe	5 enfans	marque de Jan de Croy scieur de boy
fe	2 enfans	marq de Challe Channy laboureur
fme	5 enfans	marq de Francoi Clitden laboureur
fme	1 enfan	Flipe Campion drapepier
	Jeune fils	Robert Broque laboureur
	Jeune fils	Philippe de Le ouvrier charpentier
	Jeune fille	Jenne Martin
	Jeunne fils	Piere Cornille vingeron
fe	2 enfans	Jan du Carpentrij laboureur
	Jeune fils	Martin de Carpentier fondeur de cuivre
fme	7 enfans	Thomas Farnarcque serrurier
		Pierre Gaspar
fme	4 enfans	Gregoire le Jeune cordonnier

APPENDIX. 353

1621.

fme	1 enfans	Martin Framerie musicien	
Homme a marier		Pierre Quiesnier brasseur	
fme	3 enfans	Pontus le Geay faisseur destamin	
fe	8 enfans	Barthelemy Digaud scyeur de bois	

NOTES FROM THE WALLOON RECORDS OF LEYDEN.

DE LA MARLIER. Jean de la Marlier was witness to the baptism of Philippe, son of Jesse de Forest and Marie du Cloux, in the Walloon Church of Leyden, September 13, 1620.

DAMONT. Françoise Damont, a native of Liege, was married, December 15, 1633.

GILLE. Jean Gille, a native of Lille, was married to Cataline Face, of Leyden, October 17, 1615.

MATON. Philippe Maton, a native of Fourcoin, was married to Philippotte Caron, January 10, 1599.

CATOIR. A child of Arnoul Catoire, was baptized September 23, 1618.

DESENDRE. Anthoine Decende witnessed the baptism of a child of Jean de Croi, March 28, 1621.

CREPY. Abel Crepy and Jaquemine de Lannoy presented their daughter Susanne for baptism, February 6, 1627.

BARBÉ. Adrien Barbé was witness to the baptism of Adrien, son of Jean Barbé, September 14, 1625.

LE ROY. Jérosme le Roy, a native of Armentières, was married to Susanne le Per, of Norwich, England, November 1, 1620.

GHISELIN. Claude Gyselin was witness to the baptism of a child of Grégoire le Jeune, March 28, 1621.

CENSIER. Michelle, daughter of Michel Censier, was baptized September 29, 1624.

DE CRANNE. Jean de Cranne was a witness to the baptism of a child of Grégoire le Jeune, March 28, 1621.

BROQUE. Louis Broque and Chertruy Quinze presented their son Pierre for baptism, January 30, 1622.

COINNE. Jaques Coinne, a native of Ron, near Lille, was married to Christienne Baseu (or le Baiseur), of Fourcoin, July 27, 1614. Their son Noé was baptized June 28, 1620.

LAMBERT. Henri Lambert, was received to the Holy Communion, at Pentecost, 1620, upon confession of his faith. Henri Lambert, born near Limbourg, and Anne Digan, of Noyelles in Hainault, were married November 1, 1620. (Another Henri Lambert, a native of Liege, was married November 10, 1621, to Marguerite Simon.)

DU PON. Michiel du Pon, a native of Valenciennes, was married to Nicole Billet, of Herdeyn, July 5, 1597.

CAMPION. Jean Campion, a native of Artois, was married to Isabeau Cap, August 25, 1607.

DE LA MOT. Jean de la Mote and Marie Fache, his wife, presented their son Jean for baptism, November 10, 1622.

1621.   MARTIN. Antoine Martin, born near St. Amand, was married to Prudence Hussé, of St. Amand, December 8, 1619.

LE CA. Jean le Ca, a native of Halewyn, was married to Marie des Pré, of Monvau, January 7, 1617.

DU FOUR. Theodore du Four and Sara Nicaise, his wife, presented their daughter Madelaine for baptism, July 24, 1616.

BROQUE. Gillain Broque was a witness to the baptism of Pierre, son of Louis and Chertruy Broque, January 30, 1622.

SAGE. Marie, fille de Jean le Sage, was baptized in March, 1605.

DE LECHIELLES. Jaques de Lespielle witnessed, with Jesse and Rachel de Forest, to the baptism of Henri Lambert's son Henri, August 1, 1621.

DE CROY. Two children of Jean de Croi were baptized in the Walloon Church, April 12, 1615, and March 28, 1621.

DU CARPENTRY. Jean des Carpentry, a native of Landa [Landas, in Flanders], was married to Anna Chotein, from the neighborhood of St. Amand, March 10, 1619.

FARNARCQUE. Thomas Farvarque and Marie, his wife, presented their son Abraham for baptism, August 4, 1624.

LE JEUNE. Grégoire le Jeune and his wife Jenne de Merre presented their son Isaac for baptism, March 28, 1621.

FRAMERIE. Martin Framerie and Marie François his wife, presented their son Zacharie for baptism, October 25, 1620.

QUIESNIER. Pierre Quesnée, or Quesnoy, a native of Fourcoin, and Marie le Per, of Wacka, near Lille, were married, February 27, 1617.

DIGAND. Barthélémy Digand and Françoise Fregeau his wife presented their son Isaac for baptism, March 1, 1620.

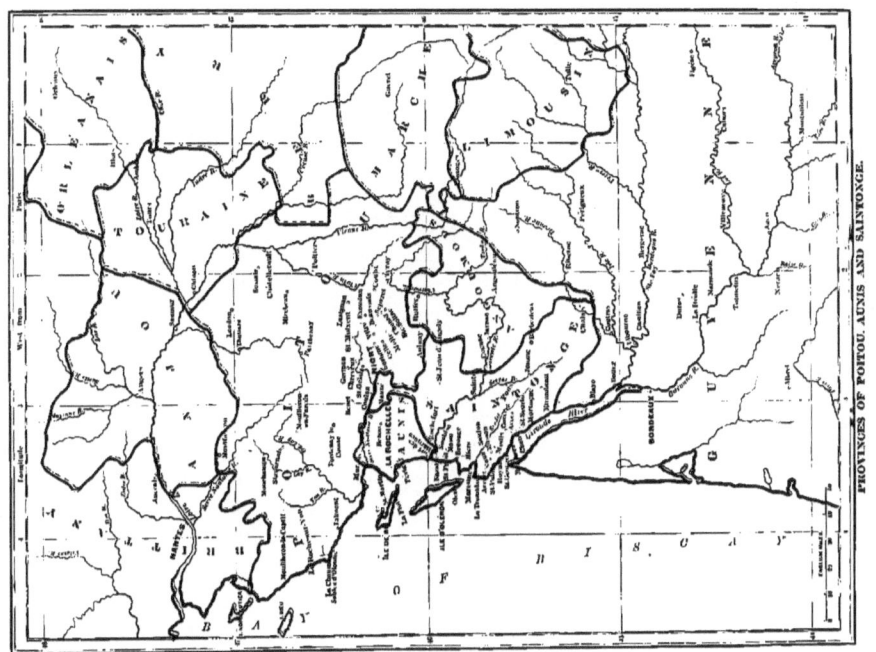

www.ingramcontent.com/pod-product-compliance
Lightning Source LLC
Chambersburg PA
CBHW031419230426
43668CB00007B/366